PHILOSOPHY, THEOLOGY,
AND HEGEL'S BERLIN PHILOSOPHY
OF RELIGION, 1821–1827

PHILOSOPHY, THEOLOGY, AND HEGEL'S BERLIN PHILOSOPHY OF RELIGION, 1821–1827

Philip M. Merklinger

STATE UNIVERSITY OF NEW YORK PRESS

Published by
State University of New York Press, Albany

© 1993   State University of New York

For information, address State University of New York
Press, State University Plaza, Albany, NY 12246

Production by Dana Foote
Marketing by Theresa A. Swierzowski

Library of Congress Cataloging-in-Publication Data

Merklinger, Philip M., 1954–
    Philosophy, theology, and Hegel's Berlin philosophy of religion,
1821–1827 / Philip M. Merklinger.
      p.   cm.
    Includes bibliographical references and index.
    ISBN 0–7914–1491–4 (hc : acid free) : ISBN
0–7914–1492–2 (pb : acid free)
    1. Hegel, Georg Wilhelm Friedrich, 1770–1831—Contributions in
philosophy of religion. 2. Religion—Philosophy—History—19th
century. I. Title.
B2949.R3M47   1993
200'.1—dc20   92–25807
                                               CIP

10 9 8 7 6 5 4 3 2 1

In memory of my brother,
Thomas Ross Merklinger (1948–1988),
who introduced me to the world of philosophy.

Human being is a cloak, which often a god throws around himself....

FRIEDRICH HÖLDERLIN, HYPERION

C O N T E N T S

A C K N O W L E D G M E N T S

I would like to thank my friend and wife, Margaret Holliston, and my friend Sean Kelly for the many fruitful discussions of Hegel we have had over the years. My thanks also go to my son, Thomas, and my daughter, Emily, who keep reminding me that "man's maturity is to have the seriousness of a child at play." Also, I express my appreciation to a number of persons who have deeply influenced my thinking: William Abbott, David Carr, Deborah Cook, Benoit Garceau, Theodore Geraets, Fred Little, Terry Males, and, especially, José Huertas-Jourda. I am very grateful to Chris Jensen McCloy for her work in the preparation of the manuscript. Without all her effort, time, expertise, and generosity, this book would not have been completed. Lastly, I offer my thanks to the editors at SUNY Press, and, in particular, Dana Foote, for the meticulous care in preparing the manuscript for publication.

RELATION OF THE PHILOSOPHY
OF RELIGION TO THEOLOGY

G entlemen! The object of these lectures is the philosophy of religion...."[1] Until Hegel wrote these words in
his 1821 lecture manuscript for his *Vorlesungen über die Philosophie
der Religion*, the lines of inquiry into religion and its knowledge of
God pursued throughout the Christian era of Western civilization
had not been unified under one simple rubric. Of course, twentieth-
century practitioners of the philosophy of religion do find the enterprise of the philosophy of religion implicit in the thinking of
philosophers before Hegel. They include such diverse thinkers as
David Hume, Benedict Spinoza, Immanuel Kant, St. Thomas
Aquinas, and St. Augustine. However, twentieth-century philosophers of religion acknowledge that there is a distinct difference
between the 'philosophy of religion' circumscribed by and within
Christian metaphysics prior to the Protestant Reformation and the
philosophy of religion implicit in post-Reformation and Enlightenment natural theology.

The 'Classical' philosophy of religion of pre-Reformation Christian thinking viewed philosophy as the handmaiden of theology,
and, as such, philosophy was considered capable of knowledge of
God through reason as long as its knowledge of God complemented,
not contradicted, the knowledge of God disclosed by faith and revelation. Thus, Classical philosophy of religion abided by an overriding hermeneutical principle: the mode of discourse employed by
philosophy in its reasoning could be 'natural'; that is, the purely

human mode of thinking about God that reasons from human being to God, unaided by revelation, could render the true speech about God and his universe as long as it was grounded in the recognition of the ontological priority of the true speech about God already disclosed through the revelatory discourse of biblical theology.[2]

After the Protestant Reformation, the hermeneutics of the knowledge of God and the universe shifted, with Enlightenment thinkers placing the discourse of natural, purely human reason before revelatory discourse as that which is most able to disclose the truth of the universe and its Creator. Freed of the restraints of the traditions of revealed theology, Enlightenment thinkers emulated the ahistorical objectivity of geometrical reasoning (e.g., Descartes, Spinoza), locating their cognition of the empirical world as the measure of all that is to be considered knowledge. This new philosophy of religion or 'natural theology'[3] pursued its reflection about God and religion by distinguishing its method of thinking from that of revealed theology. Spinoza, for example, stresses that the "end in view" of the *Theologico-Political Treatise* is "to separate Philosophy from Theology."[4] Note that Spinoza calls the treatise a 'theological' work thereby locating it within the horizon of meaning of the theological sphere; nevertheless, his emphasis on the primacy of (geometric) reason means that he will subsume the content of the 'theological' into his philosophy and redefine its content accordingly. In this way, religion, and its knowledge of God, becomes a moment in the overall horizon of meaning called *philosophy*. Moreover, philosophy freely exercised what it considered its 'natural right' to determine the conditions of the possibility of knowledge of God by the 'natural light of reason' in the form of a rationally deduced natural theology. This is most obvious in the work of Christian Wolff, who basically disavowed the legitimacy of any revelation that went against the standards of authenticity legislated by autonomous and objectively certain reasoning.[5] Thus, for Enlightenment thinkers like Wolff, religion itself, its form and content, was also open to rational and critical scrutiny by philosophy.

Although philosophy continued to reflect on the notion of God in the form of natural theology, faith, as revealed theology's ground for the methodological resolution of questions of ultimate concern, was thought to lead only to objective uncertainty and paradox. Reason, on the other hand, was believed to be capable of setting aside and transcending the limitation of the contingencies of individual experiences of faith and the prejudices of the tradition that fostered and nurtured these faith experiences.[6] But, it was not until the 1781 publication of Immanuel Kant's *Critique of Pure Reason* that the bifurcation of philosophy and revealed theology, reason and faith, was fully articulated thereby setting the theoretical parameters in which any future philosophical treatment of religion could take place.

For Kant, the primary task of his first *Critique* was to develop a "system of concepts" that "is occupied not so much with objects as with the mode of knowledge of objects insofar as this mode of knowledge is to be possible *a priori*."[7] This 'turn to the subject', and the modes of intuition and categories of the understanding inherent in the subject, limits the way in which questions about God can be addressed. Indeed, Kant demonstrated that fundamental principles of both revealed and natural theology—such as God, immortality of the soul, and free will—are not 'modes of knowledge' insofar as they are not verifiable by empirical observation. Rather, claims about God, immortality, freedom, and so forth, invariably result in antinomies, that is, contradictory conclusions that are equally reasonable and logically derived. Therefore, Kant states that his purpose in the *Critique* is to "deny *Knowledge* [of God, immortality, and freedom] in order to make room for *faith*."[8]

Both the development of the Enlightenment version of natural theology and Kant's "critical" way of saving religion for faith meant that by the time Hegel composed his lecture manuscript on the philosophy of religion in 1821, philosophy and revealed theology had become polarized into antagonistic and mutually exclusive forms of addressing claims about God and religion. Therefore, Hegel continues his opening remarks by noting that his 1821 philosophy of religion "in general has the same purpose as the earlier type of metaphysical science, which is called *theologia naturalis*. This term included everything that could be known of God by reason alone, as distinct from a positive, revealed religion, a religion that is known from some source other than reason."[9] Although his philosophy of religion has the "same purpose" as Enlightenment natural theology, Hegel distinguished his philosophy of religion from natural theology by treating religion and its knowledge of God as found in *theology in general* as his object for philosophical reflection, and not, as natural theology had done, God as he is in himself. In this way, Hegel anticipated the approach to the philosophy of religion found in twentieth-century Anglo-American analytic philosophy. This version of the philosophy of religion is predominantly a "second-order activity, standing at one remove from its subject matter....It seeks to analyze concepts such as God, holy, salvation, worship, creation, sacrifice, eternal life, etc., and to determine the nature of religious utterances in comparison with those of everyday life, scientific discovery, morality, and the imaginative expressions of the arts."[10] We will see this borne out throughout our discussion of Hegel's philosophy of religion, particularly in the tone of the lectures in general, and, especially, in the philosophy of theology that we will discover in the 1824 and 1827 lectures.

Important, for our present considerations, we must realize that Hegel knows that he, as a post-Kantian philosopher, cannot consider God as an object for philosophical contemplation without first contemplating that aspect of being human in which thought of God first arises, that is, human religious experience. Therefore, Hegel shifts his attention from God as solely an object of thought as found in natural theology to God as an objective correlate of the religious experience of human subjects. Thus, for the first time in the history of the development of the philosophical inquiry into the content of religion, a philosopher undertook a conceptual grasp of religion *as a complete modality of human experience in itself*,[11] the inner horizon of which is a concatenation of both 'nonrational' human feeling and reason: "This is the region in which all the riddles of the world, all the contradictions of thought, are resolved, and all griefs are healed, the region of eternal truth and eternal peace, of absolute satisfaction, of truth itself."[12]

Furthermore, Hegel noted that all thinking, including both the Classical philosophy of religion and Enlightenment theology, *is grounded in a common object, God*: "All that proceeds from thought— all the distinctions of the arts and sciences and of the eternal interweavings of human relationships, habits and customs, activities, skills, and enjoyments—find their ultimate centre in the *one* thought of God. God is the beginning of all things and the end of all things; [everything] starts from God and returns to God."[13]

Hegel could have followed his Enlightenment predecessors by separating philosophy and theology, reason and religion, into theoretically incompatible domains; but, because of this shared object, Hegel chose not to limit his philosophical treatment of religion by excluding certain vital components of religion, such as faith, doctrines, and tradition, as "nonrational" and hence, as unworthy of philosophical explication. Rather, God is to be explicated as the beginning and the end of all human being in the world, both in terms of thought and concrete action and, as such, must be explicated as the source or genesis of all human horizons of meaning, of all human world-views. Consequently, at the end of the last major division of the 1821 lecture series, Part Three, "The Consummate Religion," in which Hegel philosophically displays the truth of the content of the Christian religion, he stresses that philosophy *should* conceive of religion as reconciled with reason through philosophy. "Instead [of allowing] reason and religion to contradict themselves, [we must] resolve the discord in the manner [appropriate] to us— [namely,] reconciliation in [the form of] philosophy."[14]

In stating that religion and reason must be seen as reconciled in and through philosophy, Hegel moves beyond the conceptual limitations of the pre-Kantian and Kantian Enlightenment philosophical framework in which, as we have noted, religion was treated 'within the limits of reason alone', while, at the same time, acknowledging that conflict will still be present: "How the present day is to solve its problems must be left up to it. In philosophy itself [the resolution is only] partial. These lectures have attempted to offer guidance to this end."[15]

The reason that this resolution will be partial is not only due to the limitations of the Enlightenment philosophical understanding of the contents of religion and theology. Just as important is the manner in which theology came to understand itself. Indeed, post-Reformation theology did not remain unaffected by the developments in the relations between philosophy and theology. One of the key factors in this development was that many of the theologians were also philosophers[16] and thus either consciously or unconsciously submitted their theology to the rationalistic standards of Enlightenment philosophy. For some theologians, the rational questioning of the fundamental tenets of faith and doctrines of orthodox Christianity lead to an outright abandonment of faith as the ground of their theologizing, and in its place they substituted *rational theology*.[17] For other theologians, the application of reason to articles of belief and creed lead to strident reaffirmation of orthodoxy and the authority of the clergy in the form of *scholasticism*.[18] For still other theologians, the Enlightenment tendency toward favoring reason over faith lead to a renewed emphasis on the Reformation's focus on the individual's personal relationship with God. This last form, *Pietism*, rejected reason in favor of "existential participation" and feeling.[19]

Although Hegel offered these lectures on the philosophy of religion as a "guide" to the reconciliation of reason and religion, it is clear by the tone of frustration and sadness at the end of the 1821 lectures on "The Consummate Religion" that the majority of philosophers and theologians contemporary to Hegel could not conceive of, let alone enact, this reconciliation. Indeed, as a direct result of events that took place between the composition and delivery of the 1821 and 1827 lectures on the philosophy of religion—events we will be examining in greater depth in relation to the 1824 and 1827 lectures[20]—Hegel identified Enlightenment and Pietism, respectively, as the two forms of knowledge of God that continue to perpetuate the mutual exclusivity of philosophy and theology.[21] Moreover, Hegel observed that the antagonism between Enlightenment philosophy and Pietism is such that they are not only directly against each other but also opposed to the doctrines of orthodox Christianity and, hence, as we will see, against speculative philosophy.

Obviously conscious of the continuing disaffection and hostility between Enlightenment philosophy and Pietism, Hegel follows up his identification of God as the common object of all thinking with this pronouncement: "philosophy is theology, and one's occupation with philosophy—or rather in philosophy—is of itself the service of God."[22]

Both the statement of equivalence between philosophy and theology in the opening phrase and the declaration of philosophy as "the service of God" has given rise to much debate among post-Hegelian thinkers. At no time was the controversy more heated than in the division of Hegelians into Left and Right schools in the decade following Hegel's death.[23] This left-right factionalism exhibits how diverse interpretations of Hegel can be, with the atheistic Left announcing that Hegel had brought religion to an end and the theistic Right proclaiming the preservation and vindication of the doctrines of Christianity. Indeed, this division of Hegelianism parallels the weight a Hegelian can give to either side of the statement "philosophy is theology." Thus, Left Hegelians, such as Ludwig Feuerbach, D. F. Strauss, Bruno Bauer, and the young Karl Marx, emphasized the subject side, 'philosophy', to the detriment of revealed theology by desacralizing and demythologizing all things religious; whereas Right Hegelians, such as Philipp Marheineke and Karl Daub, stress the predicate by maintaining that the content of revealed religion was 'revitalized' by Hegel's philosophy.[24]

Recent trends in interpreting Hegel's philosophy of religion range from the Right, theistic positions developed in recent works like Quentin Lauer's *Hegel's Concept of God* and James Yerkes's *The Christology of Hegel*, include the more centralist positions presented at the Wofford Symposium on the philosophy of religion, held in 1967, and extend to the more 'Left'-leaning, "new orthodoxy"[25] found in a work like R. Williamson's *Introduction to Hegel's Philosophy of Religion,* which presents Hegel as a 'panentheist'. In short, to cover the various emphases placed on the relationship between philosophy and theology since Hegel's time up to and including the present, would require a new phenomenology of Spirit, a phenomenological mapping out of the complete journey of Hegel's thought through successive and coexisting communities of people who attempt to interpret Hegel. Because this task lies outside of the scope of this inquiry into Hegel's philosophy of religion, we need to set aside the various traditions of Hegel's interpretation and clarify for ourselves in what way "one's occupation with philosophy" can be construed as the "service of God."

The clue to comprehending what Hegel means by this statement lies in what, following K. Luther and J. L. Hoover, can be called Hegel's *phenomenology of religion:* "In its main lines, therefore, Hegel's approach to the philosophy of religion follows what could be described as a phenomenological method."[26] However, we must be careful to distinguish Hegel's phenomenological method from that practiced in the twentieth century by Edmund Husserl and Martin Heidegger, although Hegel can be said to foreshadow both Husserl's and Heidegger's versions of the method.[27]

Inspired by Husserl and Heidegger, twentieth-century practitioners of the phenomenological approach focus their attention on religious experience. Although religious experience can be seen as a sterile field of inquiry for philosophy because of its supposedly personal and private nature, phenomenologists start with religious experience precisely because they want to describe religion from the 'inside' to 'light up', as Heidegger would say, its internal features as an existential modality. Following Husserl, phenomenological description of the inner, lived experience of religion is made possible through the recognition of the intentionality of consciousness, that is, that consciousness is always consciousness of something. Therefore, for Husserl, the phenomenological method is a cognitive process that attempts to 'see' the 'things themselves' (*die Sache selbst*) to ground knowledge of these 'things'—that is, all phenomena which lie within the field of consciousness—apodictically while 'bracketing off' any question of their ontological nature. On the other hand, Heidegger disregards Husserl's epistemological concern and the Cartesian dualism of subject and object implied by the notion of intentionality by undertaking a "fundamental ontology" on the basis of the "existential analysis of Dasein," the being whose being is an 'issue' for itself.[28] In this way, human existence itself becomes that which is to be described. Also, there is what we can call a *generic* form of the phenomenological method, which does not adhere to the methodological restraints of Husserl or Heidegger, but does follow the methodological orientation that both Husserl and Heidegger share inasmuch as it strives to be descriptive, analytical, and empathetic in its attempt to come up with provisional 'generalizations' about the structures of religious experience.[29]

Central to all three phenomenological methods is the desire to set aside or put into abeyance (*epoché*) all presuppositions or the "encrustations of the metaphysical tradition"[30] to describe the 'things themselves'. Hegel's phenomenological method does not attempt such an '*epoché*'; rather, Hegel wants to illuminate "from within" the presuppositions and the "encrustations" that accrue to human experience through religion. However, when it comes to elucidating matters that are not embedded within our own lived experience, Hegel will seek to "understand from within" (*hineinverstehen*), a procedure we can describe as similar to the twentieth century's 'generic' phenomenology of religion insofar as it 'intellectually empathizes' with the view held by those who hold such a 'form of life' (*Gestalt*).[31]

Prior to the 1821 lectures, Hegel's phenomenological approach is best exemplified in the 1807 *Phenomenology of Spirit*. In the *Phenomenology*, Hegel displays religion in terms of the journey of consciousness to absolute knowing. Religious consciousness is the penultimate stage in this journey. As the penultimate stage, religion has not fully realized nor comprehended its own truth. For Hegel, religion contains truth *implicitly* because it thinks in terms of "representations" (or "pictures") (*Vorstellungen*):

> So far as Spirit in religion *pictures* itself to itself, it is indeed consciousness, and the reality enclosed within religion is the shape and guise of its picture-thinking. But, in this picture-thinking, reality does not receive its perfect due, viz. to be not

merely a guise but an independent free existence; and, conversely, because it lacks perfection within itself it is a *specific* shape which does not attain to what it ought to show forth, viz. Spirit that is conscious of itself. If its shape is to express Spirit itself, it must be nothing else than Spirit, and Spirit must appear to itself, or be in actuality what it is in its essence.[32]

In the lectures on the philosophy of religion, as we will see, the definition of *religion* differs from lecture series to lecture series, but religion itself, as that which 'encloses reality', is not only retained but is described consistently through the various prefaces in a manner almost identical to the 1821 formulation, which we quoted earlier.

Hence, in both the *Phenomenology* and the philosophy of religion lecture series, Hegel clearly identifies religious consciousness as the shape of consciousness that, in a genetic breakdown of the constitutive moments of consciousness, is the primordially integrated shape of consciousness. Therefore, religious consciousness is the mode of consciousness in which the notion of a self-contained totality first makes its appearance.

The gathering in of all aspects of lived experience takes place within religious consciousness through a posited center, God. Within this center, meaning structures are derived in the form of religious representations (*Vorstellungen*) which allow consciousness to grasp the world as a thematic unity. Representation not only buttresses this center, but is the active medium through which religious consciousness constitutes the 'world'.

Historically, this penultimate level forms around different centers that, in turn, generate unique, entire, content-rich, thematic fields. Both the *Phenomenology* and the lectures on the philosophy of religion depict the various religions of humankind as successive and coexisting shapes (*Gestalten*) of religious consciousness. These shapes appear as 'bursts of light' on the stage of world history. Understood successively, these bursts of light reflect the deepening awareness that consciousness has of itself as it progresses on what Mark C. Taylor describes as its "journey to selfhood."[33]

In each of these shapes of religious consciousness, the burst of light is localized and limited to particular and exclusive communities. The absolute or consummate form of religious consciousness arrives with the advent of Christianity. Christianity transcends all localized, culturally limited forms of religious consciousness with its claims to universality. From this absolute shape of religious consciousness, philosophy arises in its absolute form. Prior to this shape, philosophy was subservient to religion, articulating itself from within a particular shape of religious consciousness. But with the establishment of the Christian religion as the consummation of religious consciousness, philosophy gains the possibility of knowing the absolute. Christianity provides philosophy with access to the absolute itself through reflection on its center, Jesus Christ, who, as the incarnation of God in human form, displays the tripersonality of God, that is, the Trinity.

Most significant for Hegel's phenomenology is that through reflection on this trinitarian God, Spirit becomes self-conscious of itself as Spirit. Indeed, the entire *Phenomenology* is itself the subject matter of Spirit knowing itself as Spirit in what Hegel calls absolute knowing. In this way, absolute knowing is a self-referential, self-articulating, and self-comprehending, all-embracing totality. As such, Spirit's self-knowing affirms the prior stages depicted within the *Phenomenology* as necessary moments of its own appearance.

But, as we can see, Hegel was not yet employing the speculative method of the *Encyclopaedia of the Philosophical Sciences* and hence of his scientific system in which the explication of religion as the moment of absolute Spirit just prior to philosophy is pursued through the philosophy of religion. The thinking-through of the gradual process of development of religious consciousness into scientific, systematic knowing is also carried out in the philosophy of religion but from the point of view of an already achieved absolute knowing. As Hegel observes in the 1824 lectures: "The content is certainly *spirit* in general; the elaboration of what spirit is forms the entire content of the philosophy of religion. The different levels at which spirit is intellectualized give rise to the different religions.... This diversity of determinacy comes about as the different levels are constituted."[34] Thus, from the vantage point of absolute knowing the patterns of religious consciousness are the determinate structures of the spirituality of Spirit. And, of course, these concrete structures are to be unfolded in their determinacy 'from within'. But, the already achieved standpoint of absolute knowing distinguishes the speculative method from the phenomenological method. Indeed, as the absolute standpoint is presupposed in the philosophy of religion, then the initial task of the philosophy of religion is to present religion in its most logical and abstract form, that is, under the framework of the concept:

> It [the concept] appears as the external form grounded in spirit,
> the differences being posited within it in a determinate form
> that is at the same time an altogether simple universal, logical
> form. This form is consequently what is abstract. But this form
> is not only the external shell of this determinate spirit but also,
> as the logical element, its innermost kernel as the determinacy
> of what is inward. It combines both within itself—being the
> innermost kernel, the determinacy of what is most inward, and
> at the same time the outward form: this is the nature of the con-
> cept, to be essential and at the same time the mode of appear-
> ance, the mode of difference or of form.[35]

In this way, the concept of religion is the "outward form" that then
mirrors the inner content of religious consciousness. At the same
time, because absolute knowing develops within and arises out of
religious consciousness, it is also the "innermost kernel" of consciousness. This notion of the simultaneous 'inward' and 'outward'
forms of speculative thinking makes its first appearance in the Preface to the *Phenomenology*, where Hegel specifies that "scientific
form" is not only the nature of the project of the *Phenomenology*, but
its goal.[36] Thus, by going through the process of its own development Spirit grasps that the phenomenology of Spirit is to be understood both in the genitive sense; that is, that the activity of "phenom-
enologizing" is the source and 'possessor' of Spirit (*phenomenology* of
Spirit) and in the substantive sense—that is, phenomenology is inte-
grally Spirit's own concrete existence (phenomenology of *Spirit*, i.e.,
Spirit's generation of itself through its phenomenology of itself).[37]
Consequently, it is apparent that for Hegel the phenomenological
method "flips over" into the speculative method at the end of the
journey of consciousness through its experience when Spirit comes
to know itself as Spirit. At the same time, this turning over of phenomenology into speculation also means that this stance is to be presupposed from the very beginning (as evidenced by the speculative
nature of the Preface to the *Phenomenology*). Insofar as the 'concept
of religion' too has both this inward and outward forms, then it too
can be understood in a manner similar to the *Phenomenology of
Spirit*; that is, the turning over of the phenomenological method into
the speculative method in the concept of religion has to be understood as the result of religion's conceptualization of itself being carried through to its consummation in the conceptualization of reli-

gion from the point of view of speculative philosophy. Thus, the concept of religion can be understood in the genitive sense; that is, as the activity of humanity raising itself to God and the concept (the phenomenological side), and in the substantive sense; that is, the concept is God achieving self-consciousness in religion (the speculative side).

Now that we have a general picture of Hegel's methodological orientation in these lectures on the philosophy of religion, it is possible for us to interpret the phrase *philosophy is theology* as pointing to this outer-inner relationship found between the concept of religion and the actual content of the various determinate religions. Philosophy itself, through its ability to conceptualize religion, is the 'outer shell' that holds within its comprehensive embrace the inner content of theology, which articulates in representational thinking the content of religion. However, as we noted in our discussion of pre-Reformation and post-Reformation philosophy of religion, philosophy is also the 'inner kernel' that arises within and out of theological articulations of religious belief. We can best support this interpretation by directly examining the equation *philosophy is theology* in light of speculative thinking and, specifically, in light of Hegel's account of the speculative sentence as found in the Preface to the *Phenomenology*.

According to Hegel, a speculative sentence (or "philosophical proposition")[38] is a sentence or statement in which the subject and predicate not only refer to logical categories or universals but also articulate both the identity and distinctiveness of the two referents in a way not found in a normal sentence. Unlike a normal sentence, both terms of the speculative sentence are to be comprehended as subject terms that mutually determine each other's meaning through a "dialectical movement" between the terms themselves and also between the human subject thinking the relations between the two terms and himself or herself. Hegel contrasts this internal movement of meaning with how traditional logic understands a normal sentence. In a typical, nonspeculative sentence, a subject term (*apple*) is joined to a predicate term (*red*) through the copula is—the apple is red—in such a way that the subject is considered as the only subject term, as a fixed and isolated entity to which attributes can be assigned. Therefore, in our example, the subject *apple* denotes a particular thing and the predicate term *red* designates some attribute this thing is said to have. Quite simply then, a normal sentence asserts that a particular thing has a specific attribute. But, in the Preface, Hegel displays how a speculative sentence overcomes this traditional understanding by giving two examples, "God is being" (*Gott ist das Sein*) and "the actual is the universal" (*das Wirkliche ist das Allgemeine*):

> To illustrate what has been said: in the proposition 'God is being', the Predicate is 'being'; it has the significance of something substantial in which the Subject is dissolved. 'Being' is here meant to be not a Predicate, but rather the essence; it seems, consequently, that God ceases to be what he is from his position in the proposition, viz. a fixed Subject. Here thinking, instead of making progress in the transition from Subject to Predicate, in reality feels itself checked by the loss of the Subject, and, missing it, is thrown back on to the thought of the Subject. Or, since the Predicate itself has been expressed as a Subject, as *the* being or the *essence* which exhausts the nature of the Subject, thinking finds the Subject immediately in the Predicate; and now <having returned into itself in the Predicate,> instead of being in a position where it has freedom for argument, it is still absorbed in the content, or at least is faced with the demand that it should be. Similarly, too, when one says: 'the *actual* is the *universal*', the actual as subject disappears in its Predicate.[39]

As Hegel shows, it is now possible to view the two terms as undergoing a progressively developing modification of meaning, a modification or dialectical redefinition of meaning that takes place in the thinking of the subject. Consequently, the thinking subject grasps both the grammatical identity of the two terms of the speculative sentence (as implied by the copula) and the conceptual identity of the identity and difference of the two terms: "in the philosophical proposition the identification of Subject and Predicate is not meant to destroy the distinction between them, which the form of the proposition expresses; their unity, rather, is meant to emerge as a harmony."[40] But, when applying Hegel's notion of the speculative sentence to the philosophical proposition *philosophy is theology*, we have to be careful not to confuse the possibility of the unity and harmony of the subject, *philosophy*, with its predicate *theology* as already a fait accompli and merely posit the identity of philosophy and theology.[41] Therefore, we must "test" this proposition to display how, in fact, the terms have and do mutually define each other. Stephen Houlgate, in his recent *Hegel, Nietzsche and the Critique of Metaphysics,* suggests such a test: "The way to test speculative sentences, therefore, is to examine whether the predicate does actually render explicit what is implied in the subject, and whether the redefinition of the subject does actually follow from the identity of the categories."[42]

In light of this test we can ask, Is this statement *philosophy is theology* truly a speculative sentence? Or, to use the terms of Houlgate's test, does the predicate *theology* "actually render what is implied by the subject" and does "the redefinition of the subject...actually follow from the identity of the categories"? The answer is yes on both accounts if we recall the progressive modification of the interrelation of philosophy and theology in the history of the philosophy of the religion that we depicted earlier in this chapter. It is safe to assume that both Classical philosophy and the Enlightenment philosophy of religion interpret the relation between philosophy and theology according to the understanding of traditional formal logic. Classical philosophy of religion, as we have noted, thinks the meaning of *philosophy* is subsumed under the predicate term so that the predicate term is treated as the real subject, in effect inverting the meaning of the statement. In this way, the initial subject term "dissolves" as the primary focus of meaning in the sentence. After Classical philosophy of religion's exposition of theology as the primary subject of human thought, attention shifted back to the initial subject term (*philosophy*). Enlightenment philosophy of religion, as we observed, relocated philosophy as the loci of meaning in the relations between philosophy and theology, consequently subsuming *theology* under the modified meaning of *philosophy.* Now, with Hegel, we will have to see how this dialectical shifting and modification of meaning is mediated within his speculative philosophy of religion.

Therefore, the following study will elucidate the fundamental role Hegel's reflection on theological reflection plays in the formation of his mature philosophy of religion. Our method, however, will not take sides in the "Left-Right" debate nor will we attempt to blend Hegel's philosophy with the leading theology of his time; rather, we will undertake an empathetic description and analysis of the progressive unfolding of Hegel's mediation of theology and philosophy in the 1821, 1824, and 1827 lectures on the philosophy of religion and his Foreword to Hermann Friedrick Wilhelmm Hinrichs's *Die Religion im inneren Verhältnisse zur Wissenschaft*. Our basic thesis is that a full realization of the identity and difference implied in the speculative statement *philosophy is theology* takes place only when the assumed harmony of philosophy and theology is disrupted by the renewal of their bifurcation in the contemporary life of the religious community. We will see that this disruption comes from two sources: Friedrich Schleiermacher and his theology of feeling as found in the 1822 *Der christliche Glaube nach den Grundsätzen der evangelischen Kirche im Zusammenhange dargestellt*, and Friedrich Tholuck, who charges Hegel with pantheism just prior to 1827. To lay out the parameters of Hegel's conceptualization of religion prior to these theological challenges, Chapter One will show that Hegel takes philosophy and theology to differ only in terms of tone and mode of reflection, that is, in form not content, in the 1821 *Concept of Religion*'s comprehensive description of religious consciousness, from its genesis in religious sensibility to its sublation in conceptual cognition. With this ground set, Chapter Two will present Schleiermacher's *Der christliche Glaube* as differing from Hegel's philosophy not only in form but also in content, through its detailed rendering of a description of religious consciousness within the limits of the feeling of dependence alone. As a consequence of this renewed fissure between philosophy and theology, we will detail in Chapter Three how Hegel, in his Foreword to Hinrichs's *Religionsphilosophie*, depicts Schleiermacher as misunderstanding the pivotal interconnection of thinking and feeling in faith, an interconnection that gives rise to the witness of religious community to its own truth as Spirit and that is then confirmed as such by philosophy.[43] Chapter Four will display how Hegel, through redefining the concept of religion in light of the Foreword's insights, inaugurates both a second-order philosophy of theology and a tentative reconciliation of philosophy and theology in the 1824 "Introduction" to the *Concept of Religion*. In Chapter Five, we will display how Hegel counters Tholuck's charges of pantheism both in the 1827 *Concept of Religion* and in his speculative mirroring and subjectification of the contents of the 1827 *Consummate Religion* within the trinitarian form of the philosophy of religion. As well, we will see that this successful harmonization of philosophical form and theological content confirms that the reconciliation tentatively achieved in 1824 is now fully realized. We will conclude our study by confirming that the fissure between philosophy and theology, like that between all oppositions, is a necessary moment in the process of philosophizing about religion, a fissure that philosophy both enters into and overcomes to confirm its own truth. In this way, we will see that the "encrustations" of meaning embedded in theological reflection and religious consciousness become the signposts and spurs for philosophy's comprehension of religion and of itself.

Chapter One

THE 1821 *CONCEPT OF RELIGION*

Introduction

Hegel commences his philosophical conceptualization of religion by identifying God as the *object* of his thought. Because philosophy and theology have this object of thought in common, they also share a certain reflective tone insofar as both philosophy and theology have as their aim and purpose to explicate knowledge of God. Indeed, both Hegel's philosophy and theology do not attempt to entice their audience into religious feeling or to convert them to a certain belief system. Therefore, in the Introduction to the 1821 manuscript, *Concept of Religion*, Hegel deliberately and self-consciously states:

> First of all, the most definite consciousness regarding our aim must [be] this: that the religion present and presupposed in everyone is the stuff we merely want to comprehend. It is not [for us to] seek to produce this foundation; rather this is what must be explicitly present in everyone. <It is not a question of bringing something substantially new and alien into humanity.> That would be like trying to introduce spirit into a dog by letting it see spiritual creations, or eat witty remarks, or chew on printed matter; or like trying to make a blind person see by talking to that person about colours. Those who have never enlarged their hearts <beyond the bustle of finite life,> or looked into the

17

> pure aether of the soul with enjoyment, who have not felt the joy
> and peace of the eternal, <even if only dimly in the form of
> yearning,> do not possess the stuff that we here speak of. They
> may perhaps have an image of it, but the content is not their own
> thing; it is an alien matter they are wrestling with.[1]

In this passage, it is clear that Hegel is emphasizing the importance of having religious experience as the phenomenological ground for—and to help flesh out—the philosophy of religion. Religious experience must be the starting point of a philosophical discussion of religion;[2] but, at the same time, it is also clear that Hegel wants to keep philosophical conceptualization of religion distinct from religion and religious experience. In effect, philosophy, in its speculative mode of mirroring, has no need to existentially recreate within itself the subjective content of religion. Thus, in formulating the *Concept of Religion*, speculative philosophy *presupposes* this content; it will acknowledge that the knowledge of God can originate only in the sphere of religious consciousness. Furthermore, philosophy will recognize that the immediacy of feeling originating within religious consciousness is mediated first by reflection, and second, this reflection on religion is itself mediated by the conceptual thinking of philosophy.

Important, then, philosophical conceptualization for Hegel means a difference in *form*. However, at the same time, it is the main concern of his speculative philosophy to have the form of the concept match the content of the religious dimension of human awareness. The difficulty inherent in this speculative task is far more important than whether individual human subjects *continually feel* the truth of religion in their lives—an issue we will see Hegel directly confront in relation to Pietism in the 1827 lectures. Religious feeling, and the devotion arising out of it, may be the originary moments that allow for the possibility for the reflective thinking about God of both theology and philosophy, but both philosophy and theology extend far beyond this primary upsurge of feeling in their discursiveness. Nevertheless, it is important for us to note that Hegel contends that the worship that was once solely heart-felt adoration of God need not be considered as totally separate from thought about God. Indeed, *intellectual worship*, that is, the contemplation of God, is the continuation and transformation of what was originally felt in the medium of systematic thinking:

For religion, in which God is for consciousness initially an external object—because we must first be taught what God is and
how he has revealed himself and still does—occupies itself, it is
true, with the interior, moves and inspires the community. Still
the interiority of devotion limited to emotion and representation
is not the highest form of interiority. It is self-determining *thinking* which has to be recognized as this purest form of knowing. It
is in this that science brings the same content to consciousness
and thus becomes that spiritual worship which, by systematic
thinking, appropriates and comprehends what is otherwise only
the content of subjective sentiment or representation.[3]

Thus, what was originally 'interior' (e.g., my particular feeling
of God) becomes even more internalized by being lifted up into 'self-
determining thinking' without losing its sense of adoration. This is
possible because, as we discussed in the Introduction, religion is a
complete modality of human being, embracing both feeling and
thought, although in the form of representation. Philosophy, then,
when it reflects on religious consciousness, retains its content while
placing this content into the self-enclosed embrace of self-consciousness. This means that the worship originating in feeling and
expressed in representation is now an internal determination of self-
consciousness and is appreciated as such. Ultimately, as we shall see
in Chapter Four, this interiority of speculative thinking's comprehension of 'subjective sentiments and representations' becomes the
'witness of Spirit', a religious representation itself lifted up and transfigured by philosophy.

It is important for our present discussion to recognize that it is
also possible that just as religious feeling and faith fade and are
either forgotten or renewed in feeling or in thought or in both,
thought and contemplation of God may allow faith to evaporate as
unimportant and inessential to activity. Therefore, intellectual worship achieves its thought-filled 'adoration' of God only when it holds
its thought of God within itself by articulating its knowledge of God
to itself. Thus, as articulation of what is "held within," intellectual
worship reaches its consummation in a philosophy of religion that is
both self-conscious and conscious of the knowledge of God that has
been expressed in religion through ritual and doctrine.

For the most part, theology would agree with Hegel. Hegel's
task is to articulate conceptually what is already experienced in reli-

gion and, therefore, self-consciously construct this articulation into a philosophy of religion. Although theology does not emphasize conceptualization in the philosophically self-conscious sense that we find in Hegel's speculative philosophy, it does attempt to articulate a certain understanding of Christian religious experience.

Articulation in both the philosophical sense of Hegel and the theological sense predominant in Christianity should be distinguished from religious articulation that attempts to *edify*. Religious articulation that attempts to edify its readers has to be *indirect*, employing a hermeneutic that takes into account the reader-text relationship. In edifying works, like Kierkegaard's pseudonymous writings, for example, the author does not simply present 'truth'. Rather, the author forges a style and tone that will induce the reader into an existential encounter with the text. On the other hand, Christian theology and Hegel's philosophy of religion are more concerned with displaying a cogent, systematic picture of their subject matter. Therefore, the tension between the style and tone of writing and the reader inherent in a work of edification is not a concern for the theologian or for Hegel.

Paul Tillich summed up the purpose of Christian theology in this way: "Theology, as a function of the Christian church, must serve the needs of the church. A theological system is supposed to satisfy two basic needs: the statement of the truth of the Christian message and the interpretation of this truth for every new generation."[4]

For Hegel, the relation of philosophical conceptualization of religion to the religious feeling of the individual subject is to be comprehended in a similar manner:

> It may happen that religion is awakened in the soul through the philosophical cognition of it, and that religious feeling arise in a person thus; but this is not necessary, and it is not itself the aim of philosophy—<not what is called edification, which is the aim of preaching, directed to the heart, to the singularity of the subject, as this one person>. Philosophy does, of course, have to develop and represent the necessity of religion in and for itself, to comprehend that spirit advances and must advance from the other modes of its willing, imagining, and feeling to this its absolute mode. <[Its] necessity [is] that it is the destiny and the truth of spirit.> But it is a different task to raise the individual subject to this height.[5]

As we can see, Hegel's tone is the same as that of theology insofar as he, too, will present eternal truth directly, but *in philosophical form*. However, unlike theology and in keeping with the main motif of Enlightenment thinkers like Spinoza and Kant, Hegel delineates the difference between his mode of reflection and religious thinking. Indeed, Hegel asserts, his philosophical stance is that of reason, but unlike the Enlightenment philosophies and theologians in general, his use of reason is comprehensive reason [*Vernunft*] and as such, grasps religion as total unity unto itself. In this way, Hegel does not set reason over and against faith.

Moreover, as we noted in the Introduction, in this region or modality of human consciousness, we find that all thinking is grounded in and centered around thought about God. Hence, God is the horizon of meaning in which *all* world-views, not just the Christian world-view, are constructed. Hence, against the backdrop of this absolute horizon, the self enters into the existential modality of worship and passes over its finitude, finding "eternal rest" in a "perpetual Sunday": "In this intuition and feeling, we are not concerned with ourselves, our vanity, our pride of knowledge and of conduct, but with only the content of it—proclaiming the honour *of God* and manifesting *his* glory."[6]

By focusing the attention of the finite human subject away from the concerns and cares about self in the everyday world, consciousness of God engenders a relation of the finite human subject with an object present to human consciousness as infinite and divine or absolutely "Other"; that is, a transcendent, objectively real and eternal being, whose presence is made known to us but whose ways are ultimately inscrutable. (As such, in no way can this 'Other' be confused with the world or with other human beings or creatures.) Insofar as this relation appears *within* the awareness of the finite human subject, it presents itself to the human subject as the copresencing of the human subject with the absolute Other. This awareness is the core event on which *all* human religions are grounded. As we will see presently, Hegel treats the experiential aspect of this relation in terms of 'religious sensibility' (*Empfindung*) and 'devotion' (*Andacht*).

The Inner Dialectic of the Religious Relationship

What we have just described—the primogenial awareness of the absolute Other, or God, within human subjectivity—is similar to what Rudolph Otto, a century after Hegel, describes as *mysterium tremendum et fascinans*: "The feeling of it may at times come sweeping like a gentle tide, pervading the mind with a tranquil mood of deepest worship. It may pass over into a more set and lasting attitude, continuing, as it were, thrillingly vibrant and resonant, until at last it dies away and the soul resumes its 'profane', nonreligious mood of everyday experience."[7] Indeed, both Otto and Hegel agree that this primogenial awareness of God is the source and center of all religion; but, as we will detail in Chapter Five, Christianity gains its special status as consummate religion, for Hegel, because it is the only religion that understands this relationship as a dialectical relationship, first present in the person of Christ, and then articulated in the community through doctrine and ritual.

In the section "The Concept of Religion in General," Hegel is interested in articulating only the formal structures of this dialectical relationship. He does so by observing that when we are "considering...religion itself...we immediately encounter these two moments (α) the *object* [that is] in religion, and (β) consciousness, i.e., *the subject*, the human that comports itself toward that object, religious sensibility, intuition, etc."[8]

Of course, one could take a number of alternative paths in relation to these two 'moments' or sides of religion. The first path, Hegel observes, is to "treat merely the objects as such, God" and ignore or forget the subject side as did Enlightenment natural theology.[9] Indeed, it is this one-sidedness of Enlightenment natural theology that makes it unspiritual and ultimately unsuitable as a model for the philosophy of religion. The second path possible is "to consider and comprehend religion *only* as something *subjective*."[10] This "equally one-sided" path does "not arrive at a destination" because it only directs its thinking "toward God" but never arrives at knowledge of God, knowledge which is possible when God is contemplated as an object of consciousness.[11] For Hegel, then, the best possible path to take is that which recognizes that the two sides are united together in a dialectical relationship that is the 'totality of religion' and this two-sided path is the path to be undertaken in this philosophy of religion. Therefore, Hegel defines the concept of religion in such a way as to directly mirror both sides: "religion [is] the consciousness of *the true* in and for itself."[12] The one side is the human side, 'consciousness', which has as its object, God, who is 'the true in and for itself' and the other side, of course, is God "the absolutely self-determining true."[13] In this way, this definition attempts to mirror speculatively the dialectical correlation of the finite human subject and the infinite divine object that takes place in and through religious consciousness.

However, as we will further elaborate in our discussion of the Introduction to the 1824 lectures, the 1824 definition of the concept of religion moves beyond this dialectical phrasing by using *self-consciousness* as its pivotal term. In 1824, Hegel redefines the concept of religion as *"the self-consciousness of absolute spirit."*[14] The advantage of this formulation is that Hegel, after his dispute with Schleiermacher, no longer sees the need to articulate the two sides of the religious corelation in a strict two-sided symmetry of the subject, 'consciousness', and its object, 'God'. Instead, Hegel will emphasize *self-consciousness itself as all-embracing totality of both these sides*: "Within this its *self-consciousness*, there falls also its *consciousness*, which was previously defined as relationship. Thus in the highest idea, religion is not the affair of the single human being; rather, it is essentially the highest determination of the absolute idea itself."[15] Important to our present considerations, the 1824 definition of the concept of religion expresses the dialectical relationship of God and human, not in terms of a subject-object relationship, as does the 1821 definition, but in terms of the comprehensive grasp of self-consciousness. As we will see in our discussion in Chapter Three, Spirit is finite, singular human subjectivity raised to the level of inclusive, intersubjective subjectivity inasmuch as nothing can be thought outside the totality of the religious community. As such, Spirit is self-consciousness. Therefore, Hegel elaborates further in the 1824 *Concept of Religion*: "religion is *the self-knowing of divine spirit through the mediation of finite spirit."*[16] Even though both definitions are speculative insofar as they mirror effectively the relation of subject and object inherent in religion, the 1824 definition will show itself as being more adequate to the philosophical comprehension of religion precisely because the term *self-consciousness* unites within itself both consciousness of God and the self-consciousness of Spirit that comes through the thinking-through of what is contained within the life of the community.

Nevertheless, Hegel's 1821 manuscript will keep to the dialectical balance articulated in the 1821 definition of the concept of religion as the structure of all the determinations of the *Concept of Religion*.[17] Therefore, we find that, in the section "Distinction Between

External and Internal Necessity," Hegel shows that the religious standpoint could and has been justified in terms of external factors, for example, in the claim that "religion is useful for the purpose of individuals, governments, and states, etc.," and, indeed, Hegel notes, "it is quite correct that the purposes and intentions of individuals, governments, and states [gain] subsistence and solidity only when based on religion."[18] But, such 'external' reasoning, Hegel also comments, is not relevant to philosophy and its concerns, for it treats religion only as a "means," as "something contingent."[19] Of course, if this is how Spirit uses religion—and "spirit has the freedom of its own aims or purposes"[20]—then it would be "*hypocrisy*" on the part of Spirit, "for religion should be what exists in and for itself."[21] Instead, the *Concept of Religion*, as we have already discerned, *abstracts* from *particular* religious experience as found in the determinate moments of human history. Indeed, as concept, it need only display the *inner* necessity of religion encapsulated within it. Hegel acknowledges this when he writes: "This scientific conception means nothing else than the <portrayal> of the *necessity* of the religious standpoint—and that not as a *conditioned, external* necessity but as an *absolute* necessity. Hence we need to become aware of what spiritual process or movement it is that is advancing in that which is internal [*das Innere*] while it lifts itself up to religion."[22]

Thus, the demonstration of the external necessity of the religious standpoint is in itself superfluous to the overall unfolding of the concept of religion. Indeed, Hegel does not follow up this external demonstration with the expected internal demonstration until Section C, "The Necessity of This Standpoint."[23] In its place, we find Part Three, "The Religious Relationship as the Unity of Absolute Universality and Absolute Singularity."[24]

In Part Three, "The Religious Relationship as the Unity of Absolute Universality and Absolute Singularity," we can discover Hegel reinforcing the dialectic structure of the 1821 definition of the concept of religion when he identifies 'absolute universality' and 'absolute singularity' as the two sides of the concept of religion. Religion, Hegel reiterates, is 'consciousness of the true in and for itself' but adds that this consciousness stands "opposed to sensible, finite truth, sense perception, <etc.>."[25] Indeed, religious consciousness moves beyond the limits of finite sensibility because it is a "consciousness of the true that has being in and for itself *without limit and wholly universally*."[26] Thus, the limitless universality of the religious object, God, as 'the true in and for itself', transforms human consciousness from a natural awareness of things within its immediate sense world into an *"elevation, a rising above,* a reflecting on, a *passing over* from what is immediate, sensible, singular (for the immediate is what is first and not therefore the elevation); and thus it is a *going out* and *on* to an *other."*[27]

In these passages, we can see that Hegel is referring to an understanding of consciousness that parallels Husserl's notion of the intentionality of consciousness with its two-sided structure of consciousness and object. It is also evident in Hegel's bracketed reference to 'the immediate' as 'what is first' in the last passage we quoted that there is, prior to religious consciousness, intentionality as a natural two-sided relation between consciousness imbedded within the immediacy of sensible being in the world and the object made thematic by consciousness. As such, Husserl reinforces Hegel's already developed position that consciousness always and automatically posits an 'other' as object for itself in order to be consciousness. Therefore, we can characterize this prior two-sided relation as both natural and immediate; indeed, for Hegel, what consciousness isolates in its thematizing gaze is, as we already indicated in the previous paragraph, some *thing* within its immediate horizon of its natural being in the world. But, this prior activity of consciousness is not yet the dialectical corelation between absolute singularity and absolute universality that will arise within religious consciousness. It is, however, the *precondition* for the conjoining of universality and singularity into a particular unique modality of unification that is the religious relationship.

It follows then that religious consciousness must build on this natural intentionality of immediate, sensible consciousness. However, as the previous quotations suggest, the constitution of religious consciousness occurs through a movement of thought *out* of the confines of immediate consciousness's natural field of awareness. Although religious consciousness's inner intentional movement works *within* the two-sided structure of intentionality, its focus is not directed toward a *thing* localized in the world, but toward a thought, that is, the 'unlimited universal', the 'highest' thought, God. As such, it effectively lifts itself out of the immediacy of being in the world to the level of absolute universality because consciousness and its object are paired and, hence, united elements of thinking. Consciousness and its object are to be understood as united because in this modality,

Hegel observes, "*thought thinks itself.*"[28] Moreover, Hegel adds, "God and religion exist in and through *thought*—simply and solely in and for thought,"[29] suggesting that the *ground* for the unity of the religious relationship is *in thinking* and not in feeling or sensation.

Hegel then continues his description of religious consciousness by identifying "this thinking" as "the foundation, the substantial relation" contained within religious consciousness—a relation that may be modified later by "religious sensation," which could "[take up] this object again and the relationship to it as feeling."[30] Moreover, this thinking is not yet "thought in the regular or formal sense"; rather, this activity of thought is *devotion* [*Andacht*].[31] In this sense, devotion is the preformal, preconceptual thinking or understanding of God. But, with devotion, the two-sided relation implicit in consciousness is refigured into another more explicit shape, the shape of absolute singularity of the finite human subject. Indeed the singularity of the individual human subject becomes pronounced in juxtaposition to the absolute universality of this other (God). Consequently, consciousness, once it elevates itself into thought by thinking the highest thought, is cast back or returns to itself and perceives itself as immediate and singular, as a finite 'self' or 'I': "In religion, I myself am the *relation* of the two sides as thus defined. I the *thinking* subject, and I the *immediate* subject, are one and the same I. And further, the relation of the two sides that are so sharply opposed—<of utterly finite consciousness and being and of the infinite>—is [present] in religion for me."[32]

Hence, the devotion that arises as the base of religious consciousness is the thinking of the finite self as the relation of these two utterly disparate sides. At the same time, the internalized *otherness* of absolute universality that is present over and against the finite subject, is overcome by lifting up the self into 'infinite consciousness': "In thinking, I raise myself above all that is finite to the absolute and am *infinite consciousness*, while at the same time I am *finite self-consciousness*, indeed to the full extent of my empirical condition."[33] But, we can further see that the finite human subject's preconceptual holding together of the two sides within itself creates an inner dynamic of tension between these two sides. In essence, the subject experiences a simultaneous internal rupture and consociation:

> I am the relation of these two sides; these two extremes are each
> just me, who connect them. The holding together, the connect-

ing, is itself this conflict of self within the unity, this uniting of self in conflict. In other words, *I am the conflict*, for the conflict is precisely this clash, which is not an indifference of the two <as> distinct but is their bonding together. I am not *one* of the parties caught up in the conflict but am both of the combatant and the conflict itself. I am the fire and water that touch each other, the contact (<now separated and ruptured, now reconciled and united>) and union of what utterly flies apart; and it is just this contact that is itself double clashing relation as relation.[34]

Thus, the primal religious relation is one in which the human subject is paradoxically pulled in two directions, that is, into the divine and the human, the infinite and the finite, simultaneously, and yet paradoxically, it also pulls together in an embryonic sense of two sides touching in a healing reconciliation.[35] Hence, the religious relationship situates the divided self in the interstice between the contradictory poles of the "thinking subject" and the "immediate subject"; of the "finite consciousness and being and of the infinite," it both unites and separates.[36] But, Hegel points out that this paradoxical relation between the finite human self and its absolute other is not yet a relationship of "I as knowing and the known object." "All distinctions are as yet absent and annulled within it. Everything finite vanishes, everything disappears and is at the time included, in this aether of thought. But this element of the universal is not yet more exactly defined; out of this liquid element and in this transparency nothing has yet taken shape."[37]

Yet, because this inner conflict "exists as relation" and as "unity" and, in fact, is the grounding relation and unity of religious consciousness, it is also a 'unity-in-difference'. As such, it will temper and inform all subsequent construction of relations within religious consciousness, including that of knowledge of God.

Nevertheless, Hegel found himself compelled to spell out the dialectical interaction of the two sides of the religious relationship in terms of its genesis in thinking to help those contemporary philosophers of religion and theologians recollect this fact: "It is one of the gravest and crudest errors of our time that *thought* is not recognized to be element and essential form in all of this, as well as the sole fundamental content."[38] This criticism foreshadows the critiques Hegel will render of Schleiermacher and the Pietists, who, for Hegel, neglect, ignore, or forget the genetic priority of thinking when they attempt to ground religion and religious consciousness in feeling. But, as this section indicates, Hegel is concerned with both the thinking side and the immediate, feeling side and therefore is concerned with displaying how they dialectically interrelate in the religious life of human being. Thus, because the human being is also a sensing being, Hegel now turns his analysis to showing how devotion feeds back into natural, immediate consciousness and its sensibility [*Empfindung*], thereby forming the first shape of determinacy, *religious sensibility*.

Natural Sensibility and Religious Sensibility

In the 1821 lectures Hegel favors the term *sensibility* [*Empfindung*] over *feeling* [*Gefühl*]. After the publication of Schleiermacher's *The Christian Faith* in 1822, Hegel will prefer *feeling* over *sensibility*. Indeed, Hegel's criticism of what he calls the "theology of feeling" significantly *informs* his *reformulation* of the *Concept of Religion* in 1824. Be that as it may, what is important to our present consideration of the 1821 *Concept of Religion* is that Hegel apparently *ignores* the fine distinction he makes between *sensibility* and *feeling* in the *Encyclopaedia of the Philosophical Sciences*. In the "Anthropology" (section 402) Hegel writes:

> In the usage of ordinary language, sensation [*Empfindung*] and feeling [*Fühlen*] are not clearly distinguished: still we do not speak of the sensation—but of the feeling of right, of self; sensitivity [*Empfindsamkeit*] is connected with sensation [*Empfindung*]: we may therefore say sensation emphasizes rather the side of passivity—of finding [*des Finden*], i.e., the immediacy of mode in feeling—whereas feeling at the same time rather notes the fact that it is *we ourselves* who feel.[39]

Thus, sensation [*Empfindung*] is passive and receptive, the immediate, precognitive 'consciousness of' the objects of the external world through the senses. But, it is important to note that it is 'consciousness of' in the sense of *discovering* or *finding* "the *individual* and the *contingent*, the immediately given and present."[40] Indeed, Hegel stresses: "Sensations…are immediate and are found existing."[41]

Feeling [*Gefühl*], on the other hand, is the active constituting of self as "inward, individuality"[42] in immediate relation to the objects that are given to and found by consciousness in sensation. Therefore, feeling is the primordial activity of consciousness in which it reaches out to touch [*Fühlen*] the world. Sensation is the unorganized receptivity of objects by consciousness; feeling, however, *reverses* this relationship of consciousness to objects. In other words, where sensation is the vehicle for experience of phenomena not yet synthesized into a unified field of phenomenality, feeling is the synthesizing act by which and through which consciousness derives a single unified meaning from its sensation. In this way, sensation and feeling, as the two sides of the immediate consciousness of the phenomenal world, provide the fundamental experiential horizon in which all subsequent acts of delineation of self and other, subject and object, and so on, by consciousness will take place. As such, Hegel notes:

> The feeling individual is the simple ideality, the subjectivity of sensation. What it has to do, therefore, is to raise its substantiality, its merely implicit content, to the character of subjectivity, to take possession of it, to realize its mastery over its own. As feeling, the soul is no longer a merely natural entity, but an inward individuality. The individuality which in the merely substantial totality was only a formal being-for-self has to be liberated and made free.[43]

In the 1821 philosophy of religion manuscript, Hegel observed that "the animal has sensation and feeling" and, indeed, as a natural awareness of being in the world, sensation and feeling in both natural and rational animals is what allows for immediate relation to a world that is acted on as ordered.[44] But because devotion [*Andacht*], with its thought of 'absolute universality', is also present in human consciousness, as we discussed earlier in this chapter, then "*only human being has religion essentially*." Human sensibility, thus, is also intertwined with what Hegel calls religious sensibility: "This is the nature of [human] sensibility: it is religious insofar as it possesses a distinctive content and distinctive determinacy, and this determinacy is what was mentioned earlier. [It involves] determinacy as infinite thought of the utterly universal, determinacy as wholly empirical subjectivity, and the speculative relationship of the two of them."[45]

It is, therefore, apparent that the dialectical interaction of thinking and immediacy already established in devotion permeates sensibility and places it 'higher' than the natural sensibility found in the animal world. Therefore, Hegel says: "All that raises human beings above the level of animal consciousness is that their sensibility is at the same time knowledge and consciousness. Human beings know themselves while animals know nothing of themselves, and human beings know only of themselves precisely in consciousness, in the withdrawing [*Zürucknehmen*] from the immediate identity with the certainty [of sensation]."[46]

Hence, religious sensibility differs from natural sensibility inasmuch as the subject-object relation implicit in any form of consciousness becomes known explicitly in human religious consciousness. Through its ability to abstract from its immediate empirical surroundings (for example, to posit absolute universality), human consciousness provides for itself a medium through which this self-knowing can take place. This medium is representation [*Vorstellung*].[47] Through representation, human consciousness pictures empirical objects in images [*Bilden*] and presents them to itself. But the representation that arises out of religious sensibility, and that is thus intertwined with devotion, can also picture 'absolute universality', and consequently itself, in simplistic and complex ways. Nevertheless, it is important for us to remember that: "God is *not* the highest sensation but *the highest thought*; even when God is brought down to the level of representation, the *content of this representation still belongs to the realm of thought*."[48] Moreover, Hegel says, "Religious sensibility *must advance* to representation and doctrine."[49]

For our present considerations, it is important for us to realize that religious sensibility and its representations allow for the "negation of my particular, empirical existence."[50] In essence, representation, through image making and presentation, negates both the 'outer', empirical field of phenomenality and the inner feeling of being an individual existent in the phenomenal world that, as we have just seen, arises through sensibility. In the place of both the negated 'outer' world and the 'inner' feeling of 'being in' (and touching objects in) this world, human consciousness projects its situatedness in the world 'outside' of itself and re-presents itself as an object among other objects outside its individual consciousness. Thus, representation facilitates the movement of consciousness from simple feeling of its active presence in the world into *knowing* its presence in the world as an object for thought. In this way, representation is the means through which the human subject relates to the phenomenal world in which it is immersed as both a dependent entity and an independent entity. Thus, this negating activity inherent in human consciousness allows religious sensibility to contain within consciousness its empirical form, or what Hegel calls "empirical consciousness":

> Religious sensibility as such itself contains *both* the contrast between the determinacy of empirical self-consciousness and that of universal thought or intuition *and* their relation and unity. Religious sensibility swings back and forth between the determinacy of their antithesis and their unity and satisfaction. In the determinacy of separation together with the fact that the universal is the substantial against which the self-aware empirical consciousness also feels its essential nothingness—indeed that of its still positive <volitional> existence—this representation, this determinacy in general, is the sensation of *fear*.[51]

Because consciousness in effect can negate itself through the 'swinging back and forth' of religious sensibility between the antithesis (and separation) and unity (and satisfaction) of the 'universal' and empirical self-consciousness, the subsequent feeling of 'essential nothingness' on the part of the subject generates not only the sensation of fear, of repentance and anguish, but, as furthered, also the sensations of thankfulness, love, blessedness—all sensations that Rudolph Otto identified under his term *mysterium tremendum et fascinans*.[52]

It is at this juncture that we must point to a crucial difference between Otto's and Hegel's descriptions of the genesis of religious consciousness, a crucial difference that will underlie Hegel's criticism of Schleiermacher. Instead of sweeping the primogenial moments of religious consciousness under the general category of feeling, as do Schleiermacher and Otto, Hegel, as we have just detailed, is careful to show that the initial moment of experience of an absolute other is one that is already thought, which, then, refracts back into the feeling-sensation side of human being. Thus, unlike Schleiermacher and to a lesser degree Otto,[53] Hegel sees a human being as a being whose thinking is totally present and incarnate in its sensible experience from the outset.[54] This means that Hegel can build the concept of religion and its inner structures of spirituality as that which reveals and unfolds itself in thought from its first embodied moment in immediate consciousness of absolute universality to its explicit expression in the philosophy of religion. Therefore, we can already see from Hegel's description of devotion and religious sensibility that religious consciousness itself generates and develops the concept of religion through its own inner determination.

Indeed, Hegel is concerned with affirming the *internal* necessity and validity of the "standpoint" of religious consciousness by demonstrating how it does in fact contain within itself the two sides, whose developing determinations we have detailed thus far. Hegel writes:

> Specifically, the religious standpoint contains: (α) The *objective* and *universal*—not in any sort of determinateness (e.g., a species or right), nor [as] *a* universal ([such as] will or freedom as universals). [What it contains is] rather *the* utterly unlimited universal or concrete that encompasses utterly everything within itself—the natural and spiritual world in its full expanse and in the endless articulation of its actuality (β) The *subjective*—likewise in the full expanse of its self-consciousness (γ) The two sides are totalities only because and to the extent that each has incorporated the other within itself implicitly. The objective totality includes also the spiritual world, which [takes shape] by incorporating and subsuming the [natural] world in its imagining and thinking. For subjective consciousness shapes and deepens itself within itself by means of reciprocal interaction with its world.[55]

Notwithstanding the significance of emphasizing the reciprocal interaction of consciousness with its world through its own encapsulation of the world in the religious standpoint, Hegel now turns his attention to a direct consideration of the role of representation for the furthering of the inner dialectic of religious consciousness.

Representation and Cultus

In the last section of the 1821 *Concept of Religion*, "The Relationship of Religion to Art and Philosophy,"[56] Hegel is concerned with how representation invokes explicit knowledge of God out of the inner relationship of the subjective and objective within religious consciousness, a knowledge that will then be further cognized in speculative thinking itself. In fact, representation becomes the necessary bridge or middle ground between the immediate moments of religious consciousness and speculative thinking. For Hegel, representation leads to this explicit knowledge of God because it is a further manifestation of what we called the *interstice* or *spiritual realm* between the 'thinking subject' and 'the immediate subject', where the divided self is the relation of the two sides. Indeed, the inner dynamic of this relationship between the two sides is furthered in the very way representation brings them together:

> On this account, then, representation stands in a state of constant *restlessness* [*Unruhe*] between immediate sensible intuition and thought in the proper sense. Its determinacy is sensible in character, derived from the sensible, but thinking has gone into itself [*das Denken hat sich hineingelegt*]; in other words, the sensible is elevated by way of abstraction into thinking. But these two, the sensible and the universal, do not interpenetrate each other thoroughly; thinking has not yet completely overcome sensible determinacy, and even if the content of representation is the universal, yet it is still burdened with the determinateness of the sensible and needs the form of natural life. But it remains always the case that this moment of the sensible is not valid on its own account.[57]

This point is made quite clearly in the following passage from the *Encyclopaedia*:

> In our representations [*Vorstellungen*] a *two-sided condition* obtains so that either the content is provided by thought, but not the form; or, conversely, the form belongs to thought but not the content. If I say, for example, anger, rose, hope, I acknowledge all such things as coming to me by way of sensation, but I speak of this content in an universal manner, in the form of thought. I have left out much that is particular and only given the content as something universal; yet the content remains sensuous. Conversely, if I represent God to myself, the content is, to be sure, a product of pure thought, but the form is still sensuous in the way that I find it immediately present in myself. In representation, therefore, the content is not merely sensuous, as it is in direct examination of things;

rather, either the content is sensuous and the form appertains to thought, or *vice-versa.* In the first case the material is given and the form belongs to thinking: in the other case the content which has its source in thinking is by means of the form turned into something given, which accordingly reaches the mind from without.[58]

As we noted in the previous section, representation takes what is already present within the religious relationship and cloaks it in the garb of images drawn from the empirical world. With these images, representation deepens the awareness of the rupture or cleavage between the divine and the human already blossoming within religious consciousness. In short, these images make this gap more pronounced. Indeed, *the more God is pictured as divine other, as somehow existing outside of the field of phenomenality, the more the knowledge of the true and its reconciliation is made possible for human consciousness in its self-consciousness by picturing the finite world as God's other:* "As religion represents it, there is in God the other of God, God's *Son,* i.e., God as other, the other that remains within love and within divinity; and the Son is the truth of this finite world. Thus it is not intrinsically an other material, whose necessity would only be observed, <but rather in and for itself the same material, i.e., for the first time the truth>."[59] In this passage, Hegel is anticipating the Christian doctrine of the Trinity, which he will discuss in detail in Part Three, "The Consummate Religion" of the 1821, 1824, and 1827 manuscripts. (See especially Chapter Five.) As a representation, this doctrine takes part of its understanding of God from the natural relations of the family: "Hence we have the expressions 'Father' and 'Son'—a designation taken from a sentient aspect of life, from a relationship that has its place in life."[60] As well, the doctrine of the Trinity points to the absolute truth known by thinking in philosophy, which is already implicit in the nonsentient notion of God the Holy Spirit as unity of the Father and the Son. Therefore, the Christian doctrine of Trinity exhibits the pattern to which Hegel is alluding: God the Father is *initial unity;* the Son, the *differentiation* of God from Himself; and the Holy Spirit, as *'return'* and *'reconciliation'* of the two prior moments to each other. In this way, the Son is the 'truth of this finite world' in two senses: as that through which self-differentiation of God (the Father) into an other (the finite world) can take place, and as Jesus Christ.[61] Hegel says in 1827:

> We say that God eternally begets His Son, that God distin-
> guishes Himself from Himself, and thus we begin to speak of
> God in this way: God does this, and is utterly present to Him-
> self in the other whom He has posited (the form of love); but at
> the same time we must know very well that God is Himself this
> entire activity. God is the beginning, He acts in this way; but He
> is likewise simply the end, the totality, and it is as totality that
> God is Spirit....The fact that this is the truth, and the absolute
> truth, may have the form of something given. But that this
> should be *known* as the truth in and for itself is the task of phi-
> losophy and the entire content of philosophy. In it is seen how
> all the content of nature and spirit presses forward dialectically
> to this central point as its absolute truth. Here we are not con-
> cerned to prove that this dogma, this tranquil mystery, is the
> eternal truth; this comes to pass, as has been said, in the whole
> of philosophy.[62]

On the basis of the two senses of the "Son" that we noted earlier,
Hegel can be construed as also alluding to the ultimate realization of
the truth of unity-in-difference of God, and human being will come
in the Christian representation of the Son as the person of Jesus
Christ. In such a representation, human life is seen as containing
divine life within itself, and divine life as also holding human life
within itself. Indeed, as we will see in Chapter Five, the Son as
Christ is the divine other's life in human being that lifts human
being up into the divine life. For the unfolding of the concept of
religion, however, actual representations of Christianity and the various world religions are not what are at issue. Rather, it is of the
utmost importance to disclose to thinking how representation itself
is the implicit and explicit mediation of the thinking and the immediate sides of human being, thereby opening up consciousness's
interiority for conceptualization.

 To begin uncovering the role of representation in religious consciousness, Hegel alludes to the *Encyclopaedia's* division of the
absolute into art, religion, and philosophy; however, Hegel does not
enter into great descriptive detail about the content of these spheres
because "essentially it is a question of the *form* in which the absolute
truth is [found] in religion."[63] What is important, then, is how they
are to be seen as interrelated in a mosaic of meaning: "These [forms]
interpenetrate each other essentially because each of them, while

thus distinguished, is at the same time the totality of consciousness and self-consciousness."[64]

The mutual integration of art and religion rests on what is first distinguishable as the immediate intuition of the artist: "Truth in the genuine sense is the *correspondence of the object with its concept*, the *idea*; and this is the content of art in and for itself—a content that concerns, of course, the substantial, wholly universal elements, essential aspects, and powers of nature and spirit."[65]

At the same time, religion is "the totality of the two [art and religion]."[66] But, Hegel continues, "With respect to the consciousness of its content...it is not bound and strictly limited to the form of immediate intuition and mythical image."[67] Even though "There must be *a* religion whose intuition occurs essentially in the form of art," it is not the case that all religions must stay at this level.[68] Consequently, religious representation is distinguishable from *image* [*Bild*], but it does make use of 'pictures' and 'images' derived by immediate intuition (i.e., art) from sensation. The distinctiveness of representation over and against image lies in the *transcendence* implicit in, and which arises through, religious sensibility: "Representation [is] the image elevated into universality: [it is] thought, full of thought, and is a form for thought."[69]

Indeed, Hegel identifies various *words* as representations; for example, *God, soul,* and *world,* all of which imply transcendence through their universality; indeed, "thought is their overriding factor."[70] But, even more important, representational language combines with images in such a way as to constitute the *relational* aspect of thought in religious consciousness. Because of the 'elevation' of images in universal terms, that is, into universality, these representations express the essential relationship of the finite to the infinite. Indeed, the representational language found in religion binds together to point beyond the contingencies of finite human being. Hegel notes: "To the extent that religion gives its content essentially in the form of representation, it has a *doctrine*—namely, that of *truth*."[71]

Consequently, these doctrines and truths appear as if they are independent of humanity and therefore as *given* or *presented* to humankind. Because these doctrines and truths seem to be *received* doctrines and truths, they are understood by humanity as *objective* truth:

> Moreover, its representations have the significance of truth as *objectivity* in contrast with the other mode [of truth, that] of

subjectivity. (The sensible also is implicitly subjective, i.e., finite.) [They have the significance] of objectivity, so that the content [of religion] *is* in and for itself, [is] not something posited, remaining within me, a movement in me. In contrast with religious sensibility, [representation gives] objective duties, objective faith, the fact that there is something higher than this empirical consciousness of mine, no matter what I call "mine." Rather, in and for itself [this higher being is] secure in its substantiality against me.[72]

The affirmation of God as the source of all 'duties', of all meaning, indeed of faith itself, allows religious consciousness to lift itself out of its 'mineness' toward a life in an other. As we have noted, God is posited as the center in which all aspects of human experience activity are united, including, therefore, being with others. Important, then, objectivity is given to representation and its more formal mode, doctrine, by the *cultus*.[73] Thus, all stirrings of devotion and religious sensibility on the part of the individual consciousnesses are always situated within an intersubjective sphere. A communal mode of representation arises through discourse with other human beings, and it provides the spiritual context in which these individuals establish themselves as *cultus*. Thus the shared representations of God as the eternal totality that embraces the finitude of all human being are the concrete objectification of the self-understanding of a people. Within the contours of this collective self-awareness, these representations, understood as truth, are articulated into an ordered knowledge of God, into a theology.

As part of the objectivity of the truths of representation, the religious community imparts its spirituality to its children. "Religion can be *taught*, it can be *imparted*, starting from representation."[74] Thus, the human subject always finds itself within a particular set of beliefs, beliefs that determine how the human subject will relate to itself, to its world, and to God. However, Hegel notes, the initial moments of the religious relationship can be reenacted by the individual subject and not be confused with some other feeling or sensation, such as obedience: "[A person must] first return to love of the awesome object, but precisely by transcending oneself in it—i.e., having liberated oneself from oneself, having made oneself empty and pure, having surrendered oneself."[75] Thus, there is the religious sensation of "love," of going outside oneself into another and leaving "nothing for myself" other than "my self-consciousness in it, but as pure and lacking desire"[76] at the heart of religion and that Hegel identifies with the word *faith* as used by Luther:

> This relation is called *faith*; from my side [it is] implicitly within me, adjudicating the content to me. <Faith is the same as what religious sensibility is, [namely,] the absolute identity of the content with me; but in such a way that faith expresses the absolute objectivity that the content has for me. The church and Luther knew quite well what they meant by faith....> [Faith is] the inner testimony of my spirit, therefore not a historical, learned testimony, but one without the necessity of the concept <and [without] determination as my determination. [It is] concrete, a conjunction,> a distinctive mode of truth—the absolute content of thought and truth [in] representations.[77]

It should be clear from this discussion that Hegel is pointing to two distinct types of faith. The first type, common to all religions, is what we will call *inherited faith*. It is the system of doctrines (implicit or explicit within a particular community) that are imparted to the individual through socialization. These learned truths then become the objective correlates to the inner structures of religious consciousness that arise within every human being and are then subjectively appropriated as certainty "for me." In this way, the doctrines of inherited faith provide the medium for an objective interpretation and understanding of an individual's relation to being in the world. As such, inherited faith is a necessary determination of the concept of religion. The second meaning, displayed in the quotation just cited and peculiar to Luther, is a matter of subjective appropriation undertaken by self-consciousness in direct consciousness of its selfhood already known as constituted in relation to God as divine subject. As we will see in Chapter Three, this unique mode of faith 'subjectifies' its objective correlative and brings all religious content into the sphere of subjectivity (As well, we will see that speculative philosophy sublates this subjectifying activity by resupplying full objectivity to its objective correlative through speculative thought.) We will designate this version of faith as *existential faith*. These two modes are by no means mutually exclusive. They can mutually reinforce each other as grounds for knowing God. In short, religious faith, whether inherited or existential, is "the certainty of this content...for me."[78] As well, Hegel observes, there are many "different ways of coming to faith." "Birth, training, and custom," "miracle, the historical mode, and...the Word and the letter," all may lead to a certainty that transverses both rational and nonrational consciousness. Indeed, the universal experience of faith throughout the "history of religion" provides its own verification: "Thousands, millions, [have] found in the wondrous expansion of religion their consolation, happiness, dignity. This sort of authority based on human commonality [determines faith]. If all [believe] something, then it must very probably be correct; to cut oneself off is always perilous and perverse. [One] must think twice [before] setting one's own authority (which <is [mere] opinion>) against this general authority."[79]

However, problems may enter with reflection on what is established as true by faith. Although reflection in the form of the proofs for the existence of God "demonstrates...credibility" of faith, reflection may find the representations of religious faith tinged with a certain opacity that "can and do(es) confuse me."[80] It is, in fact, the opaqueness of religious representation that allows for the positions vis-à-vis the relation of faith to reason of Hegel's Enlightenment and Pietist predecessors and contemporaries. For the Pietists, this means a retreat from reflection back into a one-sided 'sensibility' and 'subjectivity'. According to Hegel, the Pietists follow a simple pattern in their treatment of doctrine: "[There are] two ways in which religious doctrine perishes: (α) sensibility (β) argumentation." Indeed, what the Pietists do is reduce doctrine first to "argumentation." In so doing, they then claim that doctrines are merely a "corruption" that covers and conceals what is, for the Pietists, the true ground of knowledge of God, sensibility (or 'personal experience').[81]

By singling out *argumentation* and *sensibility* as sources of the destruction of religious doctrine, Hegel is alluding to his own confrontation with the development of religious thinking up to and including his own time. As we discussed in the Introduction, Hegel found himself within a spiritual context where a mutual antagonism and exclusivity existed between reason and faith. As we saw, philosophers like Spinoza and Kant had placed religion within the limits of moral reason. We also noted in passing that Pietist theologians had placed the one-sided subjectivity of piety (which does not allow itself to admit the objectivity of the content of religious sensibility), over the positivity of the Church, its history, and doctrines.

Consequently, for *Hegel*, corruption of the truth ensues and, ultimately, its self-destruction. Therefore, in the place of a God who knows himself through a religious community, and a religious community that knows itself through its knowledge of God, Hegel will observe only memorial echoes of the divine in the rituals, language, and ethical life [*Sittlichkeit*] of his own community, a state of affairs that we noted is discussed by Hegel at the end of his lectures on Consummate Religion.

For Hegel, the momentous, central task of speculative philosophy of religion is to overcome the stumbling blocks presented to reflection by these credible (for faith) and incredible (for Enlightenment reason) representations and allow us to peer through the windows afforded by representation in order to encapsulate in thought the truths already present in it: "<The relation of philosophy to this content is different; or more exactly, the form [of this subjective vanity exhibits] a deficiency.> The requirement of philosophy is to permeate [this content] with thought. The absolute identity of the subjective and objective [is] implicit; for me it [is found] in this element. <[Philosophy has] the requirement to carry thought through to the point that it should prevail and not remain subjective vanity.>"

Thus, the sedimentation of representation in the meaning structures of the community, when thought in the true sense, is what allows philosophy to escape falling into a 'subjective vanity'. And, although the *cultus* itself may be crumbling, these residual meanings remain in the objective life of the community in general holding together the community as community. In fact, when the *cultus* builds a repertoire of representations, it constitutes for itself a horizon of meaning, or what we may call an *intellectual world,* which both circumscribes and permeates the life of the community which forms out of the *cultus.* But, what Hegel calls the Understanding [*Verstand*] dissects this content into disparate and opposing conceptual frameworks. When the Understanding applies its 'rules and standards' to "expressions that contain implicitly speculative thought"[83] (for example, the doctrine of the two natures of Christ), it jeopardizes the movement of thinking into the absolute truth. It is essential for speculative philosophy to maintain its focus on such doctrines to render an adequate conceptualization of religion and, consequently, the truth found within religious consciousness, inasmuch as representation is the point of mediation between thinking and feeling, *doctrines*, as the systematic expression of representation, *are the point of mediation between religion and philosophy*. Therefore, the discourse of the philosophy of religion requires the language of religious representation and lifts it out of the 'shape' of representation to the level of philosophy's 'conceptual cognition'. For Hegel, true conceptual cognition must recognize that the content of doctrine is true, while not "adhering to the form of representation" itself. Furthermore, true conceptual cognition affirms that these truths originate in devotion and religious sensibility; it also must affirm that once they are conceptualized they are not "remaining embedded in *sensibility*," "adhering to the forms of *representation*" or "*reflection*" as found in the Understanding.[84]

Moreover, in opposition to the 'false representations' of his predecessors and contemporaries, Hegel shows that his philosophy of religion has 'returned to love of the awesome object...by transcending oneself in it' and has maintained his 'self-consciousness in it, but as pure and lacking desire' thereby affirming the truth of all the determinations that exist in the sphere of religious consciousness. In this act of self-conscious affirmation, speculative thinking overcomes the divisive one-sidedness of human subjectivity as manifested in Enlightenment and Pietism, and conceptually cognizes the unity of finite and infinite, of consciousness and God that is found in human subjectivity as the 'totality of aspects' outside of which nothing exists. For Hegel, mirroring this truth of religious consciousness is what permits thinking to grasp all antitheses and all determinations in the domain of religion as a unified whole, as the concept of religion.

We cannot claim that the 1821 manuscript leaves out any distinctions or forgets the whole that constitutes the concept of religion. As we have shown in this chapter, the 1821 *Concept of Religion* unfolds the entire range of those elements that constitute religion as religion. But, the 1824 *Concept of Religion* drops superfluous dialectical formulations, such as the "Distinctions Between External and Internal Necessity," and emphasizes even more the inner contours of self-consciousness. As we will determine, this reformulation of the concept of religion marks a deep appreciation of the objective and central doctrines of the Christian religion, that of the two natures of Christ and the Trinity, and their conceptual interrelation, in opposition to the 'corrupting' emphasis on sensibility-feeling and argumentation to be found in Schleiermacher's 'theology of feeling'.

In this way, the 1824 *Concept of Religion* will build on the ground cleared and provided by the 1821 *Concept of Religion*. And, as we will see in our discussion of the Introduction to the 1824 *Concept of Religion*, this subsequent rebuilding and restructuring of the concept of religion in 1824 is necessitated by the continuing exclusivity perpetuated in the thinking of theologians like Schleiermacher. Thus, it will become clear that this progressive self-development of the concept of religion from lecture series to lecture series must take place.

Chapter Two

RELIGION WITHIN THE LIMITS OF FEELING ALONE: SCHLEIERMACHER'S *THE CHRISTIAN FAITH*

Introduction

As we saw Hegel intimate in the 1821 *Concept of Religion*, the grounding inner dialectic of religious sensibility—"I am the conflict"—produces a further, higher dialectic between representation [*Vorstellung*] and reflection. In fact, the discovery and the thinking through of the concept of religion would not have been possible were it not for the interrelations between religious sensibility and representation on the one side, and representation and reflection on the other side—interrelations that became enunciated within the parameters of the absolute religion, Christianity: "<The distinction of religion from philosophy and art itself first appears in the absolute religion....>"[1] As we discussed in the Introduction, the movement of thought between representation and reflection took the form of the demarcating of philosophy and its rational mode of reflection from religious sensibility and faith in theology, both natural and revealed. At the same time, we observed that religion became considered a subject worthy of rational intellectual study and analysis according to standards consciously determined by reflection. Now, in a similar fashion, Hegel's conceptualization of religion not only built on this type of reflection, but established itself as conceptual cognition of all the inner determinations of religion by distinguishing itself from this type of reflection. Consequently, the inner dialectic and oscillation of representation and reflection are now enfolded into the conceptual cognition of the philosophy of religion in general and can be seen unfolding directly in the sections on determinate religion and consummate religion where the concept of religion is displayed in its concretization in the lives of human beings.

In the 1824 lectures, Hegel would not leave his detailed consideration of the reflective activity of religious consciousness until after the concept of religion. Instead, in the 1824 *Concept of Religion*, Hegel directly engaged in building his concept of religion on the reflection taking place on the theological level by entering into the dialectic of representation and reflection. Thus, in relation to the abstract reflection of natural theology,

> Our concern here is therefore not with God as such or as object, but with God *as he is* [present] *in his community*. It will be evident that God can only be genuinely understood in the mode of his being as *spirit*, by means of which he makes himself into the counterpart of a community and brings about the activity of a community in relation to him; thus it will be evident that the doctrine of God is to be grasped and taught only as the doctrine of *religion*.[2]

To grasp God as he *appears* in the community's 'doctrine of religion', philosophy has to have "before us the mode of God's representation."

> God represents only himself, and does so only to himself. This is the aspect of the existence of the absolute. Thus, in the philosophy of religion, we have the absolute as our object not merely in the form of thought but also in the form of its manifestation. Thus the universal idea is to be grasped in its utterly concrete meaning, which involves the characteristic of appearing, of revealing itself. This aspect of existence, however, is itself to be rethought in philosophy and grasped by thought.[3]

Consequently, Hegel would look closely at the dialectic of representation and reflection as found in rational theology, orthodox theology,[4] and as the main spur for his speculative 'rethinking', Schleiermacher and his chief work of dogmatics, *Der christliche Glaube nach den Grundsätzen der evangelischen Kirche im Zusammenhange dargestellt*, the first half of which was published during Hegel's 1821 lectures on determinate religion.[5] However, in the ensuing speculative cognition and criticism of Schleiermacher and this theology, Hegel would make all the forms of theology into an object for his thought thereby determining the inner contours of the 1824 concept of religion in direct relation to the contemporary theological level of reflection. As we will see, this will not only make the concept of religion much more inclusive of the objectification of God found in the absolute religion, but, also, points his philosophy of religion toward an overall formulation that will have as its objective side God's knowledge of himself.

These considerations will help us understand the differences between the 1821 and 1824 lectures on the concept of religion. However, before we undertake this task, we need to consider what is available to us as the 1824 lectures on the philosophy of religion. The critical edition, which serves as the main source of our investigations, bases the 1824 lectures on the philosophy of religion on student transcripts. Thus, from the outset, we should note that the *initial difference* between the 1821 and 1824 lectures is that of *the difference between the written and the spoken word.*[6] Although we could speculate as to the exact philosophical meaning of this difference or limit our understanding of this difference to the level of philology, we will instead envision the 1824 lectures simply as an *oral broadening of the horizon of the concept of religion* as already laid out by Hegel in the 1821 manuscript; an oral broadening necessitated by the appearance on the theological scene of Friedrich Schleiermacher's major work of dogmatics, *The Christian Faith*. To buttress this view, we will also depict Hegel's anti-Schleiermacher polemic in his Foreword to H. Hinrichs's 1822 publication, *Die Religion im inneren Verhältnisse zur Wissenschaft*, as a *bridge* between the 1821 manuscript and the 1824 lectures.[7] Rather than undertaking an explication of the 1824 *Concept of Religion*, however, we will concentrate our efforts on the Introduction to the 1824 *Concept of Religion* where the impact of Schleiermacher on the oral broadening is most directly and obviously felt.

The importance of viewing the 1824 lectures as an "oral broadening" of the 1821 manuscript, with the 1822 Foreword as a "bridge" is not merely an arbitrary choice on our part, but rather lies precisely in the claim with which we ended Chapter One: the progressive self-development of the concept of religion must take place. Although the theology of Schleiermacher initially does come from 'outside' of the philosophy of religion and is, in no way, sympathetic to it, his theology must be considered by philosophy as within religion and therefore as a moment in philosophy's thinking of the concept. As we discussed in Chapter One, the philosophy of religion reflects on the doctrines and representations of religion, comprehending their true significance for religious consciousness. This reflection also necessitates philosophy's contemplation of all conflicting positions that arise in theology precisely because these conflicts arise out of the religious relationship, that is, from its ground in the oscillation of finite self-consciousness and infinite consciousness in the religious subject. Moreover, the oscillation of theology between theology oriented to feeling and theology oriented to reason is a furthering of this religious relationship and is part of the community's activity of developing its own nature. Thus, this self-development, on the theological level, becomes part of the self-development of philosophy in its conceptualization of religion, as we will detail in Chapter Four. Moreover, this means that the selfhood implied by the notion of self-development that we have been using is, by no means, to be identified only with a particular subject, for example, G. W. F. Hegel. The self-development of philosophy's concept of religion is an activity of *philosophy* itself, which, as we have just noted, acts, by necessity, in tandem with religion: "Philosophy," Hegel wrote in 1827, "is only explicating *itself* when it explicates religion, and when it explicates itself it is explicating religion."[8] As well, the notion of 'oral broadening' allows us to see that the concept of religion undergoes a speculative rebuilding and restructuring, not as a break with the 1821 manuscript, but, rather, as an essential moment in the progressive self-development of the concept of religion *necessitated* by the continuation of the division between philosophy and theology in the religion of the day. Hegel, on the basis of his own standards, must take into account the entire range of religious life when determining the concept of religion.[9] Therefore, he must take into account each new major development in theology—of which Schleiermacher's *The Christian Faith* is one—and adjust the structure of his philosophical conceptualization accordingly.

Moreover, our notion of "oral broadening" as "progressive self-development" of the concept of religion concurs with Hegel's own reflections at the end of the 1821 manuscript on the philosophy of religion. If we recall, Hegel ended the 1821 manuscript with the suggestion that philosophy forms its own "priesthood," which, almost in anticipation of Heidegger's later philosophy, is like a 'shepherd' of the truth of human existence but *as found in religion*, protecting and preserving this truth from those who choose to forget or conceal this truth by focusing on one-sided 'subjective reflection'. As we discussed in Chapter One, for Hegel, finite human subjectivity is an inclusive, infinite subjectivity inasmuch as it realizes itself in intersubjectivity. Therefore, the 'oral broadening' of the spoken lectures of 1824 take on a special significance; that is, the 1824 lectures are a *concrete realization of the intersubjective ground required for a successful philosophical conceptualization of religion.*[10] Not only is oral presentation a more immediate mode of articulation, it is (ideally) a *conversation* with the audience. Although it is doubtful whether any of Hegel's students ever said anything in class (according to the norms of the time), we can nevertheless note that Hegel's willingness to tackle the theology of the day reaffirms theology's reflection and representations as the pre-text of the philosophy of religion (and philosophy itself). Moreover, Hegel's willingness to do this in the presence of the "student-priests" of the class of 1824 demonstrates his desire, expressed at the finish of the 1821 manuscript, *to continue to preserve* 'the possession of truth' and to preserve it in the only way possible, within the context of the spiritual community of which the university is arguably an extension.[11] Therefore, with this notion of 'oral broadening' in mind, we will find that the polemic incursions against Schleiermacher in the introduction to the 1824 *Concept of Religion* necessitate a conceptual broadening of the philosophy of religion into a philosophy of theology. Our concern is to understand this addition in the 1824 lectures as necessitated by the theological event of the publication of Schleiermacher's *The Christian Faith*. To accomplish this, we will see in what way Hegel's speculative redefinition of the concept of religion as 'self-consciousness of absolute religion' is the direct result of philosophical comprehension of Schleiermacher. Indeed, 'self-consciousness', its content and role in human awareness and religious consciousness, will be uncovered as the issue on which Hegel's polemics and criticisms of Schleiermacher hinge. For us to understand the proper meaning of Schleiermacher's use of the term *self-consciousness* in its theological context we will examine in detail his account of the genesis of religious consciousness in the first half of *The Christian Faith*. But let us first turn to a consideration of the biographical background to this 'issue' and examine the relations between Hegel and Schleiermacher prior to the publication of *The Christian Faith*.

The Relations between Schleiermacher and Hegel

Friedrich Schleiermacher (1768–1834) was Hegel's contemporary in the theological faculty of the University of Berlin. Influenced by Pietism, Romanticism, and Rationalism,[12] Schleiermacher saw his first major work, *On Religion. Speeches To Its Cultured Despisers*, published in 1799, eight years before the publication of Hegel's *Phenomenology of Spirit*. A fervent nationalist,[13] Schleiermacher helped establish the University of Berlin in 1810 and was appointed head of the Department of Theology in the same year. Schleiermacher was also a strong supporter of the Prussian Reform Movement and the union of the Lutheran and Reformed Churches into the United Evangelical Church, established in 1817.[14] Very few would dispute the influence of Schleiermacher on theology of both the nineteenth and twentieth centuries; indeed, it is widely agreed that this theological method, his 'philosophy of religion', and his development of hermeneutics mark a watershed in the history of both Protestant theology and German philosophy.[15]

By the time of Hegel's 1821 lectures on the philosophy of religion, both Hegel and Schleiermacher were firmly established as the leading lights of the university, and, consequently, both men dominated their respective disciplines with "schools" dedicated to propagating their ideas. Not surprisingly, the relations between the two men were antagonistic from the outset.[16] Even before Hegel's move to the University of Berlin in 1818, we can find a number of sources for the animosity between these two "leading lights."

As the head of the prestigious Academy of Sciences, Schleiermacher successfully blocked Hegel's application for membership, while, on the other hand, apparently for his own reasons, Schleiermacher endorsed Hegel's call to Berlin in 1816 and 1818. Perhaps the greatest point of contention between the two was over a political event—the assassination of the poet, August von Kotzebue, by a member of a nationalist, right-wing student fraternity in 1819. Sympathy for the assassin, Karl Sand, was expressed in a letter to Sand's mother by a friend and colleague of Schleiermacher on the faculty of theology at the University of Berlin, de Wette.[17] Hegel not only endorsed de Wette's dismissal from the university but indirectly criticized de Wette through direct criticism of his mentor, the theologian Fries,[18] in the Preface to the *Philosophy of Right*.[19] Of course, Schleiermacher's support for de Wette rankled Hegel, and the inclusion of a polemic against de Wette and Fries in the *Philosophy of Right* points to the existence of a political dimension to the tensions between Hegel and Schleiermacher.

Although various attempts were made to reconcile Hegel and Schleiermacher, their disagreement over theoretical, political, and academic matters apparently did not allow for any kind of genuine rapprochement. In fact, the grounds for their philosophical-theological disagreement were already present in Schleiermacher's *On Religion*, published nearly a quarter of a century before Hegel's lectures on the philosophy of religion and Schleiermacher's *The Christian Faith*. We will therefore go back to Schleiermacher's *On Religion* to trace the origins of the "theology of feeling," which, in Hegel's 1824 lectures on the philosophy of religion and 1822 Introduction to Hinrichs's *Religionsphilosophie*, we find as the main *object* of Hegel's speculative comprehension of theological reflection.

Schleiermacher: On Religion

Schleiermacher, like Hegel and most of their generation, inherited the conceptual framework of Kantian philosophy. To this generation, Kant's three *Critiques* and his *Religion Within the Limits of Reason Alone* marked the advent of a new era in philosophizing. Indeed, the radical nature of Kant's transcendental, or critical, philosophy opened up the possibility of philosophical and theological reinterpretation. As we noted in the Introduction, Kant's philosophy allowed the new generations to perceive that they were piercing through the oppressive cultural screens and false objectivity of previous ways of thinking to the truth of the subject. For the theologians, Kantian philosophy provided the epistemological justification for their moral reinterpretation of Christian truths or of the doctrines of orthodoxy, depending on their prior bias.[20] For a philosopher like Jacobi, Kantian philosophy illustrated the need for a philosophy of faith;[21] whereas, for idealistic philosophers like Fichte, Schelling, and Hegel, the contours of Kantian philosophy *without* phenomena-noumena dualism permitted the construction of systematic, holistic philosophy grounded in a conception of human subjectivity and consciousness in general. As Rudolph Otto eloquently put it, the post-Kantian period was "the high noon of that stirring springtime which saw the germination and the blossoming of modern intellectual life."[22]

However, for Schleiermacher, the trend toward reinterpretation of Christian belief tended to diminish what was essential to religion. To counter this calumny, Schleiermacher wrote his first major work, *On Religion*. Addressed to religion's 'cultured despisers', specifically, his friends in the *Sturm und Drang* movement, *On Religion* criticizes any thinking that finds "the only sacred things to be met with are the sage maxims of our wise men, and the splendid compositions of our poets."[23]

According to Schleiermacher, this mode of thinking ascribes meaning only to secular modernity by believing "that nothing new, nothing convincing can any more be said on this matter."[24] Therefore, Schleiermacher undertook the composition of *On Religion* to repudiate directly the antireligious attitudes and conclusions of his contemporaries.

Schleiermacher commenced the argument of *On Religion* with an appeal to experience. He asks the "cultured despisers" whether they have truly set aside their antireligious prejudices in their dismissal of religion: "whether you have rightly observed all these phenomena and have rightly comprehended their content."[25] Schleiermacher claims that the evidence shows otherwise: "With the cry of distress, in which most of them join over the downfall of religion, I have no sympathy, for I know no age that has given a better reception than the present."[26]

Thus, Schleiermacher directly accuses the cultured despisers of ignoring empirical data, while, at the same time, revealing his main methodological principle. Indeed, Schleiermacher's reference to "phenomena" and "content" indicates a methodology concerned with only the "thing itself," religion, and not with any preconceived notion of religion. In a manner that *foreshadows* twentieth-century phenomenology[27] he attempted a type of reduction by bracketing off prejudice and attempting to lead or point the reader to the religious phenomena themselves: "I do not seek to arouse single feelings possibly belonging to it, nor to justify and defend single conceptions, but I would conduct you into the profoundest depths whence every feeling and conception receives its form."[28]

With the object of his investigation clarified and all prejudgment suspended, Schleiermacher took the 'reduction' one step further "by regarding it [religion] from within."[29] Consequently, any reader following this investigation into religion "would have to admit that these thoughts"—the thoughts generated *within* religion—"are at least in some way based on human nature."[30] By situating the 'profoundest depths' of religion in human nature, Schleiermacher described not only the genesis of 'every feeling and conception', but also the manifest content of religious consciousness, and at the same time, held it open for the reader to compare these descriptions with his or her own experience.

As a product of human nature, Schleiermacher uncovered "religion" as "a kind of activity,"[31] an activity distinct from other modes of activity rising from human nature like "ethics and metaphysics."[32] Religion, and consciousness of religion on the part of the living individual, is activated by a unique aspect of human being, piety [*Frömmigkeit*]. Piety, or religious *feeling* [*Gefühl*], is the natural fount and source of religious consciousness and, as such, holds *all experience* together in a thematic field of consciousness.[33]

In keeping with this 'binding' effect supplied by religious piety to consciousness, Schleiermacher determined that ethics and morality are only abstractions of *action* and *knowledge* that arise within human life. By *abstraction*, Schleiermacher means the type of analytic thought that arises in reflection, thought that makes distinctions and divisions on what is experienced originally as a living unity. To abstract is to separate the living unity of human experience into "fragments," a natural enough activity also found in human beings, but to focus only on abstractions is to "not acknowledge religion as the third" element among action and knowledge; that is, the "unity" of which we have already spoken. Indeed, this living unity is missed because "you do not deal with life in a living way."[34] So, if one focuses on what is living and experiential in religion, Schleiermacher maintained, then one has to recognize that "religion is essentially contemplative";[35] contemplative of the piety that swells within and seizes human awareness in such a way that "the contemplation of the pious is the immediate consciousness of the universal existence of all finite things, in and through the Infinite, and of all temporal things in and through the Eternal."[36] Therefore, the essence of religious activity "is to seek this and find in it all that lives and moves, in all growth and change, in all doing and suffering."[37]

Consequently, Schleiermacher saw religious consciousness as the primary consciousness of human beings. This means that, for

Schleiermacher, religious consciousness is a faculty of human aware-ness essential to humanity's living in the world. And, as we have already noted, the two other faculties, knowledge and action, are grounded in this faculty. As originary, Schleiermacher's description of religious consciousness indicates that piety *ontologically* encom-passes the content of human awareness within an inner horizon that yields immediate self-consciousness. Immediate self-consciousness arises with and is, in fact, identical with, piety. Piety, or religious feeling, constitutes itself as self-consciousness precisely because it serves as the vehicle through which the Eternal is experienced as copresent with the individual human subject. Piety supersedes the other faculties as *the* form of organization of human experience insofar as its predominant *feeling of absolute dependence* on an Absolute Other is dialectical in nature thereby allowing the individ-ual human subject to apperceive itself as a unique, distinct, individ-ual human subject.

Schleiermacher's emphasis on piety and immediate self-con-sciousness marks a significant turn in the study of religion. As we noted in the Introduction, the pre-Kantian emphasis on reflection about religion had been on the existence and nature of God. Schleier-macher, on the other hand, turned toward the human subject, focus-ing on its innate capacity for religious experience. Although this 'turn' opens the human subject itself for contemplation and study, it also tends to obscure the possibility of determinate, objective knowledge of God. Indeed, fundamental Christian doctrines, such as the two natures of Christ, are not dealt with in *On Religion*; they fall outside of the range of what is derived directly from religious feeling. All humans experience the feeling of absolute dependence and different cultures objectify and interpret it differently, thus no particular set of religious doctrines has priority over another. By adopting the rhetorical and polemic terminology of his Romantic contemporaries, Schleiermacher indirectly demonstrated the relative unimportance of objective doctri-nal formulations for religion. Hence, in *On Religion*, Schleiermacher utilizes, quite eloquently, other names for God, such as Highest Being, the Infinite, the Deity, the Whole, the Inexhaustible, World-Spirit, the Eternal, the Great Spirit, and many others, too numerous to list.

Underlying these many names of God is what we can best describe as a 'generic monotheism' much like that we find in Spin-oza, ultimately lacking in determinations.[38] Although Schleierma-cher did not predicate any attributes to this 'God' other than what is already implied in terms like *the Infinite* and *the Eternal,* he did add, as we have seen, the (post-Kantian) condition that the notion of the 'Infinite', and so on, is to be understood first and foremost as an object for a subject. Thus, the *"sense* of the Infinite" that underlies any notion of God, effectively reverses Spinoza's focus (and that of the natural theology of Wolffian philosophy) from the object to the subject, while maintaining a Spinozistic notion of God as something on which human beings can and do place their variegated understandings of God.

On the surface, Schleiermacher's generic monotheism would imply that all religions are equally valid forms of religiosity if they are grounded in this 'sense of the Infinite'. But Schleiermacher does admit that out of many expressions of religiosity found in human history, that which calls itself *Christian* is significantly unique: "The original intuition of Christianity is more glorious, more sublime, more worthy of adult humanity, penetrates deeper into the spirit of systematic religion and extends further over the whole Universe."[39] Schleiermacher accorded Christianity this status because of its central figure, Jesus Christ. For Schleiermacher, this person reveals this 'more glorious', 'sublime', 'original intuition', or 'sense of the Infinite'. But why this particular person is a question that Schleiermacher will not answer:

> When, in the mutilated delineations of His [that is, Christ's] life I contemplate the sacred image of Him who has been the author of the noblest that there has yet been in religion,…the truly divine element is the glorious clearness to which the great idea He came to exhibit attained in His soul. This idea was, that all that is finite requires a higher mediation to be in accord with the Deity, and that for man under the power of the finite and particular, and too ready to imagine the divine itself in this form, salvation is only to be found in redemption. Vain folly it is to wish to remove the veil that hides the rise of this idea in Him, for every beginning in religion, as elsewhere, is mysterious. The prying sacrilege that had attempted it can only distort the divine.[40]

What is important, then, is only that Jesus Christ was a person imbued with true religious piety and a concomitant sense of the Infinite, which was 'higher' and 'clearer' than any prior to his time. By locating Christ in this manner, Schleiermacher aligns himself with the rationalist theological enterprise in general, by finding this 'idea in Him', a notion that we will discuss later in conjunction with *The Christian Faith* and Hegel's 1824 Introduction to the *Concept of Religion*.

Although *On Religion* is a theological statement, we must remember that it was not intended to be a work of systematic dogmatics like *The Christian Faith*. *On Religion* should be considered as a polemical tract written for religious skeptics and atheists that nevertheless prefigures *The Christian Faith* in its emphasis on feeling and immediate self-consciousness. On the other hand, *The Christian Faith* was written under the rubric of Christian dogmatic for a Christian audience within the tradition of systematic theology. Thus, as we'll now see, the subject matter of *The Christian Faith* is the content of the Christian religion in light of and verified by religious feeling.

The Purpose of The Christian Faith

Schleiermacher's *The Christian Faith*, with its commencement in a discussion of the term *dogmatics*, verges on the philosophical insofar as Schleiermacher was being self-conscious about the essence of the task he was about to undertake. However, Schleiermacher's reflective consciousness of himself in relation to this 'dogmatics' is, according to his own terms, a theological self-reflection that arises through its foundation in the immediate self-consciousness of absolute dependence. As we have seen in the previous section, the immediate self-consciousness of absolute dependence is what allows for the understanding of 'world'. It is only appropriate, then, for the theologian of feeling to commence with the 'world' (or world-view) of Christianity as found in the dogma of the Church. Therefore, *The Christian Faith* is designed to reflect not only the structures of immediate self-consciousness but, also, the universal, mediated self-consciousness of the Christian community. Its conceptions, then, should be understood as the self-expression of the communal piety of a people.

As Paul Tillich notes in his *A History of Christian Thought*, originally "*dogmata* are the differentiating doctrines of the different late Greek schools of philosophy."[41] Thus, dogmata are the means through which various schools of thought defined and distinguished themselves from other schools of thought. The formation of the Christian 'school of thought' was completed by various councils of the fourth and fifth centuries (e.g., Nicea, 325 A.D., and Chalcedon,

451 A.D.) that established various dogmas (e.g., the Trinity and the two natures of Christ) as the set of official beliefs, or doctrines, subscribed to by a "Christian." In *The Christian Faith*, Schleiermacher will not alter this ancient notion of dogma. But, it is Schleiermacher's intention not only *to display* to his audience the *importance of the immediate self-consciousness of absolute dependence for Christian belief*, but also, *to reconstruct Christian dogma out of the immediate self-consciousness of absolute dependence*. Therefore, immediate self-consciousness becomes the measure of meaningfulness of doctrine and dogma. If this were not to be the case, then Schleiermacher's treatment would have the same consequence as past treatments of dogmatics, such as those Schleiermacher claimed to have found in Scholasticism: "The result inevitably was that Dogmatic was overloaded with a multitude of definitions, which have absolutely no other relation to the immediate Christian self-consciousness than that indicated by the history of controversy."[42]

Therefore, for his treatment of Christian dogmatics to ferret out what makes the Christian religion different from other religions, Schleiermacher must illuminate that aspect of Christian self-consciousness of absolute dependence that marks Christian religiosity as Christian. Indeed, Schleiermacher concentrated his efforts on identifying that qualitative state of being that undergirds the Christian experience. In this way, *The Christian Faith* is best understood as a phenomenology of the Christian religion.[43] As we will see, *The Christian Faith* (as was Hegel's 1821 *Concept of Religion*) was constructed on the basis of a conception of consciousness that foreshadows Husserl's formulation of consciousness as intentional. With this methodological presupposition, Schleiermacher presented in *The Christian Faith* what amounts to a description of the genesis of self-consciousness as manifest in the present life of the Christian community. Consequently, the contemporary Christian experiential world is, for Schleiermacher, the precondition of his description; it is what is to be understood empathetically. Thus, Schleiermacher inscribes as the 'motto' of *The Christian Faith*, the following: "No one will understand unless he has experienced."[44]

The Relation of Philosophy to Religion

Having situated *The Christian Faith* as a work of dogmatics grounded in the feeling manifest in contemporary Christian self-consciousness, Schleiermacher took steps to avoid the tendency of human thinking to 'fit' Christian religious phenomena into premade theoretical forms. Accordingly, as part of his introductory discussion of 'dogmatics', Schleiermacher demarcates and, in essence, brackets off reason:

> the present work entirely disclaims the task of establishing on a foundation of general principles a Doctrine of God, or an Anthropology or Eschatology, either, which should be used in the Christian Church though it did not really originate there, or which should prove the propositions to be consonant with reason. For what can be said on these subjects by the human reason in itself cannot have any closer relation to the Christian Church than it has to every other society of faith or life.[45]

Indeed, as a unique manifestation of immediate self-consciousness of absolute dependence, Christianity has determined its own manner of objectifying the content of this feeling. This self-objectification is what Schleiermacher calls *theological science*; but, we have to be cautious in understanding what Schleiermacher intends by this term because, as the preceding quotation indicates, he assumed that none of the products of reason can shed light on the Christian faith as it is in itself:

> The peculiarity of the Christian Church can neither be comprehended and deduced by purely scientific methods nor be grasped by mere empirical methods. For no science can by means of mere ideas reach and elicit what is individual, but must always stop short with what is in general. Just as all so-called *a priori* constructions in the realm of history come to grief over the task of showing that what has been in such-and-such wise deduced from above is actually identical with the historically given—so it is undeniably here also. And the purely empirical method, on the other hand, has neither standard nor formula for distinguishing the essential and permanent from the changeable and contingent.[46]

Thus, the methods constructed within the limits of reason alone cannot explicate what lies within the realm of religious feeling. Reason imports into its methodological reflection ideas that arise from outside of feeling's parameters. Consequently, Schleiermacher will not allow himself the methodological vantage point of an 'objective' or 'transcendental' observer peeping into and dispassionately analysing the Christian religion, as we might find in Husserl, for example, if he had gotten past writing introductions to phenomenology. Rather, the most reason can do is to assist in the demarcation and definition of what is essentially a *science of the feeling of dependence*.[47] Thus, "since the preliminary process of defining a science cannot belong to the science itself, it follows that none of the propositions which will appear in this part can themselves have a dogmatic character."[48] With this recognition of what is essentially a limitation inherent in any methodological definition of a subject matter, Schleiermacher will 'let down' the brackets he has set around his subject matter and 'borrow' propositions "which belong to other scientific studies, in this case to Ethics, Philosophy of Religion, and Apologetics."[49] By borrowing propositions from these three 'outside' perspectives, Schleiermacher had available to him provisional linguistic intermediaries between his reflection and the content of feeling to help him shed light on and illuminate the inner parameters of his science of feeling. Indeed, these 'borrowings' allow Schleiermacher to construct his science of feeling in the form of what has been traditionally called a *dogmatics* or what Schleiermacher himself will also call the *doctrine of faith* [*Glaubenslehre*]. One suspects that if he did not accept some notions from reason he would have had to remain mute, especially because, as we will see, thinking itself lies outside of the inner sphere of feeling.

As we can see, Schleiermacher thought he could now justifiably use as the focus of *The Christian Faith*, the 'church', a term that Schleiermacher says he borrows from the philosophical field of ethics:[50] "Now the general concept of 'Church', if there really is to be such a concept, must be derived principally from Ethics, since in every case 'Church' is a society which originates only through free human action and which can only such continue to exist."[51]

At the same time, Schleiermacher observes, if his science is to keep itself centered on what is unique in Christian religious feeling, it should look at the Christian 'church' as that 'form of organization' or 'society' in which the peculiar type of Christian religious feeling is manifested. Therefore, we can see it is Schleiermacher's intention to 'borrow' the term *church* from ethics only to point to the 'form of organization' that circumdates the collective religiosity of a group of individuals who join together to share their peculiar religiosity, that is, their religious self-consciousness. Schleiermacher wrote: "Every such relatively closed religious communion, which forms an ever self-renewing circulation of the religious self-consciousness within certain definite limits, and a propagation of the religious emotions arranged and organized within the same limits, so that there can be some kind of definite understanding as to which individuals belong to it and which do not—this we designate a Church."[52]

Schleiermacher took further care in establishing the limits of his provisional use of the term *church* by observing that it could be understood in conjunction with the term *state*. For Schleiermacher, this connection is obvious because both the church and the state are concrete formal expressions of community that arise *sui generis* out of its collective experience. But, because his science is concerned only with the inner life of religious community, the correlation of church and state as expressed in the civil side of a community's life is not an issue. Therefore, for Schleiermacher, the outer, civil life of the community falls outside of the range of his concern and must be set aside as an area of interest belonging properly to the domain of inquiry called the *philosophy of right*.[53] Also, the other main consideration that comes to mind when one thinks about the "church"—that it stands in relation to other similar 'churches' to which it should be compared—is to be excluded from the considerations of dogmatics proper:

> the task of thus exhibiting in a conceptually exhaustive way, according to their affinities and gradations, the totality of all those 'Churches' which are distinguished from each other by peculiar differences of basis—this would be the task of a special branch of historical science, which should be exclusively designated Philosophy of Religion; just as, perhaps the name of Philosophy of Right would best be reserved for an analogous critical study which, as bearing on the general conception of the State, is developed in forms of civic organization.[54]

In addition, such an activity would best be undertaken, Schleiermacher points out, in conjunction with the theological field of apologetics, which "would lay down as foundation a description of the peculiar essence of Christianity and its relation to other 'Churches'."[55] Therefore, apologetics is similar to the philosophy of religion—they "take the same road"—but with the important methodological difference that apologetics drops all considerations that do not "directly contribute to the purpose of ascertaining the nature of Christianity."[56] Indeed, in Schleiermacher's view, the philosopher of religion could not possibly understand the actual genesis of the feeling of a religious community not his or her own, let alone know what goes on inside the religious consciousness of an individual member of a particular religious community.[57] On the other hand, apologetics undertakes precisely this task; it presents the contents of the religion as truth from inside the religion. This inner, experiential side, or what Schleiermacher calls *subjective* or *inward religion*, must be understood alongside its "common," outer side, "objective" or "outward religion."[58] Indeed, objective religion as "the organization of the communicative expressions of piety in a community" needs to be scrutinized as the outgrowth of "the total content of the religious emotions, as they actually occur in individuals," that is, subjective religion.[59] Thus, for Schleiermacher, the term *church* is now to be understood as signifying the "outer" form of organization through which the "inner" personal and individual religious feeling is publicly articulated and constellated. Hereafter, Schleiermacher would intend this term to mean only the "objective" or "outer" superstructure that encapsulates within its scope all aspects, both inner and outer, of the lives of its constituent members: "Each particular form of communal piety has both an outward unity, as a fixed fact of history with a definite commencement, and an inward unity, as a particular modification of that general character which is common to all developed faiths of the same kind and level; and it's from both of these taken together that the peculiar essence of any particular form is to be discerned."[60]

This means that it is important for us to remember that, for Schleiermacher, the objective and subjective are two aspects of one overall unity, and therefore, his dogmatics will not talk of the superstructure of the 'church' without first seeking its infrastructure in the 'peculiar essence' of its religious feeling. Indeed, for Schleiermacher, doctrines, the lines of ecclesiastical authority, rites, and all other outward manifestations of a communal religiosity are not to be conceived as rooted in some transcendent reality, 'outside of the community' and its life, but, rather, as emanating from within the actual religious feeling of its individual constituents. Thus, for Schleiermacher, any discussion of the dogmatics of the Christian church must take as its starting point the peculiar essence of feeling found in individual Christians and that, taken together, form the Christian church. However, the commonality of the piety experienced by Christians does not rule out that there may be other, non-Christian forms of religious feeling. Consequently, Schleiermacher observes: "Our proposition does not assert, but it does tacitly presuppose the possibility, that there are other forms of piety which are related to Christianity as different forms on the same level of development, and thus so far are similar. But this does not contradict the conviction, which we assume every Christian to possess, of the exclusive superiority of Christianity."[61]

Now that Schleiermacher has identified the religious feeling of the individual Christian as the fount and source of the Christian church, this religiosity and its epiphenomenon, the church, are now open to systematic and scientific explication and as "material for scientific knowledge," can be described and "their proper place in the total field of human life" determined. Indeed, the Church must be examined in light of its "essential business," "piety."[62] But, to accurately understand the relationship of piety and the church at its most fundamental level, the relation of piety to other aspects of human being must be explicated. These are (1) Feeling, Doing, and Knowing and (2) immediate and mediate self-consciousness.

Feeling, Doing, and Knowing

At the beginning of the section, "The Conception of the Church: Propositions Borrowed from Ethics," Schleiermacher sets forth the following: "The piety which forms the basis of all ecclesiastical communions is, considered purely in itself, neither a Knowing nor a Doing, but a modification of Feeling, or of immediate self-consciousness."[63] Thus, Schleiermacher 'lets down' his methodological brackets to discuss piety in relation to three fundamental faculties of human being: feeling, doing, and knowing. Within the Christian context, the faculty of feeling is equivalent to piety, knowing to Christian belief, and doing as Christian action. Schleiermacher, however, excludes what he calls the *traditional fourth*, thinking, because he construes it as lying outside of the triad of inner relations readily identifiable within the scope of expression of the Christian church. According to Schleiermacher, the interrelation of feeling-piety, knowing-belief, and doing-action constitutes the whole of a human life. Life, Schleiermacher posits, "is to be conceived as an alternation between an abiding-in-self and a passing-beyond-self on the part of the subject."[64] On the basis of this alternation of "abiding-in-self" and "passing-beyond" Schleiermacher then allocates specific functions to each of these three constitutive moments of human life: knowing and feeling are modes of "abiding-in-self," that is, they are interior to the subject; whereas doing is a mode of "passing-beyond-self," that is, it is open to the scrutiny of other feeling and thinking subjects. Although the internality of both feeling and knowing appear to stand over and against the externality of doing, Schleiermacher notes that knowing passes over into doing insofar as "Knowing" is "possession of knowledge," an "act" that becomes "real" by concretizing itself by informing and directing action in the external world. Feeling, on the other hand, remains unique in its exclusive, subjective form of 'abiding-in-self', that is, as receptivity (which we will discuss in terms of immediate self-consciousness). As we mentioned earlier, Schleiermacher found that the possibility of a fourth faculty (thinking) or, he adds, a third form that embraces "abiding-within-self" and "passing-beyond-self," would be to mistake how these aspects of human being interact with each other:

> the unity of these is indeed not one of the two or the three themselves; but no one can place this unity alongside of these others as a coordinate third or fourth entity. The unity rather is the essence of the subject itself, which manifests itself in those severally different forms, and is thus, to give it a name which in this particular connection is permissable, their common foundation. Similarly, on the other hand, every actual moment of life, in its total content, is a complex of these two or three, though two of them may be present only in vestige or in germ.[65]

Because there is the possibility of these 'three' or 'two' interacting in a mutual 'complex' of ways, we must see how Schleiermacher conceives of their interaction as originating in a common underlying experiential ground that binds them together. Of course, of these three faculties, feeling is this ground. It is the primogenial source of doing and knowing, in the same way as sensibility is the ground of representation and reflection in Hegel.

Feeling, Piety, and Immediate Self-Consciousness

As we all experience and know, there are many 'dispositions' and 'determinacies' of 'feeling' of which piety is but one; for example, affective feeling, attitudinal feeling, specific localized feeling. By *piety,* Schleiermacher has in mind the mode of feeling found in both Spinoza and Spener as the center of religion; that is, piety as devotion, reverence, and obedience to God.[66] As such, the feeling-tone of the pious disposition is determined by its sense of dependency on an absolute Other, on God: "What is common to all pious emotions, hence the essence of piety, is this, that we are conscious of ourselves as utterly dependent, i.e., that we feel ourselves to be dependent on God."[67]

Therefore, the essence of piety, like that of any other 'determinacy of feeling', hinges on and is conditioned by its relation to a distinctive object. Phenomenologically, all dispositions and determinacies of feeling arise from consciousness of something, something whose presence to consciousness is passively received as an individual something over and against consciousness, as we saw in Hegel's description of sensibility. No cognition (knowing) or action (doing) need take place nor are they necessarily present. But, unlike other feelings, "pious feeling, in all its configurations, however varied, is always a pure feeling of dependence" and, consequently, consciousness cannot and does not set itself in a "relationship of reciprocal action" and, thus, into an "equalization with the codeterminer."[68] Indeed, consciousness's reaction to its feelings and its objects is not the same in every case; there are degrees of 'equalization' of the feeling of consciousness with its 'codeterminer', and this means that there are degrees of the intensity of feeling on the side of consciousness. These gradations of feeling are due to the degree of the intensity of the 'influential action' of the object on consciousness. Thus, the more intense the action of the object on consciousness, the more consciousness finds itself in a subordinate position to its object and its reaction less in strength to that of its object. Piety, as the 'pure feeling of dependence', denotes the greatest degree of intensity.

At the same time that an object, regardless of its intensity, is present to feeling, the immediate awareness that feeling brings to consciousness folds back into itself as consciousness of being conscious of itself. Thus, this enfolding of consciousness into self-consciousness is itself immediate. In this way, immediate self-consciousness is a self-contained region of human being. Indeed, immediate self-consciousness, as an aspect of human being, encloses all other aspects of human being, all its experiences and knowing and doing, within a totality, or 'world' as we called it in our discussion of *On Religion*. Therefore, we can see that for Schleiermacher feeling configures the sense of the 'world' of consciousness for self-conscious-ness on the basis of its reception of objects: "There is no pure self-consciousness which comes forth as filling a portion of time, no self-consciousness in which one would be conscious only of one's pure I in itself, but, rather, always in reference to something, whether that something may be one or many, whether determinately grasped or indeterminate."[69]

As we can see, it is important for us to realize that for Schleier-macher the consciousness of self has to be always described as in relation to its object and not as some thing, reified as 'pure' or as independent of and prior to feeling. Thus, self-consciousness is only the presentation of the "being for itself of the individual" repre-sented as centered around an 'I' or 'Ego'.[70] But, this self-positing through representation of an 'I' or 'Ego' is not part of immediate self-consciousness proper because immediate self-consciousness in itself "is not representation but in the proper sense feeling."[71]

Now that Schleiermacher had established that immediate self-consciousness is equivalent to feeling in general, he observed that some of "these feelings approach pious feelings" inasmuch as the essence of piety is to be found in the feeling of dependency on its object, God. Indeed, the more the determination of a feeling is weighted toward a one-sided emphasis and dependency on its object as something greater than it is in and by itself, the more it is pious.

> In this gradation such feelings stand nearest to pious feelings, and are founded on a relationship of the purest possible dependence, such as that of the child on the father and that of the citizen on his native land and its rulers. Nevertheless, that dependence is also felt already as a gradually diminishing and self-extinguishing dependence, and the individual, without cancelling the relationship, can even to some extent react to, and to some extent exert a governing influence on, his native land and its rulers; and this dependence is thus felt as a partial dependence, compatible with reciprocal action, if only in a transitory way.[72]

Thus, even as some feelings approach the intensity of piety, con-sciousness finds itself only in 'partial dependency' on its object in relation to its ability to act on its object. Even the "world as the totality of all bodily and spiritual finite being" can be reconfigured by consciousness's reaction to it and not solely by the primordial configuration that arises through the moment of immediate self-consciousness of an object in feeling. This feeling of partial dependency is then also a 'consciousness of freedom'. Moreover, in this "freedom," consciousness can express its reconfiguration of its over-all world through concrete action in the world and through its knowing, which, as we have seen, can pass over into concrete action by influencing and directing action. However, when it comes to the feeling of dependency on God found in piety proper even the possibility of a slowly evaporating sense of dependency vanishes. In its stead is a sense of something that lies outside the parameters of the 'world' as totality of all finite being, something which is infinite:

> As regards the identification of absolute independence with 'relation to God' in our proposition: this is to be understood in the sense that the *Whence* of our receptive and active existence, as implied in this self-consciousness, is to be designated by the word 'God', and that this is for us the really original signification of that word. In this connection we have first of all to remind ourselves that, as we have seen in the foregoing discussion, this 'Whence' is not the world, in the sense of the totality of temporal existence, and still less is it any single part of the world.[73]

Because of the experiential reality of the 'simple and absolute' presence (of God), the sense of 'infinity' felt by immediate self-con-sciousness falls outside the self-enclosed 'infinity' of the 'world' of self-consciousness. But, we must remember that because it is experi-enced through pious feelings, Schleiermacher will maintain that it is still experienced as prior to knowing and doing:

> Piety in itself is neither a knowing [*ein Wissen*] nor a doing [*ein Tun*], but a disposition and a determinacy of feeling....I main-tain only that feeling is the seat of piety. However, the claim that feeling is only an accompaniment, is contrary to experi-ence. Rather, I expect that everyone will recall that there are moments in which all thinking and all acts of the will take sec-ond place to a self-consciousness which is determined in some specific way.
>
> The term 'in itself' implies that some knowing or doing may emerge from piety as an expression or effect of that piety. Piety

can then be known in both, but is itself neither of them, either in its beginning or in its proper essence.[74]

The term *in itself* thus points to Schleiermacher's realization that some knowing or doing may well emerge from piety in the same way as they do from other forms of feeling. Similarly, it can be found underscoring action and thought, but, yet, is neither knowing nor doing, neither in its beginning nor its production of a 'world' for consciousness. And, like feeling in general, the apprehension of a correlation between a finite self and an infinite other (God) can and does underlie and condition knowing and doing but solely as 'effects' of piety. But with piety, a qualitative difference enters in, a difference that distinguishes its products or effects from those of all the other forms of feeling. Where feeling in general is the receptivity of "abiding-in-self," and therefore passive receptivity, piety has an active side in that immediate self-consciousness's feeling of utter dependence is generated not from itself and its world but from consciousness of a transcendent infinity. As we can see, then, for Schleiermacher, the pious immediate self-consciousness contains within itself a feeling that points to the presence of an absolute other, God, as actively independent of the self and its 'world'. Thus, this God appears on the boundary of immediate self-consciousness as that which is totally outside of its own self-presencing. This qualitatively different object for consciousness uproots the prior relationship of self and world. Indeed, the lived-world of immediate self-consciousness is now modified in relation to what experientially amounts to an ontological reestablishment of self-consciousness. To use Paul Tillich's phrase, a *new being* ushers forth with immediate self-consciousness and subsequently becomes the new horizon of consciousness, a field of self-consciousness in which all other forms of feeling and immediate self-consciousness are subsumed: "Piety is the highest level of human feeling, the level which assimilates the lower levels within it, but does not exist apart from them."[75]

It is important for us to clarify at this point in our discussion that Schleiermacher is describing piety in general, not a specific modality of piety, like that found in Christianity, just as Hegel did in his description of religious sensibility in the 1821 *Concept of Religion*. For Schleiermacher, all particular manifestations of piety share a common essence, the sense of dependency on God as the outside 'infinite' whose presence impinges on self-consciousness. But, it also must be noted that, because piety has its 'seat in feeling', its tone varies according to the empirical factors involved in a given moment of consciousness. Indeed, this feeling of dependence is superimposed on the already present sensible consciousness and its feeling of partial freedom from and partial dependence on the empirical world. Thus, Schleiermacher said:

> it thereby becomes a particular religious emotion, and being in another moment related to a different datum, it becomes a different religious emotion; yet so that the essential element, namely, the feeling of absolute dependence, is the same in both, and thus throughout the whole series, and the difference arises simply from the fact that it becomes a different moment when it goes along with a different determination of the sensible self-consciousness. It remains always, however, a moment of higher power.[76]

Because of piety's seat in sensible self-consciousness, another major set of antitheses, pleasure and pain, which are grounded as well in immediate self-consciousness and which accompany its feeling of dependency and freedom, are in turn modified in light of the pious feeling of dependency and freedom. As existential modalities of feeling, pain and pleasure now are cast as religious feelings accompanying each other and elevated into a dialectic of 'joy' and 'suffering':

> And thus it is by no means that the case that the pleasant and the unpleasant, which exist in the sensible feeling, impart the same character to the feeling of absolute dependence. On the contrary, we often find, united in one and the same moment (as a clear sign that the two grades are not fused into each other or neutralized by each other so as to become a third) a sorrow of the lower and a joy of the higher self-consciousness; as, e.g., whenever with a feeling of suffering there is combined a trust in God. But the antithesis attaches to the higher self-consciousness, because it is the nature of the latter to become temporal, to manifest itself in time, by entering into a relation with the sensible self-consciousness so as to constitute a moment. That is to say: as the emergence of this higher self-consciousness at all means an enhancement of life, so whenever it emerges *with*

ease, to enter into relation with a sensible determination, whether pleasant or unpleasant, this means an easy progress of that higher life, and bears, by comparison, the stamp of joy. And as the disappearance of the higher consciousness, if it could be perceived, would mean a diminution of life, so wherever it emerges *with difficulty*, this approximates to an absence of it, and can only be felt as an inhibition of the higher life.[77]

Therefore, we can see that Schleiermacher finds a new form of consciousness has been circumscribed by the feeling of dependence. This new consciousness, the "higher" consciousness Schleiermacher alludes to in the just-quoted paragraph, is God-consciousness. Because it is structured on the basis of consciousness of God, this "higher" consciousness structures all other relations within its terms. However, there is another level of consciousness, the "lower," finite, and sensuous consciousness. Its contents may, in fact, become transfigured into the contents of the higher consciousness or it may find itself not concerned with, even alienated from, 'God' to the extent that 'God' may be totally absent from it. This "lower" consciousness therefore corresponds to what theologically has been called the *natural* side of human beings; "higher" consciousness corresponds to what has been traditionally designated the *spiritual* side of human beings.

For Schleiermacher, it would be wrong to hold that the higher, spiritual consciousness that arises from the God consciousness of the feeling of dependency must always bear the same intensity or be expressed in the same ways. As we noted earlier, sensible self-consciousness (feeling) is everpresent. Consequently, because the lower consciousness quite 'naturally' comes on the absence of an empirical object called *God* in its lived experience, higher self-consciousness does not always coincide with lower self-consciousness, or to put it another way, higher self-consciousness simply does not cancel lower self-consciousness. Rather, the alternation between higher self-consciousness and lower self-consciousness "forms the feeling-content of every religious life."[78] Thus, "in its actual occurrence" higher self-consciousness "is never separated from the lower, and through its combination therewith in a single moment it participates in the antithesis of the pleasant and the unpleasant."[79]

By thus describing sensible and religious consciousness Schleiermacher's description does not attempt to suppress the impact of natural consciousness as the most primordial consciousness of reality that is human being in the world. To do so, would be to misconstrue consciousness's need to intend empirical objects in order to exist as consciousness. But, even though lower consciousness, with its finite object, is the source of the human self-awareness in relation to a natural world, it is not the source of the natural world as far as "higher" consciousness, with its infinite, 'outside' object, God, is concerned. And, even though higher consciousness finds God in its feeling of absolute dependence, it does not feel itself to be the source of this God-consciousness. For Schleiermacher, to think that feeling is the sole source of God-consciousness would involve making the mistake of identifying consciousness of God with God himself. Hence, God would no longer be truly an infinite infinite, but a finite infinite, a mere projection of consciousness. To think this would defeat Schleiermacher's purpose in rendering a dogmatics based on the ontological ground of the feeling of dependence.

The Relations of Religion and Cognition in Dogmatics

So far we can see that Hegel's and Schleiermacher's descriptions of the ground of religion differ not only in terminology, but, most important, in terms of their understanding of when thinking and knowing occur in relation to feeling. This difference now becomes manifest in the difference in purpose in their respective enterprises. As we saw in Chapter One, Hegel not only wanted to describe religion as a complete concatenation of human being, but also that he wants to show how reason and religion are to be considered as reconciled in philosophy's conceptual thinking. Schleiermacher's purpose in writing a dogmatics, on the other hand, was to demarcate what is actually contained in higher consciousness, on the basis of deliberately retaining the integrity of consciousness of God as found in the feeling of dependence. This means that for Schleiermacher, unlike Hegel, his concepts cannot and do not capture the nature of God in their grasp. For God is both inside and outside of human consciousness, as we noted at the end of the last section. Indeed, Schleiermacher assumed that "religious men know that it is only in speech that they cannot avoid the anthropomorphic."[80] Therefore, he admits that human beings cannot help but cast God in their own image, which they then systematize in the form of dogmatics. However, it is clear that for Schleiermacher any work of dogmatics is inherently limited because the experience of God falls outside of the natural range of self-consciousness's self-containment, unlike Hegel whose philosophy of religion finds for itself that the experience of God can be fully described only by philosophy as within the enclosure of "self-consciousness of absolute spirit."[81] As we can surmise, then, the necessity of anthropomorphism is apparently not an obstacle for Schleiermacher, but, presumably, a part of the reality of human being that dogmatics reflects. Indeed, Schleiermacher assumed that the language of dogmatics can *point to* the true infinity of God: "Dogmatic propositions are doctrines of the descriptively didactic type, in which the highest possible degree of definiteness is aimed at."[82] Therefore, Schleiermacher proposes that human beings can create descriptions (which instruct) but also can order scientifically [*wissenschaftliche*] their talk about God. He therefore asserts: "Dogmatics is essentially a systematic configuration which must be exhibited in the dialectical character of language and in the methodical [*systematischen*] character of ordering."[83]

Dogmatics thus attempts to be the form of knowing that remains closest to what is experienced in the feeling of absolute dependency at its highest level. At the same time, it scientifically and systematically orders what is pointed to by the anthropomorphisms used by language in its speech about what is contained in higher consciousness. Thus, it is Schleiermacher's opinion that dogmatics can open itself up to all that is generated by religious feeling and explicate this content.

In a direct reference to philosophy and, presumably, to Hegel, Schleiermacher makes it clear that his systematic explication will not indulge in 'speculative' thinking or in logical deduction of the truths it is describing because "no philosophical proofs and no falling back on speculative doctrines can occur in dogmatics."[84] These activities fall outside of the scope of what legitimately belongs to higher self-consciousness. Indeed, speculation and logical proofs may be part of that of which the human being is capable, but they do not keep to what is contained in higher self-consciousness. All the predicates that human beings have predicated of God—such as his omniscience, omnipotence, eternal and infinite nature—can be and have been thought of as objective qualities of God, which exist 'out there', independent of our experience. Yet, those who engage in speculation and the proofs of God's existence (like Hegel) talk as if these predicates are totally comprehended by human being. As we have noted, Schleiermacher feels that our talk of God cannot correspond directly to the true nature of God as he is 'in himself', because God consciousness occurs in the nonrational core of religion, piety. Therefore, God cannot be 'known'. As José Huertas-Jourda said, in pinpointing the starting point of Heidegger's *Being and Time*, "Being overflows the categorical glance";[85] so, for Schleiermacher, consciousness of God truly grounded in the pious feeling of absolute dependency cannot fully grasp God in language. Thus, for Schleiermacher, contra Hegel, *God overflows the boundaries of human consciousness*.

Schleiermacher will acknowledge that God is "eternal," which is a synonym for the more anthropomorphic conception of 'timelessness' that is opposite to our own experience; that is, God is not subject to motion or change. As well, Schleiermacher allows that God is "omnipresent," if this term is understood as 'spacelessness' above and beyond finite location. Indeed, God's omnipresence can be said to be also that of permeating the world with his presence. But Schleiermacher qualifies this sense of omnipresence by holding that the presence of God is itself dependent on the human experience of God as he who situates himself within human experience independent of any rational effort of consciousness. Indeed, Schleiermacher said, God discloses himself as suprarational. Therefore, this suprarationality of God limits Schleiermacher's discourse in *The Christian Faith* to explicating *religion within the limits of feeling alone*: "Therefore this supra-rationality implies that a true appropriation of Christian dogmas cannot be brought about by scientific means, and thus lies outside the realm of reason: it can only be brought about through each man willing to have the experience for himself...it can only be apprehended by the love which wills to perceive. In this sense the whole of Christian doctrine is supra-rational."[86]

Mediate Self-Consciousness and the Christian Church

In section 42, Schleiermacher provides what amounts to a summary of his descriptions of religious consciousness as he has determined thus far. Also included in this summation is an affirmation of the basic methodology he has employed so far in *The Christian Faith*: "Insofar as our self-consciousness, as that which feels itself dependent, includes the world, and on the other hand, insofar as we feel ourselves dependent because of the supreme Being coestablished within this self-consciousness; the relation of the world to God is expressed in this state of mind itself, and God can only be described to the extent that this relationship is described."[87]

As we can see, Schleiermacher's method will continue to be descriptive, but with the added advantage that its subject matter, "relationship with God," has been distinguished from all other divergent subject matters and that the path that it will follow, describing Christian dogmatics in light of this relationship, has been cleared of unnecessary philosophical (and theological) obstructions. Moreover, this description is now to be seen as arising from, yet remaining inside, Christian religious consciousness, innocent of speculative philosophy and other nonrelevant ideas and ideologies. However, the innocence of this inner descriptive articulation has to be maintained with the greatest diligence: "But, if our presentation is to remain pure, we must everywhere be on our guard not to assert anything about God or the world which cannot be immediately demonstrated as a content of our self-consciousness."[88]

Important, Schleiermacher uses the third person, *our*, in this last quotation to indicate that what he is about to describe as Christian dogmatics is the result of a self-consciousness whose knowledge of the Christian religion is mediated in, with, and through the presence of other self-consciousnesses. Indeed, in talking about the origin of the Christian Church, Schleiermacher contended:

> at the same time a mutual influence is provided for, is due not only to the fact that in each there remains much of the world, against which the common activity of the rest must be brought to bear; but also to the fact that, as none credits himself with a complete and perfect apprehension of Christ, each individual regards that of others as complementary to his own; and so a mutual and reciprocal presentation results. From this everything must be derivable that can be represented as an element in the life of the Church.[89]

Schleiermacher's Christian dogmatics, in this sense, *is not only the science of feeling of what is disclosed to the individual, immediate self-consciousness but also the science of what is disclosed through the intersubjective religiosity of mediated self-consciousness as expressed in the church.* Even though feeling of absolute dependence and the consciousness of relation to God is 'inside' of each individual self-consciousness, as Schleiermacher has shown, it is now necessary for

Schleiermacher to display that it is also revealed through apperception of and empathy for the religious feeling of others, which *appears* as analogous to our own religious feeling. Indeed, the God-consciousness and God-relationship of others is revealed to us through what amounts to what we can call a *phenomenological physiognomy*; that is, what the other person feels (not only religiously, but in other ways as well) is made apparent "by means of facial expression, gesture, tones, and (indirectly) words; and so becomes to other people a revelation of the inward."[90] Thus, an individual's inwardness is brought into view for other people insofar as other people see an individual's inwardness 'inscribed' in, with, and through the phenomenon of the body. But, what is divulged through this public phenomenon is also disclosed as a *personal* configuration. In this way, continuous unveiling of personal configurations and perspectives not my own constitutes intersubjectivity. Intersubjectivity, in this sense, is like a blanket of perspectives laid over the 'world' of immediate self-consciousness. Indeed, individual, immediate self-consciousness is both encircled by the perspectives of other self-consciousnesses contemporary to it and continually immersed in and affected by these subjectivities. Thus, the field of awareness of the immediate self-consciousness enlarges to include in its scope what is deemed meaningful within the 'our' of intersubjectivity. What had previously presented itself to immediate self-consciousness as a complete constellation of experience, that is, of God consciousness, is no longer a private, isolated pocket of individual, immediate self-consciousness. Now, it is mediated through the presence of others and becomes mediated self-consciousness, that folding over of the self upon the self that can occur only through the intercession and revelation present in the appearance of other selves. In this way, the self's knowledge of its relationship with God also becomes mediated through its knowledge of God's relationship to these other selves.

Having recognized the communal scope of religiosity, Schleiermacher adjusts his description to encompass it. This, then, is the place of the church in dogmatics. The church is the expression of communal piety. But to maintain the innocence of his descriptive methodology is a difficult task in light of the many variations of religiosity expressed in the churches of the human world. Monotheism, polytheism, even atheism are all articulations of relationship to God. As we have seen, Schleiermacher has indicated that his descriptive methodology reduces the many different paths of inquiry into religion possible to the description of the inward character of religious experience. But, now, the other aspect of this methodology—not to appeal to any experience that falls outside of a 'relationship to God'—comes into play. There must be identifiable a common core of religiosity, a unique experience of the feeling of absolute dependence that marks off Christian communal piety from all other communal pieties and that pulls individuals together into the Christian church. Schleiermacher is unequivocal about what that unique, core experience is: "There is no other way of gaining participation in the Christian communion than through faith in Jesus as the Redeemer."[91]

Thus, the Christian church is formed on the basis of the personal relations of conscious subjects who share a common object of faith, Jesus Christ. As we will discuss in relation to Hegel's 1824 Introduction to the *Concept of Religion*, Schleiermacher's christology will display 'Jesus Christ' as the 'archetype of humanity'. But, let us now examine Hegel's Foreword to Hinrichs's *Religionsphilosophie*, in which Hegel responds to those sections of *The Christian Faith* we have just discussed.

Chapter Three

UNVEILING FAITH AND SPIRIT: HEGEL'S CRITICISM OF SCHLEIERMACHER IN THE FOREWORD[1]

Introduction

With the publication of the first half of Schleiermacher's *The Christian Faith* in June 1821, Hegel found it necessary to address Schleiermacher's "theology of feeling" directly. As we noted at the beginning of Chapter Two, Hegel had indirectly addressed Schleiermacher in his 1821 publication, *The Philosophy of Right*, when he attacked Fries over the Koetzebue-Sand affair. Hegel also indirectly responded to Schleiermacher in a number of comments and criticisms intertwined in his discussion of determinate religion in the 1821 lectures.[2] Hegel's first direct response to Schleiermacher comes in his 1822 Foreword to Hinrichs's *Die Religion im inneren Verhältnisse zur Wissenschaft.* "If religion in man is based only on feeling, then such a feeling rightly has no further determination to be the *feeling of his dependence*, and the dog would then be the best Christian, for the dog feels most strongly in himself and lives mainly within this feeling. The dog also has feelings of redemption, whenever his hunger is satisfied by a bone."[3]

This commonly cited[4] criticism of Schleiermacher by Hegel is a useful entry into Hegel's conceptual cognition of theology's reflection. But we must avoid the temptation to treat Hegel's criticism of Schleiermacher, especially as articulated in the "dog passage," as a matter of personal animosity or political differences.[5] To do so would not shed any light on Hegel's philosophy as it develops in

75

relation to religion and theology in the interim between the 1821 and the 1824 lectures on the philosophy of religion.

The best way to begin to understand Hegel's criticism of Schleiermacher is to recall the notion of "oral broadening," which we discussed earlier in terms of the 1824 lecture series and the dynamics of lecturing, and apply it to the dynamics of writing a Foreword to a book about to be published. Indeed, we can say that the notion of "oral broadening," as already implied in the dynamics of lecturing, when applied to the act of writing a Foreword, is based on the assumption that the lecturer or writer takes into thoughtful consideration the audience and then adjusts the scope of discourse accordingly. Therefore, we can assume only that Hegel was more than mindful that his students, Schleiermacher's students (and the students that they had in common), Schleiermacher's and his own colleagues in the theology and philosophy department, members of the Historical School and Academy of Sciences, as well as the minister of education, Karl von Altenstein, and, of course, Schleiermacher himself, would be reading and interpreting the Foreword as a response to *The Christian Faith*. Obviously, then, Hegel's criticism and, especially, the "dog passage" can be construed only as Hegel's philosophical response to the theology of his time, that is, a response that required graphic criticism to drive home the implications of a theology based on feeling. Indeed, Hegel depicts Schleiermacher's theology, and any other thinking based solely on feeling, as the "malady of our time": "This *malady*, the *contingency* and *arbitrary will* of *subjective* feeling and its opining, combined with the *culture of reflection* which claims that spirit is *incapable* of the *knowledge of truth*, has since ancient times been called 'sophistry'."[6]

Lest his audience remain unaware of who and what mode of thinking exemplifies this contemporary sophistry, Hegel adds the following pointed reference to Schleiermacher, translator of Plato,[7] in conjunction with a summation of the contemporary intellectual climate in which Hinrichs's book will be read:

> I believed that in this foreword I should remind the author himself of the sort of reception and favor he would have to expect from a state-of-affairs where what calls itself "philosophy," and indeed is always talking about Plato himself, no longer has any inkling of the nature of speculative thinking, of the contemplation of the idea—where in both philosophy

and theology there swagger the *beast-like ignorance of God* and the *sophistry of this ignorance* which put personal feeling and subjective opining in the place of the doctrine of religious belief as well as in the place of fundamental principles, laws, and duties.[8]

Hegel's audience could not fail to note the severity of these charges against Schleiermacher. To equate the feeling of absolute dependence with the feelings of a dog to its master, and then to continue to link this 'beast-like ignorance' and 'sophistry' with the thought of a person who translates Plato would be the ultimate opprobrium in the eyes of Hegel's readers, especially because, as we have seen, both Hegel and Schleiermacher place animal awareness at a distinctly lower, solely natural, level. It should also be obvious to Hegel's audience that Hegel thinks that Schleiermacher's theology of feeling reduces and limits the reality of religion to a single subjective faculty, feeling, and is thus capable of nothing more than "subjective opining." By itself, this philosophical charge of subjectivism (and, by extension, relativism) would be a serious enough censure of Schleiermacher's claim to be scientifically expounding Christian faith as it is—"Dogmatic Theology is the science which systematizes the doctrine prevalent in a Christian Church at a given time"[9]—but to add that his theology amounts to unthinking ("beast-like ignorance") would be sufficient reason for Hegel's audience to sit up and carefully consider the thinking behind these charges. Thus, as Hegel's audience would (and we should) conclude, Hegel thinks that Schleiermacher's theology is at best a tenuous theoretical relationship to God and, decidedly, does not even resemble what Hegel considers to be objective knowledge of God.

As we can see, Hegel's central task in the Foreword is to confront Schleiermacher's theology in terms of its knowledge of God. Indeed, Schleiermacher's account of feeling and its relation to knowledge of God falters on one principal point: *it simply does not distinguish animal (natural) sensibility and human (religious) sensibility finely enough.* Therefore, Hegel finds himself compelled to clarify the ground of human knowledge of God, which, as we shall presently see, is *faith as the concurrence of subjective feeling and objective content in the life of the individual.* In this way, Hegel's criticism of Schleiermacher is also a sublation of the theology of feeling.

The Foreword

As the last section intimated, Hegel's Foreword to Hinrichs's *Religionsphilosophie* continues the discussion of reason and religion that we found at the end of the 1821 manuscript on consummate religion,[10] with the difference, however, as we have noted, that Hegel is no longer addressing only an "isolated order" of "student-priests," but, also, a larger audience, including the "theologians of the present day." With Schleiermacher's *The Christian Faith* in mind as chief representative of the theology and malady of the present day, Hegel addresses the issue of the relationship of subjectivity and objectivity, religion and reason, in terms of the opposition of faith and reason; that is, in terms of the classical expression of the opposition that, as we have seen in Chapter One, underscores the relations of philosophy and religion in the Christian world.

Because of the long discussion of relations between faith and reason in the history of the philosophy of religion, the term *faith* not only has certain technical and existential resonances within the language of his general audience—undoubtedly part of what apparently is a strategy of stylistic and terminological simplicity—but it also directly signifies to his audience that he, too, as a philosopher of religion, has decided to engage Schleiermacher in a dialogue about 'faith' as the foundation of what is contained within the horizon of religion. As well, Hegel is reappropriating the term *faith* with a specific need of the time in mind—to revivify for his audience a term that had become so routine and decolorated as a signifier of a basic human reality that a theologian like Schleiermacher could reinterpret it with apparent impunity. But lest we suspect that Hegel is teetering too far into the theological side of knowledge of God, it is clear that Hegel has a definite philosophical purpose in mind as well; that is, to set into motion a crucial distinction between *faith* as philosophy comprehends it in its lived actuality and Schleiermacher's notion of *feeling*, a notion that philosophy will also reappropriate as part of its speculative mirroring of a contemporary expression of theological thought.

Indeed, Hegel sees the problem of reconciling reason to faith and faith to reason continuing in much the same manner as he described it at the end of the 1821 lectures; that is, that present in the thinking of many of his contemporaries is either a notion of this opposition as irredeemably bifurcated or a notion of the opposition as not really existing, as if the differences between faith and reason could be and should be collapsed into each other. Either way, for Hegel, is unacceptable. As Richard E. Brandt puts it, in his short appendix on Hegel and Schleiermacher in *The Philosophy of Schleiermacher*: "It is desirable that there should be some reconciliation of this conflict, but it must be a reconciliation in which the claims of both reason and faith are really satisfied."[11] For Hegel, this satisfactory reconciliation is already implicit in the originary moment of religion, religious sensibility, as we discussed in Chapter One. It is now a matter of re-cognizing this essential truth and bringing it to the attention of others, especially to an influential theologian like Schleiermacher. For Hegel, this was not an unrealistic goal. He himself had come to this truth as a theology student in Tübingen: "the Ideas of Reason enliven the whole web of human feeling—their operation penetrates everything, like subtle matter and gives a peculiar tinge to every inclination and impulse."[12] In 1822, this was still how Hegel conceived of the essential relation of reason and feeling.[13] Feeling and reason are codeterminants of human being as whole, complete being. Whereas a thinker like Schleiermacher, while engaging at various times in translation of Plato, philosophy of religion, ethics, aesthetics, and a host of other philosophical activities, would not admit the possibility of reason coinstantaneously informing religious feeling and thus leaves only "the empty shell of subjective conviction."[14] Consequently, Schleiermacher's theology of feeling is only the flip side of Enlightenment reason that, in its post-Kantian form, "renounced the cognition of truth, and has left to spirit only an issue, partly of appearances, partly of feelings."[15] For Hegel, this present state of affairs constitutes a paradoxical 'discord', a discord that is not really a discord insofar as what is essential to disagreement, a common theme or object of disagreement, is missing. He asks (somewhat rhetorically): "How then could there be a great discord between faith [*Glaube*] and reason, if neither has objective content any longer, so that there is present no object of dispute."[16]

To pierce through this illusory veil of discord around knowledge of God made by thinkers like Schleiermacher, Hegel set for himself what Merold Westphal identified as a "Platonic-Aristotelian task": to combat the sophistry that, through the subjectivism of pietistic theology of feeling and the post-Kantian 'skepticism' about the possibility of knowledge of God, has reached an illusory peace in regard to the discord between faith and reason.[17] For Hegel, as for

Plato and Aristotle, it is pure intellectual folly to base any knowledge claim on subjectivism and skepticism. And, like Plato and Aristotle, Hegel argues that any attempt to do so knowingly is a sophistry that must be combated with thinking anchored in objective and absolute truth. But, rather than aiming for an objective and absolute knowledge of God conceived as independent transcendent reality that exists beyond the grasp of our cognitive abilities, as did Socrates, Hegel centers his discussion on what is immanent in, and thus is available to, self-consciousness; that is, that knowledge of God which, as we discussed in Chapter One, exists when human thought thinks itself and elevates finite human consciousness into infinite divine self-consciousness.[18]

For Hegel, reflection on and explication of 'faith' and its content provides the most suitable entry point to that knowledge of God which already exists within the human being. Indeed, *faith* already contains within its horizon of meaning the conditions for a genuine objective knowledge of God as well as providing the ground for a 'genuine' reconciliation of the opposition between faith and reason. Hegel wrote:

> By faith, of course, I do not understand either the merely subjective state of being convinced, which is limited to the form of certainty and still leaves undetermined whether it has content, and if so, what content it has—or, on the other hand, only the creed, the church's confession of faith, which is set down in words and in writing, and can be admitted orally, in mental imagery, and in memory, without penetrating the inner man, without having identified with the certainty which a man has of himself, or with human self-consciousness. I consider faith, according to the genuine sense of the term, as involving both phases, the one just as much as the other, and I place them together, bound up in a differentiated unity [*in unterschiedener Einheit*].[19]

As we can see, Hegel locates faith as "differentiated unity," or unity-in-difference; that is, at the commencement of religious consciousness. Indeed, in the 1824 *Concept of Religion*, he states explicitly that "What has emerged as religion, and is a product of the divine spirit, shows itself first as faith."[20] Following the dialectic of thought and sensibility set out in his discussion of the religious relationship in the 1821 *Concept of Religion*, although changing its terms, Hegel states that there are two elements within this differentiated unity: the 'feeling' side of conviction that something is the case, and the objective 'content' side, that is, the 'case' affirmed by feeling. With the two sides of this inner division identified as the two sides of faith's unity-in-difference, Hegel now proceeded to describe them.

Simply stated, the objective content of faith is the system of belief that has been articulated and encoded into a set of creeds and doctrines by the religious community. Furthermore, this objective content exists regardless of whether or not specific individuals have, as we said in our consideration of the 1821 *Concept of Religion*, 'subjectively appropriated' this 'inherited faith'. As we can see, this aspect of faith should not be construed as purely subjective, regardless of its origin in the thought of members of a religious community. Rather, faith is to be comprehended as holding within its purview content, which is objective insofar as it manifests itself as *the* doctrine of truth. And, Hegel wrote, "The doctrine of truth is no more and no less than this: to be a doctrine of God, and to have revealed His nature and occupation."[21] As is now apparent, this objective content of faith arises through interaction with others, but what is significant for Hegel is that it presents itself as the divine plan in whose terms the religious community constructs its world as world. Accordingly, these creeds and doctrines also present themselves to the individual as the eternal framework in which one is to think, feel, and act.

We must, however, emphasize that in depicting the content of faith in this way, Hegel no longer conceived the doctrines of the church as something simply 'inherited'. Rather, here, Hegel is placing more stress on the objective nature of creed and doctrine than he did in the 1821 manuscript, an accentuation necessary in light of Pietist and Schleiermacher's attempts at theologizing: "But regarding the *requirement* of our time, it is the case that the *common* requirement of *religion* and *philosophy* is directed toward a *substantial, objective content of truth*."[22]

However, this 'objective faith' is what is forgotten or ignored by contemporary theologians like Schleiermacher:

> It is the quite symptomatic appearance of our time to have reverted, at the pinnacle of its culture, to that old mental image which holds that God is uncommunicative and does not reveal

His nature to the human spirit. This assertion of the jealousy of God must be much more conspicuous within the sphere of the Christian religion, because this religion is said to be nothing other than the *revelation* of what God is, and the Christian community is supposed to be nothing other than the community into which the spirit of God is sent and in which this spirit— just that spirit which, because it is spirit, is not sensuous and feeling, not a mental imagining of something sensuous, but, rather, thinking, knowing, cognizing; and because it is the divine Holy Spirit, is only the thinking, knowing, and cognizing of God—guides its members toward the cognition of God. What ever would the Christian community be without this cognition? What is a theology without a cognition of God? Precisely what a philosophy is without a cognition of God: a resounding brass and tinkling cymbal.[23]

On the other side of faith, in acknowledgment of Schleiermacher's description of feeling, Hegel affirms that the certainty and conviction of feeling is of utmost importance to fulfilment of faith. Indeed, the immediate certainty of feeling is that which allows the creeds and doctrines to "penetrate," as Hegel explained, to the core of the inner person thereby maintaining faith as a living unity. Of course, as soon as the two sides are distinguished through reflection, one side can be emphasized over the other. Indeed, emphasis on the objective, doctrinal side negates the importance of the subjective, feeling side (Pietism's and Kierkegaard's complaint), whereas overemphasis on the subjective, feeling side can negate the importance of the objective, doctrinal side (Hegel's complaint). Therefore, we can see that for Hegel both sides are important: one side of 'faith' without the other does not provide any possibility of the realization of the truth of the God-human relationship. Thus, 'true faith', for Hegel, is the holding together and interpretation of the "subjective state of being convinced" and the objective side, the "church's confession of faith," which, as we have seen, is also immanent insofar as it is produced and shared by the religious community.

The Inner Dynamics of Faith

In terms of the "subjective state of being convinced," this side of 'faith' can be called *belief*. Indeed, what Hegel finds on the subjective side is the *natural belief* that underlies and permits coherent living in the world. For Hegel, belief is that most fundamental, everyday form of human understanding of the life world. It can range from the immediate sense-certainty of what is given to consciousness in the living present of the 'here' and 'now' (for example, the 'here' of standing before a tree and the 'now' of being in the night) to beliefs based on past experience (for example, that the sun will rise tomorrow) to more sophisticated, theoretical beliefs (such as the law of gravity always affecting the trajectory of a projectile), and so on. In this sense, natural belief is that which underlies all other more sophisticated forms of human knowledge. Although Hegel holds that there is distinction between (natural) beliefs and the subjective beliefs that are formulated on the basis of inner conviction, as is meant by Schleiermacher's notion of feeling, he maintained that the distinction is inconsequential. In fact, Hegel claims that natural beliefs and subjective convictions are essentially manifestations of the same primordial mode of being in the world.

> belief is generally a *taking-as-true*; what is claimed to be true may be organized according to its inner nature, in any way whatever. It is this same taking-as-true which is and is valid in its place within the everyday things of ordinary life, its conditions, relations, events, or other natural existences, properties, and qualities. If the criteria on the basis of which belief in such things emerges are sensuous external direct beholding, or internal immediate feeling, the testimonies of others, and trust in their witness, etc., then doubtless hereby a conviction as a taking-as-true mediated through *grounds* can be differentiated from belief as such. But this differentiation is too insignificant to maintain that such a conviction has an advantage over mere belief; for the so-called grounds are nothing other than the indicated sources of what is here called belief.[24]

Thus, for Hegel, not every belief is determined by sensibility and solely the result of the apprehension involved in our everyday consciousness and understanding of our world. There are beliefs that are the result of subjective appropriation of grounds for believing that such and such is the case and, as such, become a matter of conviction. Of course, as the preceding passage makes clear, belief in and of itself is simply inadequate a mode of human being to be taken alone as the sole signifier of what is involved in faith. For Hegel, as we have already noted, one side of the two moments of the differentiated unity of faith without the other does not provide any possibility of the comprehensive realization of what is unique to the human-God relationship that the word *faith* has traditionally signified.

Hegel's interpretation of faith thus rests on the question of the relation of subjective conviction (belief) to objective creeds and doctrines. Without the collective religiosity of creeds to frame belief as *religious* belief, belief is an accidental momentary state of the finite human subject. In fact, creeds and doctrines condition what is believed. They shape sensibility and transmute it into *religious sensibility* through already-existing categories of knowledge of God. On the other side, the creeds and doctrines thought by the finite human subject are only rote, aimless and floating unsubstantiated inklings of the objective content of human knowledge, if they are not brought into concurrence with the subjective conviction that there is a God. Thus, Hegel agrees with Schleiermacher to the extent that the manner in which knowledge of God becomes manifest to the finite human subject is determined by feeling. But, this agreement, as we can see, is only partial, for, as we have shown, Hegel sees that this feeling is also determined by the sociohistorical religious milieu in which the finite human subject finds itself.

Significantly, neither 'creed' nor 'subjective conviction' have chronological priority over the other in the differentiated unity of faith. Rather, it is clear that Hegel perceived faith as that mode of religious consciousness in which religious consciousness appears to itself as religious precisely because it is framed as such by its own objective religious content. Thus, faith produces its own inner hermeneutic. And, on the basis of this self-hermeneutic, we can see that *faith's actualization of the intermixture of subjective feeling and objective content depends on the simultaneous self-interpretation of this subjective feeling as religious.* This hermeneutic is itself possible only through the religious community and the institutionalized pedagogy of its church:

> The internal activity of the church will consist principally in the education of the human being, in the business of internalizing the truth which, at first, can be given only to representation and to memory, so that the mind may become captivated and permeated with it, and self-consciousness may find itself and its

essential stability only in that truth. However, as a part of the appearance of the permanent process of education, there is a separation of immediate self-certainty from the genuine content, and these two are united with each other neither immediately nor permanently and firmly in all of their determinations. Self-certainty is, to begin with, natural feeling and natural will, as well as the opinions and vain imaginings which correspond to this feeling and will; but the genuine content comes to spirit externally at first, in the word and the letter. Religious education brings about a unity of the two, so that the feelings, which are immediate to man only when they are natural, lose their force, and what was the letter grows into its own living spirit.[25]

Therefore, feeling and faith can be seen as separate if we are discussing the genesis of faith in terms of the immediate self-consciousness of the individual. Again, to an extent, Schleiermacher is correct. The individual human subject can be considered as a feeling subject who has a vast array of dispositions that arise through empirical sensibility. And, Hegel adds, these feelings are natural and thus prior to religious feeling. Therefore, they may not link up with the creeds of the church inculcated into the individual. In fact, the immediate self-consciousness of subject may reach out to a system of belief that exists as 'letter', as something outside of itself and thus may be interpreted willy-nilly. But, for Hegel, faith itself is a matter of mediated self-consciousness, and its differentiated unity is possible only if there is representation provided to it and inculcated into its rote memory by religious education. To understand how the differentiated unity of faith can spiritualize the letter of the imagery of the church, we must now examine how consciousness mediates subjective feeling and objective content.

The Relationship of Feeling and Thinking in Faith

As we have just seen, the differentiated unity of faith is possible only when the 'letter' of religious imagery is already present within the prereflective 'world' in which the finite human subject finds itself and that is inculcated into the memory of the finite human subject by religious education. Through religious education, all the experience of the finite human subject becomes understood in terms of the imagery of religious language. Hegel's notion of faith, then, presupposes that this letter of the imagery of religious language is already present in the life of the individual so the spiritualization of these presuppositions can occur (if and when the finite human subject responds to the truth inherent in this imagery as its own truth). In this way, through faith, the content of religious language becomes incarnate, embodied in the conscious life of the subject as its very fabric and essence. However, on the basis of what amounts to a dichotomy between the 'letter' and 'spirit' of 'the Truth', the 'letter' of the creed and its content is epistemologically prior to the 'spirit' or inwardness of the belief side of the unity of faith. Ontologically, however, the finite human subject must first be considered in its naturalness as a feeling subject who has within itself a vast array of dispositions that arise through empirical sensibility. These feelings, as we have said, are natural and because of their ontological priority the "modification and unification of what is at first external material...instantly encounters an adversary with which it must deal: there is an immediate opponent in the natural spirit, which the modification and unification must presuppose, precisely because it is free spirit which is to be engendered, not a natural life, because free spirit exists only as a reborn spirit. Nevertheless, this natural adversary is overcome in its very origin, and free spirit set free, through the divine idea."[26]

This struggle is the conflict of opposites that Hegel identified in the 1821 concept of religion as implicit in the religious relationship's unity of absolute singularity and absolute universality. Now, with the additional knowledge of Schleiermacher's analysis of immediate self-consciousness, Hegel saw that the problem of the conflict between the 'natural', finite self-consciousness and the 'spiritual', infinite self-consciousness is precisely a matter of the 'absolute singularity' of the sensibility and the natural beliefs of the finite individual *over and against* the absolute universality of the 'pure thinking' that comes through the objective content of faith as 'the consciousness of the true in and for itself'. Indeed, without the original overcoming of the natural side of which Hegel speaks in the preceding quotation, the natural side of human feeling may never link up with the spiritual side of human being as imparted through religious education. Moreover, the finite individual subject may maintain an intellectual distance between the belief system in which it was born and only reach out to touch it (but not grasp it) through the "supersensuous essence" of human being, thinking.[27] Because of the human capacity for "independent thinking," thinking not grounded in the recognition of its "divine origin" and that therefore declares its own autonomous ground, the 'spiritual' side itself of human being may give rise to "an even greater and more obstinate struggle."[28] In general, Hegel finds that human being, because of its ability to think itself in isolation, can lean too far into what he calls "finite reason" and concentrate only on human ends, imposing on its world only its own shape of truth, to the detriment of that 'divine thinking,' which is contemplation of "the infinite and the eternal as that which alone has being" and which should be affirmed as such.[29] Such 'divine thinking' would entail the embracing of what is already divine in human thinking, the infinite reason already accessible to the human mind in the form of the objective doctrines inherited through religious education.

Keeping all of this in mind, Hegel discerned yet another way finite thinking may approach the religious creeds and doctrines of religious faith. Finite thinking may attempt to understand the contents of the objective side of faith, not by taking an adversarial and negative attitude to it, but by illustrating this content through its own imagination:

> it will...take the trouble within this doctrine, allegedly for the benefit of religion, to embellish, support, and honour the doctrine with its discoveries, curiosities, and ingenuities. In such an endeavour it may happen that the understanding ties a multitude of determinations to the doctrine of faith, as deductions or presuppositions, foundations and aims—determinations which, although they are of finite import, are easily attributed a dignity, significance, and validity equal to that of the eternal truth itself, because they appear in an immediate association with this truth. At the same time, since they have only finite import, and hence are susceptible to counter-arguments and objections, they are likely to require external authority for their maintenance; thus they become a battlefield for human passions. Produced in the interest of what is finite, they are not supported by the testimony of the Holy Spirit, but by finite interests.[30]

At this point in the Foreword, we can see that Hegel is broadening his description of the relationship of finite thinking to faith as a concrete human modality to incorporate allusions to the history of Christian thought and the various orthodoxies and heterodoxies that have been advocated in the course of this history. But, setting aside this historical side for present, we can see that for Hegel this thinking remains finite and one-sided if it remains rooted in natural belief. Indeed, its thinking becomes that of the Understanding [*Verstand*], importing into its horizon of meaning all sorts of derivations and supports, such as the authority of the Church, impassioned logomachies and sophistries, and as Kierkegaard would say, all sorts of *"approximation-processes"*[31] that attempt to challenge, correct, or, at minimum, refine thought about God ever present in human being as thinking being. Thus, the Understanding sets itself up as arbitrator of what is absolute truth; furthermore, it replaces faith's absolute conviction of the truth of its objective doctrines with provisional truths. In this way, the Understanding can hold sway over human thinking and prevent it from realizing its potential in the two-sided sense of faith. Such is the veil cast by the 'theologians of the Understanding' over knowledge of God.[32]

Notwithstanding this criticism of the 'theologians of the Understanding', Hegel does not seem to be outright condemning this intrusion of the Understanding into the domain of infinite reason. In a way, Hegel was saying, this intrusion is inevitable because of the way absolute truth appears: "Absolute truth itself, however, when it appears, passes over into temporal configuration, and into its external conditions, associations, and circumstances."[33] Indeed, the unfolding of the (divine) Idea, already alluded to in the rebirthing and overcoming of the natural side of human being "through the divine idea," as we saw earlier in this chapter, falls by necessity into the historical experience of the human being. And, although various historical interpretative configurations accrue to the divine Idea, the divine Idea remains the thematic center for religious consciousness. At the same time, however, all the vagaries of finite human thinking arising within the course of human history create a thematic field, "a multiplicity of local, historical, and other positive material"[34] around this thematic center. Subsequently, we find crystallized within the domain of religion belief systems that not only contain "absolute Being and eternal history," but also "finite histories, events, circumstances, mental images, commandments, etc."[35] It is this field of belief that becomes encrusted through the socialization of the finite human subject as part of the true religious education that passes on what is truly transcendent and eternal. Again, Hegel did not reject these external encrustations; indeed, this "sphere of histories and doctrines which surrounds the eternal truth...deserves, at the very least, the greatest attention and a respectful treatment."[36] They, however, may obstruct the possibility of ascent to absolute truth if the finite human subject learns to mistake the 'ancillary', external encrustations of the Understanding for the absolute truth. Hegel saw this happening in the dogmatic, close-minded thinking that attempts to impart its own particular understanding to others:

> Now it is one thing if such a sphere is innocently taken by pious sentiment alone, and utilized for the sake of this sentiment; but it is something else if it is grasped by one understanding offered to another understanding in the way in which it is grasped and fixed by the first understanding, so as to be valid to the second understanding as the standard and as a solid basis for taking-as-true; in so doing this second understanding is supposed to subjugate itself only to the first understanding, providing that this subjugation is demanded in the name of divine truth.[37]

By subjugating itself to its own authority, the Understanding confines itself in the thematic field of the divine Idea without ever knowing the divine Idea itself. This misunderstanding thus becomes the whole basis of the theology of the Understanding in which, perhaps, some true knowledge of God and human existence may seep through—but that which ultimately is engaged in perpetuating epicycles of thought that circle around the true center, the divine Idea, and that, like the epicycles necessitated by the Ptolemaic geocentric view of the universe, obfuscates cognition of the center. However, one further ingredient is necessary for this to happen, and this ingredient is the 'witness of the Spirit'.

Hegel called this third moment in which faith finds itself in the 'inner testimony of the Spirit', *Luther's faith* in 1821, as we noted in Chapter Two, and it is what we alluded to as *existential faith*. Indeed, because 'Luther's faith' can take place only in the life of the individual finite human being, it is existential in orientation. Moreover, the existentiality of what Hegel later called *the principle of subjectivity*, arising with Protestantism, arrives late on the religious scene. In fact, the existential realization of the truth of the whole spiritual process that is grounded in faith is the 'last moment' in the consideration of the *cultus*. As Hegel noted in the 1824 *Concept of Religion*: "The final [moment] of the *cultus*, then, is precisely that individuals work through this process on their own and so remain members of the community in which the spirit is living."[38]

Luther's Faith: Its Source and Ground

Luther's faith is grounded in an ontology of difference between God and the human being that, at the same time, is a difference that has been overcome through the life, death, and resurrection of Jesus Christ. Nevertheless, it is central to Luther's faith that we first clearly understand how Luther viewed humanity and God as radically distinct from each other. For Luther, God is the Creator of human beings, and human beings, precisely because they are created beings, can never equal their Creator. Thus, in this Creator-creature relationship lies the crucial dissimilarity between God and humankind about which Luther wrote in his *Sermons on the Gospel of St. John*: "For God is not created or made as we human beings are; He is from all eternity. No one has given Him His Speech, His Word, or His conversation. What He is, He is of Himself from eternity. But whatever we are, we received from Him and not from ourselves. He alone has everything from Himself."[39]

Indeed, Luther believed that before the creation of humanity and its world, God was a unity unto himself, a unity that at the same time is inwardly differentiated into three persons: the Father, the Son, and the Holy Spirit. Because this divine unity also contains within itself these three distinct persons, Luther suggested that it is proper to think that this tripersonal God was involved in an inner conversation with himself before the generation of the world:

> God...in His majesty and nature, is pregnant with a Word or a conversation in which He engages with Himself in His divine essence and which reflects the thoughts of His heart. This is as complete and excellent and perfect as God Himself. No one but God alone sees, hears, or comprehends this conversation. It is an invisible and incomprehensible conversation. His Word existed before all angels and all creatures existed, for subsequently He brought all creatures into being by means of this Word and conversation. God is so absorbed in this Word, thought, or conversation that He pays no attention to anything else.[40]

But, Luther noted, we can also conceive of this inner conversation and its inner Word as exteriorized through the act of creation: "The created Word is brought into being by the uncreated Word. What else is the entire creation than the Word of God uttered by God, or extended to the outside? But the uncreated Word is a divine thought, an inner command which abides in God, the same as God and yet a distinct Person. Thus God reveals Himself to us as the Speaker who has with Him the uncreated Word, through whom He created the world and all things with the greatest ease, namely, by speaking."[41]

This 'created' and 'uncreated' Word is, for Luther, Jesus Christ, the Word made flesh. In his commentary on John 1:3, Luther made this connection between the Word as Christ and creation explicit:

> this text is a strong and valid attestation of the divinity of Christ. St. John includes every creature in his expression, for he says: "All things [for he who uses the word *all* does not exclude anything] were made by the Word, who was in the beginning." Now Creator and creature are two distinct entities. He, the Word, already existed in the beginning when all things were made. From this fact the evangelist concludes that He not only antedated all creatures, but also that He was a coworker and equal Creator of all things with the Father....All that is made, is made through Him; He is the Creator of all creatures. Thus, so far as Their divine nature is concerned, there is no difference between Him and the Father....According to His divine nature, He is the true God, who was in the beginning and was with God. This He actively demonstrated in the work of creation; for all creatures, angels, heaven, and earth were made by Him.[42]

Because God preexisted before creation in an immanent Trinity so completely self-enclosed, its inner conversation transcends humanity's ability to comprehend its essence. Humankind can come to know of God's preexistence, but, as we will see, only through the activity of God as economic Trinity; that is, through the saving work of the Son, Jesus Christ, and the witness of the Holy Spirit in the heart of the believing individual. But, as Luther noted, this state of ignorance was not always the case. Rather, it is the result of human self-exclusion from God's inner dialogue, a self-exclusion caused by sin in the event of the Fall. Before the Fall, human beings were not outside of God's inner conversation, but were absorbed in and sustained through God's Word, and thus were able to attend to God's Word, precisely because it was and continues to be the source of their being. Indeed, through the Fall, the difference between Creator and creature becomes highly pronounced, accentuating the initial ontological difference between God and humankind. Luther found that this alienating distance between God and humankind is evidenced by the truth that "this Word in God is entirely different from my word or yours."[43] What this difference in word indicates, for Luther, is that fallen humanity has become absorbed in its own conversation, a conversation caught in the vortex of fleshly existence and hence restricted to a fleshly circuit between the human heart and human reason.

Indeed, for Luther, reason cannot be located anywhere else than within the flesh, regardless of what reason may think about itself. As Merold Westphal succinctly put it:

> As the enemy within us, an ally of the law in opposition to the gospel of grace, reason is often identified by Luther with the flesh in its opposition to the Spirit. This identification made it clear that Luther has no Platonic, gnostic, dualistic view of the flesh, as if it represented the lowest in us against the highest, the bodily and animal side of our nature against the mental and divine side. His is instead a Pauline view, according to which the flesh includes even the highest in us whenever it declares its autonomy in relation to God's sovereignty. Thus reason as an expression of the flesh is human thought uninformed by, and independent of, the Word and Spirit of God. It is by no means unreligious, but its religion is based on the presumption of self-chosen forms of worship, and these deserve to be called superstition.[44]

Indeed, Luther asserts that a human being is not to be understood as divided into a rational, objective, and divine part over and against an irrational, subjective, and human part, which somehow coexist. Rather, Luther referred to reason as being embodied as a "word of the heart":

> When, for example, we think about some thing and diligently investigate it, we have words; we carry on a conversation

within ourselves. Its content is unknown to all but ourselves until such words of the heart are translated into oral words and speech, which we now utter after we have revolved them in our heart and have reflected on them for a long time. Not until then is our word heard and understood by others....For a word is not merely the utterance of the mouth; rather it is the thought of the heart. Without this thought the external word is not spoken; or if it is spoken, it has substance only when the word of the mouth is in accord with the word of the heart. Only then is the external word meaningful; otherwise it is worthless.[45]

Insofar as reason is embodied, Luther was suggesting, all it can know and think is its life from within, from the subjective realm of its inner conversation. Indeed, because knowing can take place only through the alignment of thought and the heart, this means that human thinking is incapable of objectivity. Nevertheless, Luther affirmed that the rational aspect of human being, in its reflection on its 'word of the heart', can and does separate its word from its heart. In this way, yet another difference arises: the rational part of humanity, the mind, flatters itself into thinking itself separate and superior to its own heart and flesh. Such a bifurcation is not only symptomatic of the rupture between God and humankind engendered in the Fall, but it accentuates the God-human difference by assuming what Luther noted becomes a "normal human pattern"[46] of self-righteousness and self-centeredness. Indeed, by granting itself autonomy and authority, reason presumes that it is capable of knowing eternal truth. But, Luther proposed, this presumption is ultimately dangerous:

nothing is more dangerous than to stray into heaven with our idle speculations, there to investigate God in His incomprehensible power, wisdom, and His majesty, to ask how He created the world and how He governs it. If you attempt to comprehend God this way and want to make atonement to Him apart from Christ the Mediator, making your works, fasts, cowl, and tonsure the mediation between Him and yourself, you will inevitably fall, as Lucifer did, and in horrible despair lose God and everything. For as in His own nature God is immense, incomprehensible, and infinite, so as to man's nature He is intolerable.[47]

In contrast to reason's idle and dangerous speculations, Luther believed that true thoughts about God can issue from human beings if and only if they have entered the heart from a source other than the heart. Indeed, nothing of any eternal consequence can come out of humankind's conversation with itself unless the Holy Spirit breaks into the human conversation by affecting the heart: "No man can accept it unless his heart has been touched and opened by the Holy Spirit."[48] Once the Holy Spirit opens the human heart then it can be lifted into the circle of God's inner conversation where the immanent and economic activity of the Trinity becomes revealed:

> Any attempt to fathom and comprehend such statements [about the preexistence of the Word of God] with human reason and understanding will avail nothing, for none of this has its source in the reason: that there was a Word in God before the world's creation, and that this Word was God; that, as John says further on, this same Word, the Only-begotten of the Father, full of grace and truth, rested in the Father's bosom or heart and became flesh; and that no one else had ever seen or known God, because the Word, who is God's only-begotten Son, rested in the bosom and revealed Him to us. Nothing but faith can comprehend this. Whoever refuses to accept it in faith, to believe it before he understands it, but insists on exploring it with his reason and his five senses, let him persist in this if he will. But our mind will never master this doctrine; it is far too lofty for our reason. Holy Writ assures us that faith alone can appropriate it. Let anyone who refuses to believe it let it alone. In the end only the Holy Spirit from Heaven above can create listeners and pupils who accept this doctrine and believe that the Word is God, that God's Son is the Word, and that the Word became flesh, that He is also the Light who can illumine all men who come into the world, and that without this Light, all is darkness.[49]

Thus, we can see that for Luther to have faith is to hear and participate in God's Word as witnessed to and verified by the Holy Spirit. Moreover, it is quite clear that this faith is not a product of human reason. Indeed, Luther concluded, "the knowledge of Christ and of faith is not a human work but utterly a divine gift; as God creates so He preserves us in it."[50]

Let us now look at how Luther and Lutherans understand how the Word made flesh in Jesus Christ affects the human heart.

The Subjectification of Objective Doctrine

At the heart of Luther's theology is the belief that "God and man are united in one person"; that is, in Jesus Christ. Even though Luther did not formulate this belief into a precise theological doctrine, it became the foundation of Lutheranism, especially as enacted in the Lutheran observance of communion. It is with Martin Chemnitz,[51] an influential sixteenth-century Lutheran thinker, in *On the Two Natures of Christ*, that the notion of the conjoining of divine and human natures in the form of a single personality, Jesus Christ, became encapsulated in the theological phrase *communicatio idiomatum* (literally, "communion of properties"). This doctrine, *communicatio idiomatum*, states that there is an intimate union of the two natures of Jesus Christ but "no commingling, conversion, abolition, or equating" of the divine and human natures.[52] Chemnitz explained: "The natures are not poured together, but each nature with its properties remains intact and distinct. For Christ is both God and man, and He is and remains co-substantial with the Father according to the deity but of the same substance with Mary and with us according to the humanity [human nature]."[53]

As we can see, Lutheran christology retains the basic claim of Christianity, proclaimed from the council of Chalcedon onward,[54] that divine and human natures are united in the person of Christ. Indeed, the Lutheran doctrine of *communicatio idiomatum* articulates in precise terminology the notion of the Church Fathers that there is an intimate union of the divine and human, infinite and finite, and that they are brought together in the *personality* of Christ, fused but not confused, separate and distinct, yet unified in difference.[55] Moreover, Chemnitz's formulation, *communicatio idiomatum*, provides the theoretical underpinnings for the fundamental thesis of Luther's theology of the cross, that God Himself died on the cross. Luther can assert that God is dead precisely because the simultaneity of the two natures, the divine and human, in one person, means that the human side is subsumed under the divine side, and thus, in effect, God was crucified on Golgotha.

By focusing on the death of God in the person of Christ, Luther was stressing the importance of these truths for the feeling side of the human subject. Indeed, this notion of the death of God is a powerful, pathos-ridden notion that fills the heart of the finite human subject and, as such, becomes the frame of reference for the human subject's understanding of the divine activity of the Trinity. Luther wrote:

> We Christians must know that unless God is in the balance and throws his weight as a counterbalance we shall sink to the bottom of the scale....If it is not true that God died for us, but only a man, we are lost. But if God's death and God dead lies in the opposite scale then his side goes down and we go upward like a light and empty scale. But he could not have sat in the pan unless he became a man like us, so that it could be said: God dead, God's passion, God's blood, God's death. According to his nature God cannot die but since God and man are united in one person, it is correct to talk about God's death when that man dies who is one thing or person with God.[56]

By subjectively appropriating this idea in feeling, the believing subject no longer sees Christ as standing at an historical distance, a distance mediated by church and tradition. In setting aside these external forms of mediation through an act of faith in the truth of the death of God in the person of Christ, an internal mediation between God and the finite human subject is effected and the finite human subject appropriates itself as standing before God in an immediate relationship. Indeed, the death of God on the cross discloses Christ to the human subject as the "mirror of the Fatherly heart" because this death is the concrete realization of the reconciliation of humanity with God through the self-sacrifice of God. Moreover, the resurrection of Christ demonstrates to humankind how God has overcome the rupture that exists between God and humankind. At the same time, the human subject knows Christ as the means of reconciliation, not because of its own effort, but because this knowledge is "put into our hearts by the Holy Spirit."[57]

In this way, 'Jesus Christ' points to the presence and the activity of the other two divine persons; God the Father and God the Holy Spirit. Indeed, the feeling of the believing subject invokes the doctrine of the Trinity as set down by the Church Fathers at the Council of Nicea (325) as the eternal superstructure in which it abides. Moreover, this invocation is also felt and known as objective insofar as the subject comes to know itself as absorbed into the intraactivity of the Trinity as a finite human subject, separate and distinct from the Trinity itself.

Indeed, not only do the objective doctrines of the incarnation, death, and resurrection of Jesus Christ address the individual in his or her subjectivity for Luther, but, just as important, they are made a *problem for the individual subject by the subject's own understanding*; the individual human subject feels estranged from God because of the rupture between its natural self and God's selfhood. Moreover, the natural human subject found the whole notion of the Incarnation an irreconcilable paradox. Therefore, for Luther, its natural mode of objective reasoning (philosophy) falls to the wayside: "Philosophy understands naught of divine matters. I do not say that men may not teach and learn philosophy; I approve thereof, so that it may be within reason and moderation. Let philosophy remain within her bounds, as God has appointed, and let us make use of her as of a character in a comedy; but to mix her up with divinity may not be endured."[58]

As we can see, for Luther, the resolution of this problem comes not by rational argumentation and judgment but by the activity of the Holy Spirit in the heart of the individual which then allows for the individual to *subjectify* these objective doctrines; that is, the *subject takes objective doctrine into itself, subsuming the objectivity of these doctrines in the embrace of its subjective conviction*. In so doing, its alienation is overcome; it is now in pure relation to God, a relation that is personal. Indeed, the very act of bringing God into view in this way changes the sense of the infinite from that which lies outside of finite human experience to that which now resides within the subject in a *subject to subject* relationship. Nevertheless, because the subject knows itself as grounded in the divine nature, it still defines itself in a dualistic fashion; as a created being, it is still in the flesh. Therefore, the subject resides in a dialectical tension between its original condition (sin) and its redeemed state (sainthood). In this way, the simultaneity of two natures, in this case redeemed and fallen, permeates the *living* of the finite human subject. For Luther, this dialectical tension is the state in which the subject continually realizes itself; it perpetually found itself acting within a set of oppositions as it applies itself to the finite world: law and gospel, Church and State, faith and reason. In this last set, faith is again to be understood as the only mode through which we can come to know God and His grace; for Luther, reason is a "whore," a "source of mischief," and an "enemy of God," although he does admit of the possibility of its reclamation.[59]

From the preceding, we can see that Luther has, in effect, 'existentialized' the notion of personality. For Luther, the individual finite subject knows itself as a particular finite being whose being is ultimately grounded in God thus gaining substance for its own self. Indeed, the human subject isolates and individuates itself as a natural self over and against God thereby knowing itself as this singular self. However, because of the natural rupture between the two sides of the religious relationship, the natural self feels itself as insignificant. But, simultaneously, the human subject hypostaticizes this self-knowing into a new sense of self as spiritual self. Thus, the individual subject found itself split into two selves, a natural self set off as an entity that stands in relation to a spiritual self. With this internal split, the individual found itself as a spiritual self 'moving away from' and 'above' the natural self into deeper, more substantial ground of knowledge of God. Thus, an inner sanctum is formed within human subjectivity in which the 'higher', spiritual self watches over and tries to direct its 'lower', natural self by subsuming this lower self as a moment in its own substantial existence. In other words, the subject now *knows* itself as two-sided: it distinguishes itself from itself but yet remains identical with itself; that is, it has become *self-conscious*.

Moreover, this two-sided subject confronts in Christ a mirror of the paradoxical nature of its own existential situation—of being 'deep in the flesh' like Christ in his humanity yet transcending this embodiment in its spiritual side. For Luther, this means that in our naturalness we are incapable of comprehending this truth:

> The minds of men arrive at these foolish conclusions when they
> are determined to do their thinking about such lofty matters
> without the Word. Yet indeed we lack knowledge about our
> very selves, as Lucretius says: "It is so far unknown what the
> nature is." We feel capable of forming judgments, of assigning
> numbers, of distinguishing quantities and spiritual creatures (if
> I may call them so), what is true and what is false; but we are
> still incapable of giving a definition of the soul. How much less
> knowledge are we going to have of the nature of God? We do
> not know how our will is aroused; for it is not aroused qualita-

tively or quantitatively, and yet it is aroused in some way. Much less, then, could we know anything of divine matters.[60]

Where the natural self can 'form judgments', 'assign numbers', use the categories of objective reasoning and so on, these are to no avail in overcoming this paradox. But inasmuch as the human subject sees Christ as mirror of its own existential situation, it surrenders its sense of individuation and isolation and becomes transparent to the Word thereby negating its naturalness. Indeed, the death and resurrection of Jesus Christ not only mirrors the negation of the natural self by the spiritual self, but also the affirmation of the spiritual self as true self, as a 'new work of creation' situated in, with, and under God: "For a Christian should be a new creature or a newly created work of God, who in all things speaks and thinks and judges differently from the way the world speaks or judges. And because he is a new man, everything here in this life should and must become new through faith."[61]

Hegel's Philosophical Confirmation of Luther's Faith

Hegel identified himself as a Lutheran a number of times at the University of Berlin. In the Introduction to the *Lectures on the History of Philosophy* (1823, 1825, and 1827) he stated: "We Lutherans (I am and will remain one) have a better faith."[62] In a letter to Karl von Altenstein, Minister of Religious and Educational Affairs, April 3, 1826, Hegel wrote: "I have there explained and expressed Luther's teachings as true, and as recognized by philosophy as true."[63] Later, in the same letter, Hegel noted that he is a professor "who prides himself on having been baptized and raised a Lutheran, which he still is and shall remain."[64] As well, in a letter to the Pietistic theologian, Friedrich Tholuck, Hegel identified Lutheranism as the theological underpinning for his speculative rendition of the doctrine of the Trinity: "In your entire publication I have not been able to feel or find any trace of a native understanding of this doctrine. I am a Lutheran, and through philosophy have been at once completely confirmed in Lutheranism."[65] Obviously, whether or not Hegel attended church, prayed, tithed, and so forth, is of no concern for our consideration of Hegel's philosophy unless we follow Lou-Andreas Salomé into the realm of the ad hominem when she proposed to Nietzsche "the reduction of philosophical systems to personal dossiers on their authors."[66] Rather, what is important to our consideration is that Hegel emphasized that it is philosophy that confirms Lutheranism and not his Lutheranism that confirms his philosophy. Indeed, for Hegel, even though the theological thinking of the Christian religion, especially as it is found in Luther's notion of faith and the witness of the Spirit, allows for the conceptualization of religion by philosophy, philosophy is not subservient to any particular religion or theology. Indeed, once it has attained its position of scientific cognition, "Thinking is the absolute judge, before which the content [of faith] must verify and attest its claims."[67] At the same time, philosophy does confirm that: "In faith the true *content* is certainly already found, but it still lacks the form of thinking. All the forms that we have considered earlier—feeling, representation, etc., are indeed capable of having the content of truth, but they themselves are not the true form, which made the true content necessary."[68]

As we will now see, what Luther brought into fruition for Christianity and ultimately for philosophy is the recognition that: "Faith itself is the divine Spirit that works in the subject."[69] For Hegel, this is exactly what Luther realized in his notion of faith:

> Faith [for Luther] is by no means a bare assurance respecting mere finite things....In fact it is not a belief in something that is absent, past and gone, but the subjective assurance of the Eternal, of Absolute Truth, the Truth of God. Concerning this assurance, the Lutheran Church affirmed that the Holy Spirit alone produces it—i.e., that it is an assurance which the individual attains, not in virtue of his particular idiosyncrasy, but of his essential being.[70]

As we can see, for Hegel, Luther's faith signifies the movement of finite subjectivity away from externality. Indeed, as we saw, for Luther, faith can be only a spiritual gift, manifested in the inner life—the 'heart'—of humankind by the Holy Spirit. Thus, the external orientation of Catholicism and the obstruction it places for enactment of the 'subjective assurance of the Eternal' is, for Hegel, "overcome" by Luther's view of faith. In this way, the spiritual relationship between infinite subjectivity (Christ) and finite subjectivity (the believing subject), can be properly realized:

> Luther's simple doctrine is that the specific embodiment of Deity—infinite subjectivity, that is true spirituality, Christ—is

in no way present and actual in an outward form, but as essentially spiritual is obtained only in being reconciled to God—in faith and spiritual enjoyment [*Glaube und Genuss*]. These two words express everything. That which this doctrine desiderates, is not the recognition of a sensuous object as God, nor of something merely conceived, and which is not actual and present, but of a Reality that is not sensuous.[71]

Moreover, the inner, spiritual relationship of the finite subject with infinite subjectivity achieved through Luther's doctrine of faith also brings forth, according to Hegel, the 'principle of subjectivity':

> This, then, is the Lutheran faith, in accordance with which man stands in a relation to God which involves his personal existence: that is, his piety and the hope of his salvation and the like all demand that his heart, his subjectivity, should be present in them. His feelings, his faith, the inmost certainty of himself, in short, all that belongs to him is laid claim to, and this alone can truly come under consideration: man must himself repent from his heart and experience contrition; his own must be filled with the Holy Ghost. Thus here the principle of subjectivity, of pure relation to me personally.[72]

Indeed, we can surmise that, on the basis of our account of Luther's theology the 'principle of subjectivity' enters religious consciousness through the Lutheran faith because not only did Luther recognize that the objective doctrines of the incarnation, death, and resurrection of Jesus Christ address the individual in one's subjectivity, but, as Hegel noted, the individual human subject becomes the arbitrator of truth insofar as one is empowered by the Holy Spirit to examine it for oneself.

> Each [individual human subject] has to accomplish the work of reconciliation in his own soul—Subjective Spirit has to receive the Spirit of Truth into itself, and give it a dwelling place there....Subjectivity therefore made the objective purport of Christianity, *i.e.*, the doctrine of the Church, its own. In the Lutheran Church the subjective feeling and the conviction of the individual is regarded as equally necessary with the objective side of Truth.[73]

But, as we can see, this last part of the quotation indicates that Hegel was not merely applauding Luther's emphasis on subjectivity, but, as well, confirming Luther's contention that the central doctrines of Christianity, as found in Catholicism, have to be upheld as objectively true. Hence, Hegel observed that "The Lutheran doctrine therefore involves the entire substance of Catholicism, with the exception of all that results from the element of externality."[74] In other words, Hegel affirmed that in the Lutheran version of Christianity "all externality disappears in the point of absolute relation to God; along with this externality, this estrangement of self, all servitude has also disappeared."[75] Consequently, what we called, in Chapter One, the *interstice* between the human and the divine in which the divided self dwells opens to embrace itself as also containing the paradoxical reconciliation of these two conflicting sides. This is, then, the realm of the spiritual, the place where God is copresent with the human subject and the human subject, copresent with God. Hegel describes it in this way:

> Thereby a place has been set apart in the depths of man's inmost nature, in which alone he is at home with himself and at home with God; and with God alone is he really himself, in the conscience he can be said to be at home with himself. This sense of being at home should not be capable of being destroyed through others; no one should presume to have a place therein. All externality in relation to me is thereby banished, just as is the externality of the Host; it is only in communion and faith that I stand in relation to God.[76]

With the creation of this spiritual home, the core religious relationship of absolute universality and absolute singularity has now been filled out with the objective content inculcated into the human subject through religious education. Moreover, the subject, by subjectifying the contents of inherited faith, reconstructs this content in conformity with the two sides of the religious relationship. Therefore, the notion of the simultaneity of the two natures of Christ pervades the world-view of the individual subject and, consequently, undergirds the Lutheran world-view. It is the new center, that is, the relation of God and human being viewed christocentrically, of religious consciousness in which the individual subject and, as we will see presently, its community, derives everything particular from

God. Hence, when the individual human subject grasps itself as subject in relation to God, it grasps its self in a manner parallel to the doctrine of *communicatio idiomatum*: it perceives itself as containing both human and divine nature conjoined in an intimate union, yet not commingling these two natures. However, one more element is needed to complete our account of the importance of Luther's faith for Hegel: the witness of the Holy Spirit.

The Principle of Subjectivity and the Witness of the Spirit

Perhaps the clearest window of the suitability of the application of the term *personality* to the finite human subject as well as to Jesus Christ comes through the significance Hegel attached to Luther's translation of the Bible for the development of the 'principle of subjectivity'. Hegel hailed Luther's translation of the Bible into German as the sociohistorical and theological moment in which the 'principle of subjectivity' found its deepest expression.[77] For Hegel, this translation establishes the conditions in which the 'principle of subjectivity' can be fully realized by opening up the possibility of the individual subject confronting and appropriating the words of the Bible for itself. Prior to this translation, according to Hegel, the discordant 'principle of disharmony' marked the Christian world insofar as the Bible was controlled and read only by a select few. The Latin Bible of the Catholic Church, Hegel noted, ensured blind obedience to the authority of the church, which reserved for itself the right to interpret this text to its constituents. Thus, for Hegel, Christianity itself engendered the very alienation and estrangement that the Christian message of reconciliation was to overcome. Because of this institutionalized discord, all aspects of life, including philosophy and theology, were enslaved to the will of the ecclesiastical elite. However, Luther's translation allowed for a renewal of religiosity within the 'heart' of the individual by allowing the individual subject to encounter this text and internalize its truth. In this way, the Christian religion became a matter of the individual subject entering into an immediate, personal relationship with God by centering on the Bible as the only legitimate "*external*" source of knowledge of God.

As a result of Luther's innovative approach to the Holy Scripture of Christianity, authority is granted to the subject's reading of this text. However, Luther also recognized that assigning *complete* authority to the individual subject could result as well in the sacrifice of the central doctrines of Christ and Trinity. Of course, it is just this capriciousness of subjectivity that Hegel found troublesome in the writings of the theologians contemporary to his own philosophy of religion. Therefore, for Hegel, the 'principle of subjectivity' must be understood as always standing in relation to objective content, and in Luther, this problem was adequately met. For Luther, and subsequently, Lutheranism, the structural features of personal study and interpretation of the Bible demand an hermeneutic that will provide for conformable continuation of those truths already articulated in orthodox Christianity. At the same time, Luther appreciated that the relationship that ensues between reader and text has to be defined in such a way as to underscore the relationship of God and the finite human subject found in the christocentric faith that, as we will see, actually arises concurrent to the reading of the text. And, as we have indicated earlier, this christocentric faith is itself first and foremost a gift of God activated within the finite human subject through the witness of the Spirit. Thus, this witness of the Spirit furnishes the hermeneutical framework in which the reader-text relationship can be explicated.

Not surprisingly, for Luther, the witness of the Spirit involves an hermeneutic in which the reading of the Bible is the horizon through which the Spirit witnesses to the truth of Christ and the activity of the Trinity. In so doing, the possibility of looking outside of the Bible for verification of these truths is excluded.[78] For Luther, *Scripture interprets itself (sola scriptura)*, and hence, the text authenticates itself. That it can do this is due to the hermeneutical assumption that "the Spirit...does not operate apart from scriptural word, but is mediated through it";[79] indeed, through the subject's reading of scripture, Spirit witnesses to itself (*testimonium Spiritus Sancti internum*).[80] This means that because the subject can receive and orientate itself to this truth only through faith (*sola fide*) bestowed on it by the grace of God (*sola gratia*) this hermeneutic entails that *for the subject the truth of Christ and the Trinity is simultaneously required and given by the Holy Spirit*. Therefore, the finite human subject, by undertaking a reading of the biblical text, is enclosed within the circle of Spirit's self-enclosure, or inner testimony.

The totality of this reader-text relationship disclosed to the subject through faith—in such a way that faith itself belongs to the context of Spirit's self-disclosure—takes place and is enacted within human subjectivity. For Luther, and subsequently, Lutheranism, the witness of the Spirit endows human subjectivity with the spiritual insight that not only does the infinite contain the finite, but also that the finite must be capable of the infinite (*finitum capax infiniti*). In this way, for Luther, human subjectivity must always realize its true self in and through an other, an other whom, as we have seen, as Christ is the concrete personification of the relation of the infinite and finite. Thus, through continual appropriation of the Bible the finite human subject does not remain isolated and exclusive in its subjectivity, but becomes inclusive in the Lutheran sense of *finitum capax infiniti*, and, therefore, like Christ and worthy of the significa-tion, *personality*.

But, we must note that, without the hermeneutic of the witness of the Spirit, it is still possible for the finite human subject to inter-pret the biblical text as it would any other text and still, in some sense, explicate Christ. Spinoza, for example, used a hermeneutical principle—*Scripture should be judged by Scripture*—that is remark-ably close to the Lutheran notion of *sola scriptura* but that, at the same time, neglects the notion of subjectivity and the tripersonality of God.[81]

Therefore, one further aspect of the inclusivity arises through the witness of the Spirit. This aspect is pointed to by Edward Schillebeeckx in his discussion of personality, found in his major work, *Jesus*:

> He [Hegel] concedes [to Fichte] that 'person' implies an 'oppo-site', but not *per se* 'outside itself', as a delimiting of one's own 'I'. On the contrary, it belongs to the essential being of the per-son so to be involved with an opposite that this 'I' 'exteriorizes' itself in an opposite, in order thus to recover itself in the other thing (other being), either in the thing which the 'I' composes or recognizes or in the 'Thou' with whom the 'I' is conjoined in love and friendship. A person discovers himself in the other to the degree that he has surrendered and yielded himself to the other. So it is in personal living that the opposition or contrast to other—finitude itself, therefore—is cancelled out and over-come. Person *qua* person, that is, the very nature of being-a-person, entails infinity.[82]

If we accept Schillebeeckx's description, personality should not remain exclusive *vis-à-vis* other finite human subjects *precisely because they are 'other'*. Indeed, for Hegel, the human subject as personality does not subsist as an attenuated and alienated subject. In the 1827 *Consummate Religion* he commented:

> But as far as personality is concerned, it is the character of the person, the subject, to surrender its isolation and separateness. Ethical life, love, means precisely the giving up of particular personality, and its extension to universality—so, too, with friendship. In friendship and love I give up my abstract personality and thereby win it back as concrete. The truth of personality is found precisely in winning it back through this immersion, this being immersed in the other.[83]

For Hegel, this immersion in the other is most fully manifest and expressed in the Christian notion of *love*. Hegel wrote in 1821:

> It [love] becomes objective in Christ as the focal point of faith at an infinite distance and sublimity, but [at the same time] in an infinite nearness, and with a relevance that peculiarly belongs to the individual subject. <Humanity, death, infinite limitation [are] taken up into the divine idea.> But it is not for the [individual] (the latter is nothing particular but, in regard to the idea, is itself universal), but rather for [all] individuals, and *as thus actual in their subjectivity*, that the divine idea is spirit—the *Holy Spirit*. The Holy Spirit is in them; they constitute the universal Christian church, the communion of saints.[84]

Therefore, the dialectical opposition implicit in what Schillebeeckx called the *contrast* between self and other, like that between the infinite and finite, divine and human, is overcome through the witness of the community of human subjects to each other of their relationship with God as objectified in Christ. Indeed, Luther contended that, if the finite human subject enters into dialogue with other human subjects about the truth witnessed to it by the Spirit, then full knowledge of the truth personified in Christ will be incarnate in humankind as well. He claimed: "We are all one body of Christ the Head, and all members one of another. Christ does not have two bodies, one temporal, the other spiritual. There is but one Head and one body."[85] Consequently, with Christ as the communal center all distinctions between human subjects fall away. As Hegel confirmed, "Before God all human beings are equal."[86] All distinctions, of gender, class, race, politics, and the like that separate human beings from each other are mediated through "the life, suffering, death, and exaltation of Christ. This subjectivity is implicitly universal, not exclusive, and the relation of the many, to each other, is the unity of faith in the representation of faith in this third [the community of Christ]."[87]

We can see that for both Hegel and Luther human subjectivity as a whole 'universal' communal subjectivity is itself exalted to what both call the *Kingdom of God* or *community* of Christ. Consequently, the finite human subject, to be lifted out of itself into a relation fully inclusive of the other—in both senses of God as absolute other and other finite human subjects—that is, to be a personality, it must have an *intersubjectivity*. For Hegel, this intersubjectivity is what he calls the *cultus* in 1821:

> But since God is the absolute essence for the subject—the substance or the absolute subject—the singular being knows itself to be only an accident or a predicate, something vanishing and transient over against it—a relationship of might, the sensation of fear, etc. But equally the relationship is not a negative one but also a positive one: <love>. The subject [is] <implicitly> identical [with the absolute essence], which is its substance, *its* subject and [this essence] is *in* the subject, is *its* essence, not the essence of another. This unity, this reconciliation, this restoration of oneself, giving oneself, from out of the previous cleavage, the positive feeling of sharing, of participating in this oneness, partaking of one's positive character, <fulfilling oneself, [achieving] divine knowledge> —this is a form of doing or acting that can at once be more external or internal in character; in general it is the *cultus*.[88]

As an intersubjective constellation of thinking and witnessing about God, the *cultus* itself becomes the dwelling place of God; that is, through the mutual witness of the community to its belief in a God who reveals Himself as Trinity through Jesus Christ, the *cultus* actualizes the presence of Spirit in its communal life:

> Spirit is the infinite return into itself, infinite subjectivity, not represented [subjectivity] but as actual divinity, as divinity that is *present*, not the substantial in-itself of the Father or of the

Son and of Christ, who is the truth in the shape of objectivity. The Spirit is rather what is subjectively present and actual; and it is only through this mediation [in the community] that it itself is subjectively present as the divestment into the objective intuition of love and its infinite anguish. This [is] the Spirit of God, or God as the present, actual Spirit, God dwelling in his community.[89]

Thus, the *cultus is the concretization of Spirit.* It is 'infinite return into itself' or 'infinite subjectivity' insofar as the intersubjectivity of the *cultus* is a *self-enclosed* totality, witnessing to its own truth. In this sense of self-enclosed self-actualization, inclusive subjectivity is a context or totality within which the finite subject receives its full sense of 'going over' to and 'giving to' other human subjects in inter-subjectivity.

The Birth of the Science of Spirit out of the Science of Faith

As we have seen, Luther rejuvenated the orthodox notion of Jesus Christ as the 'God-man' as the ground of his hermeneutic of the inner witness of the Holy Spirit to itself. At the same time, we can see that this inner witness in turn grounds Jesus Christ as the truth of the infinite-finite relationship. Because this mode of reasoning is circular, we can say that through the witness of the Holy Spirit, faith in Jesus Christ creates its own self-enclosed knowledge of God. Moreover, this hermeneutic means that faith's knowledge of God is also a sui generis knowledge of God insofar as God is producing this knowledge of himself. In this sense, we can see that faith creates its own science, a science that authenticates itself within its own horizon of meaning. As such, this science of faith need not admit any other mode of discourse or reasoning into its thinking. Indeed, in its self-enclosed self-actualization, human intersubjectivity as inclusive subjectivity keeps its inner authority restricted.[90] But for Hegel, Luther's use of the principle of subjectivity in a science of faith needs to be expanded beyond just religious objects: "Now this principle [of subjectivity] was first grasped in relation to religious objects only, and thereby it has received its absolute justification, but it has not been extended to the further development of the subjective principle itself."[91] By not extending the subjective principle beyond religious objects, Hegel found that "into this spiritual freedom, the beginning and the possibility of the unspiritual mode of regarding things has thus entered. The content of the Credo, speculative as it is in itself, has, that is to say, an historical side. Within this barren form the old faith of the church has been admitted and allowed to exist, so that in this form it has to be regarded by the subject as the highest truth. The result then follows that all development of the dogmatic content in a speculative manner has been set aside."[92] Consequently, Hegel here preferred Catholic theology: "The connection of Philosophy with the theology of the Middle Ages has thus in the Catholic Church been retained in its essentials; in Protestantism, on the contrary, the subjective religious principle has been separated from Philosophy, and it is only in Philosophy that it has arisen in its true form again."[93] Thus, the Protestant theology that arises as the science of faith only subjectifies the objective relation of God and human articulated in doctrine. It does not realize that there is one further step to take in the knowledge of God: to cognize conceptually the relation of subject and object in theological reflection itself. Hence, although Hegel, in the 1821 manuscript, confirmed the significance of Luther's contribution, he also criticized its onesidedness: "Certainly, it is infinitely important to have emphasized this subjective side so much, the side which Luther called *faith*, but it is not the only aspect. It is vain and in itself empty and incomplete; and the truth is that it should equally contain the objective content—<as the object [is], so [is] the subject, and vice versa>."[94]

According to Hegel, this vain one-sidedness does not permit the human being to see that it is "essentially thinking spirit."[95] Instead of unspiritual truncating thinking, "Thought as such must also develop itself therein, and that essentially as this form of inmost unity of spirit with itself, thought must come to the distinction and contemplation of this content, and pass over into this form of the purest unity of spirit with itself."[96]

Nevertheless, Lutheranism, as the 'mystical' and 'churchly' mode of religious consciousness "defines this connection between God and subjective volition and being more precisely, and brings it to consciousness in the specific form that we [have] seen—i.e., the speculative [form] of the nature of the idea."[97] Now, it is a matter of making this inner relation an explicit object for thought thus relieving it of Luther's one-sided stress on the subject side. And, Hegel did precisely this in the philosophy of religion: he made the theological content of Christian religious consciousness an object for philosophy's thinking thereby making this content philosophy's own content. In this way, the structures of selfhood established in theology now become the structures of Spirit's own selfhood as articulated in philosophy. Indeed, by embracing theology in philosophy's thought as an object for philosophical thinking, philosophy thinks the reconciliation of opposites produced by faith in its witness of the Spirit. Indeed, through thinking, the self-enclosure of the self within itself, implicit in the science of faith and the witness of the Holy Spirit, now becomes the explicit self-enclosure of Spirit which is systematically explicated by philosophy as its own spiritual self-relating. Thus, philosophy found itself as totally self-conscious subject, as Spirit, in which relations between self and God, self and self, self and other selves are inner relations, moments of its own knowledge of itself. And, for philosophy, this is an absolute relationship. Hence, faith has become the witness of the Spirit to itself as absolute spirit: *"Faith is the witness of spirit concerning absolute spirit.* It is the certainty of the truth of the divine intrinsic connectedness of spirit within itself and in its community; it is the community's knowledge that this is its essence. This is the substantial unity of spirit with itself. It is not the abstract unity, but the unity that is essentially, infinite form, knowledge self-contained."[98]

Thus, philosophy does not treat contents of theology as 'other'; indeed, the 'otherness' of theology is itself overcome in this absolute self-relating thereby creating a subject-subject relation between the two, a relationship that we already noted is implied in the speculative statement, "philosophy is theology." Thus, for Hegel, the reconciliation of philosophy and theology, and the transformation of theological content into the speculative knowledge of God of the philosophy of religion, is made possible by conceptually cognizing the Christian community's christological self-understanding articulated in its science of faith through the witness of the Spirit and elevating it to the level of the "speculative midpoint"[99] of the Incarnation. Hence, not only are the feeling and doctrine sides of faith mediated through the knowledge of God as personified in Christ, but the theological and philosophical sides of thinking are mediated through this knowledge as well. As James Yerkes observed: "Hegel's philosophy of religion is clearly intended to be *a philosophy of religion based on, i.e., epistemologically and methodologically normed by, Christian fact.* And by the 'Christian fact' I understand Hegel to mean the historic revelational incarnation of God in the event of

Jesus as the Christ and the church's subsequent witness of faith about revelational events in Scripture, creed, and cult."[100]

Thus we can see that for Hegel Christianity found its final consummation in this philosophical thinking about religious consciousness that, although it may not admit it, Christianity itself produced.[101] Furthermore, we can see that, for Hegel, theology and philosophy reveal to each other Spirit. This is precisely what Schleiermacher's *The Christian Faith* had done for Hegel. It spurred him to solidify in his philosophy of religion the role feeling plays in faith in a manner unarticulated before *The Christian Faith* came on the scene. And, in the same way, this is what Hegel's Foreword did and what the 1824 lectures would do for consciousness: they point out that two sides are involved in faith and that these two sides are reconciled in faith's witness of the Spirit. Now we are ready to see how this philosophical recognition leads to the further accommodation, modification, and enhancement of the relations between philosophy and theology in both Hegel's *Concept of Religion* and the concept of the consummate religion.

Chapter Four

PHILOSOPHY, THEOLOGY, AND THE INTRODUCTION TO THE 1824 *PHILOSOPHY OF RELIGION*

Introduction

The 1824 concept of religion does not achieve the full subject-subject relationship that should ensue between philosophy and theology when the science of spirit arises out of the science of faith. In fact, this subject-subject relationship is attained only in 1827 where philosophy has interiorized the trinitarian structure of orthodox theology's inclusive subjectivity (or personality) as the structure of its own inclusive subjectivity. Of course, the uppermost matter on Hegel's mind in constructing the 1824 *Concept of Religion* is to internalize and disclose all the contents of religious consciousness as interrelating determinations within the *"self-consciousness of absolute spirit."*[1] But, as we will see, in the 1824 *Concept of Religion*, Hegel concentrated on solidifying the role of faith in religious consciousness as disclosed in the Foreword by continuing his criticism of Schleiermacher and all theological cognition that utilizes the Understanding; that is, Schleiermacher's theology of feeling, natural and rational theology, and as well, orthodox theology when it ignores its own science of faith and its hermeneutic of the witness of the Spirit. In so doing, Hegel did display these theologies as moments within the self-consciousness of absolute spirit, but only as *objects* for philosophical reflection. As we will see, this objectifying of the theologies of the Understanding in the Introduction to the 1824 *Concept of Religion* clears the way for the full subjectifying of the content of theological reflection in *Consummate Religion*.

In light of philosophy's need to interiorize and criticize theological reflection, Hegel commenced his unfolding of the Introduction to the *Concept of Religion* by directing his audience's attention to the relations between philosophy and religion as a present issue within philosophy: "I have deemed it necessary to devote a separate section of philosophy to the consideration of religion. Let us first consider how philosophy of religion is connected with philosophy in general; this is tied up with the question of our present-day interest in religion and philosophy; and this in turn is linked to the relationship of the philosophy of religion, and of philosophy, to positive religion."[2]

With this issue established as thematic for conceptual cognition, Hegel continued by describing what is intended by the word *religion* in an almost identical fashion to the 1821 manuscript: "the region in which all riddles of the world, etc." But unlike the 1821 manuscript, Hegel did not follow his description of religion by depicting how philosophy and religion intersect in a common object, God. Rather, he inserted an observation on the role of faith in knowledge of God gained from his 1822 criticism of Schleiermacher:

> This image of the absolute that religious devotion has before it can have a greater or lesser degree of present liveliness, certainty, and enjoyment, or can be presented as something longed or hoped for, something far off, otherworldly. But it is never isolated, for it radiates into the temporal present. Faith is cognizant of it as the truth, as the substance of present existences; and this content of devotion is what animates the present world, what operates effectively in the life of the individual, ruling over one's commissions and omissions, over one's volition and action. This is the representation that religion has of God in general, and the philosophy of religion made this content the content of a particular treatment.[3]

With the Foreword's cognition of the significance of the two sides of faith for religious consciousness reaffirmed, the 1824 Introduction to the *Concept of Religion* takes a new path and undertakes the explication of thinking itself. Thought is not only copresent with subjective feeling in faith, but, as we outlined in the last chapter, it also thinks about the relations between thought and feeling. But, this is precisely the area where thinking may stumble, misconstruing the relations of thought and feeling already present in faith. Thus, Hegel found it of the utmost importance to distinguish his mode of philosophical thinking about religion embodied in his lectures from other modes of thinking (philosophical and theological) about religion.

Natural Theology

The first instance of thinking about religion that Hegel considered is natural theology. As in the 1821 manuscript, Hegel found both a similarity and a difference between his philosophy of religion and natural theology. However, unlike the 1821 manuscript, which included this discussion of the similarity between the two as part of the description of the philosophy of religion, the 1824 Introduction's treatment focuses on the main difference. Indeed, in 1821 he was concerned to introduce the philosophy of religion to his students by noting the similarity of his philosophy of religion to a mode of endeavor with which they were already familiar. But, Hegel now saw a discussion of the differences between modes of knowledge of God as the best way to enter the mode of thinking articulated in the philosophy of religion. For Hegel, natural theology and the philosophy of religion differ on how thinking found content. Indeed, Hegel proposed that natural theology does not understand the significance of the intersubjective aspect of knowledge of God manifest in the doctrines of the religious community for the initiation of thinking about God. Indeed, where natural theology completely ignores this aspect of the knowledge of God, the 1824 philosophy of religion found itself to be a concrete realization of the intersubjective ground of religion as found in the religious community, a realization that, as we have seen, is made possible by faith as having an objective side which was described in the Foreword:

> Our concern here is therefore not with God as such or as object, but at the same time with God *as he is* [*present*] *in his community*. It will be evident that God can only be genuinely understood in the mode of his being as *spirit*, by means of which he made himself into the counterpart of a community and brings about the activity of a community in relation to him; thus it will be evident that the doctrine of God is to be grasped and taught only as the doctrine of *religion*.[4]

Thus, the doctrines of the religious community must be the place in which thinking about God orientates itself. However, for Hegel, natural theology's "content and object was God as such."[5] Indeed, by ignoring the intersubjective, objective doctrines of faith, the thinking found in natural theology amounts to a 'science of the Understanding' in which God is thought in (logical) abstraction from the thinking about God already existing in the community and thus is not "grasped as spirit."[6] In this way, natural theology is the apex of rational detachment from, and setting aside of, the contents of religion that so mars the thinking about religion in the theologies of the Understanding.

Because the mode of thinking expressed in natural theology is so one-sided in its thinking, it is to be set aside in favor of balance between contemplation of God as he is in himself ("the essence grasped in the concept; and this meaning is in common with the logical idea") and how God is "*for* himself," as absolute spirit, "as what appears, what endows itself with revelation and objectivity."[7] In 1827, Hegel would achieve this balance, viewing the logical idea as one side of the knowledge of God as manifested in Christianity and revealed doctrines as the other side.

Rational Theology

Continuing his concern about the relation of his philosophy of religion to other modes of thinking about God, Hegel pointed out that the philosophy of religion must be compared with another mode of thinking that it closely resembles, rational theology: "If we call the cognition or knowledge of God 'theology' generally, whether we approach it from the standpoint of philosophy or from that of theology in the narrower sense, we appear for the present to be treading the same path as the theology that used to be called rational theology. It is the universal high road or the universal mode in which what is known of God is said of God."[8] As we can observe from this passage, Hegel was stressing that reconciliation is already implicit in the relations between philosophy and theology insofar as they both cognize and express knowledge of God and thus share the same thematic center. In this sense, philosophy 'treads' the 'same path' as rational theology. But, in noting this similarity, Hegel underscored the key problem philosophy has with contemporary theology; that is, unlike post-Kantian theology in general, his philosophy of religion (like rational theology), is willing to claim that it actually possesses rational knowledge of God. This 'high road', Hegel went on to note, is also characteristic of mainstream orthodox theology: "We know namely that in the Christian church and chiefly in our Protestant church there was set down a *doctrinal system* [*Lehrbegriff*], a content that was universally valid and universally accepted as the truth, as [stating] what God's nature is. This content has generally been called the creed: in the subjective sense, what is believed, and objectively, what is to be known as content in the Christian religion, what God himself has revealed that he is."⁹

Having aligned himself with this mode of thinking (confirmed by the Foreword's account of the inner relation of creed and content), Hegel proceeded to criticize the theologies of the Understanding, including rational theology and Schleiermacher's theology of feeling in the same manner as we saw in the Foreword, by concentrating his analysis on the relations between creeds and subjective conviction and then by noting, in an apparent reference to Schleiermacher's *The Christian Faith*, how the content of 'faith' is called "*dogmatics*: the doctrinal system of the church, the content [of its teaching] concerning what God's nature [is] in relation to humanity and in the latter's relationship to God."¹⁰

Thus, Hegel accentuated (contra Schleiermacher) that dogmatics is the doctrinal system of the church as worked out by the Christian community and not by an individual like Schleiermacher. Moreover, this doctrinal system is to be considered as objective insofar as it reflects what is believed in terms of the God-human relationship by the community in a systematically organized fashion that, in turn, becomes the standard by which 'what is believed' itself is guided. As such, dogmatics is theological reflection fundamentally rooted in the subjective side of faith, but articulated intersubjectively. This dialectical interaction is what is forgotten by all theologies of the Understanding.

It is worth our while to note that in the Foreword Hegel observed that the presence of thought in subjective conviction even allows for the construction of theology: "If, however, the element of universal principles [*Grundsätze*] has infiltrated the religious requirement [that is, subjective conviction], then that requirement is no longer separate from the requirement and the activity of thought, and religion demands, according to this aspect, a *science* of religion—a theology."¹¹ Unlike Schleiermacher, Hegel recognized that theology, by virtue of its reflective activity, already involves thought about God and, as thought, has contained within it 'universal principles'. Therefore, for Hegel, doctrinal systems and dogmatics are formed on the basis of 'universal principles' already embedded in human being. Consequently, for Hegel, even Schleiermacher's 'theology of feeling' which rejects the value of any 'outside' rational way of thinking in working through the content of Christianity still has to make use of certain 'universal principles' imported into its conception of feeling. In the Foreword, Hegel claimed that this *double-standard* underlies "the prejudice against which philosophising on the subject of religion in our time has to fight, namely the prejudice that the divine cannot be conceived."[12] Not only does contemporary theology's skepticism (especially, Schleiermacher's) about the possibility of knowing and cognizing God outside of feeling dissociate itself from any true sense of objectivity, but it is also incoherent: why would Schleiermacher undertake a dogmatic theology when its main subject matter, God, cannot be found in thought? Indeed, a dogmatic theology based on such a prejudice must flounder on its own impossibility. Moreover, it is self-contradictory—a sure sign that in this instance the Understanding is struggling to maintain itself in the absence of the true understanding of the self and self-consciousness as it has arisen and manifested itself through the Christian religion.

Because of the confusion about the role of thinking in the Understanding's knowledge of God, Hegel realized that the 'universal principles' the thinking subject brings to its theologizing must be identified and explicitly cognized in thinking. Thus, Hegel's philosophy carries out what amounts to a philosophy of theology. As a second-order activity, this reflection on theological thinking and reflection permits the philosophy of religion to *differentiate* its mode of thinking from that of theology while, at the same time, thinking the *same* content. For Hegel, this *identity-in-difference of philosophy and theology* enacted by conceptually cognizing is the methodological position his philosophy of religion must take in relation to the theology of his time. Indeed, the 'universal principles' thought in the doctrines of the Trinity and of Christ of orthodox theology are the standard against which even the thinking of orthodox theology can be measured.

Important, Hegel asserted that there is a *supposition* (not a 'universal principle') arising with Protestantism that creates the possibility of the cleavage between theology's thinking and its awareness of the ground of thinking. This supposition is the authority invested in the Bible: "In the Protestant church the doctrinal system is at the same time *supposed* to be based essentially on the Bible; it does not exist merely in the spirit of the church but also has an external footing in the Bible."[13] Hegel would now use this supposition to center his discussion of the identity-in-difference of philosophy and theology.

The Letter and the Spirit

In our discussion of Hegel's conception of faith in Chapter Three, we found that faith's 'epistemologically' and 'ontologically' 'prior' conditions for the witness of Spirit can be equated with the 'letter' of religious imagery inculcated by socialization into the finite human being, and the 'naturalness' of the range of dispositions experienced by the finite human subject (respectively). Furthermore, we described how Hegel thought Luther's emphasis on faith created the possibility of the Spirit witnessing to itself in the self-enclosed hermeneutic of reading the Bible. But, as we shall see presently, Hegel expanded the notion of the witness of the Spirit from an hermeneutic expounding Scripture into a wider 'enlivening' process.

As we discussed previously and in Chapter Three,[14] Luther elevated the Bible to the center of theological reflection as the sole vehicle through which God could be known. With this new thematic center, philosophical and theological reflection both tapers and narrows the contours of its knowledge of God according to how it believed the Bible should be interpreted. Therefore, Hegel said, Enlightenment thinking, under the "guise of exegesis," "sought to *interpret* the word of God in a different way."[15] Thus Hegel identified this mode of theological thinking as essentially an interpretive endeavor, a rational theology, that "draws on reason for counsel" but that, in fact, is "opposed to the doctrinal system in the form established by the church."[16] Hegel went on to confirm that some of the responsibility for this state of affairs lies with the Protestant church itself: "In part, this was the church's own doing, in part it was the doing of [the thinking] to which the church is opposed. In this rational theology it is exegesis that plays the primary role. Here exegesis takes over the written word, interprets it, and professes only to make the understanding of the word effective and to remain faithful to it."[17] But, this claim of rational theology betrays the problem that is present if anybody undertakes the exegesis beyond the rather limited approach of replacing the words of a text with their synonyms; that is, that exegesis is always interpretation and as interpretation it is always laden with presuppositions. Indeed, regardless of how presuppositionless one strives to be, one is still faced with the presupposition of presuppositionlessness:

> But where interpretation is not mere explanation of the words but discussion of the content and elucidation of the sense, it must introduce its own thoughts into the words that form the basis [of the faith]. There can only be mere interpretation of words when all that happens is that one word is replaced by another with the same scope. If interpretation is *elucidation*, then other categories of thought are bound up with it. A development of the word is a progression to further thoughts. One seemingly abides by the sense, but in fact, new thoughts are developed.[18]

By elucidating the 'words that form the basis of faith', other presuppositions filter in, transforming exegesis into interpretation. These other presuppositions may come from a genuine concern with knowledge of God, but there always remains the likelihood of hypostaticizing some subsidiary or tangential concern over and against the true central concern, God. Indeed, the problem exegesis presents for knowledge of God originates with the Protestant Church's core presupposition of the *inerrancy* of the words contained in the Bible. Not surprisingly, this presupposition presupposes yet another presupposition: divine inspiration. Divine inspiration itself allows for the presupposition that the text is literally true, and that, consequently, the text can be read like an objective, infallible, and omniscient history of both God and human beings. In this view, every word, punctuation mark, grammatical mistake (contra Wolff) are as they are supposed to be, inscribed by God in his eternal wisdom through a number of human 'recording machines'. Moreover, this presupposition assumes that internal inconsistency in the text is not an inconsistency, every internal contradiction is not a contradiction. Instead, they are to point even more forcibly to the inscrutability of the ways of God and the fallibility of human reason. Thus, looking back at the history of the development of Protestant theology, Hegel saw that schisms broke out and positions became entrenched over what constituted the proper interpretation of the text, each group asserting that it alone rendered the most accurate, literal reading of the Bible: "The most sharply opposed views are exegetically demonstrated by theologians on the basis of scripture, and in this way so-called holy scripture has been made into a wax nose."[19] Indeed, concern over the 'letter' of the word of God rapidly turns theological reflection away from God to their 'wax noses' such that the objective truth of the Christian doctrines are obfuscated in favor of subjective, factional concerns. Consequently, other presuppositions of the time surface, a tendency Hegel indicated is already built into the process of exegesis. "Bible commentaries do not so much acquaint us with the content of scripture as with the mode of thought of their age."[20]

This also indicates that for Hegel this type of theological reflection is limited in its knowledge of God insofar as it is not conscious of the relation of its thought to thinking. It demarcates its own knowledge of God through its one-sided understanding of the power and range of reason and, moreover, is satisfied by this one-sidedness. It is not surprising then that the Enlightenment philosophers and theologians generally adopt the main presupposition of Protestant exegesis, the Bible as the center of knowledge of God, and use it without the orthodox doctrines of the Christian faith:[21]

> Since a so-called theology of reason arose and was produced in this manner we can on the one hand say that we find ourselves on common ground [with it], that reason has to be a factor; and if the interpretation that emerges is supposed to be in accordance with reason, then we can here claim the right to develop religion freely and openly out of reason, without taking as our starting point the specific word [of scripture]. It is therefore at this point that we consider the nature of God and of religion in general.[22]

In this way, Enlightenment thinking paved the way for the conceptualization of religion as finally articulated in the philosophy of religion. However, although the use of reason is the common ground between the philosophy of religion and rational theology, as we noted earlier, Hegel went on to state that the types of theological reflection found in both Enlightenment thinking about God and its counterpart, Pietism and Schleiermacher's theology of feeling are limited in their knowledge of God. Indeed, both modes of theological reflection unite in their lack of consciousness of the relation of the subjective to the objective. Thus, on the one side, rational theology shuns the subjective in favor of an unbalanced objectivity. On the other side, a theology like Schleiermacher's is easily satisfied by immersion in the subjective. Hence, Hegel stated:

> This rational theology has on the whole been called the theology of the Enlightenment. Pertinent here, however, is not merely this kind of theology but also the kind that leaves reason aside and expressly rejects philosophy, and then erects a religious doctrine from the plenitude of its own argumentative power. Though biblical words lie at its basis, to be sure, *private opinion* and *feeling* still remain the controlling factors. It very often happens that philosophy is set aside in the process, that philosophy is represented as something ghostlike that must be ignored because it is unsafe [*nicht geheuer*]. Philosophy, however, is nothing other than cognition through reason, the common feature in the cognition of all human beings; and to the extent that one rejects philosophy, one rejects with it the very principle of the common rationality of spirit, in order to leave the door open to private reason.[23]

As we can see, Hegel asserted Schleiermacher's theology of feeling as theological reflection that does not sufficiently pull away from its own opinion and feeling to achieve a true reflective distance on itself. Consequently, its exegesis of the Bible must remain isogesis, an elaboration of its subjective thinking only. On the other hand, the theology of reason's exegesis is an isogesis of what it, in its own one-sidedness, thinks is objectivity. In both cases, the spirit of the word of God is forgotten; the letter of the word is emphasized in such a way as to cause thinking to wander from the true theological center, God. Indeed, such meandering results in God being nothing more than a "vacuum of abstraction" for the theology of reason and, by implication, for the theology of feeling.[24] Hence, we can see that not only did Schleiermacher eviscerate his own thinking about the objective content of religious consciousness, but he did so in the same manner of the "rational theology of more recent times," that is, by "bringing reason into the lists against itself and combating philosophy on the grounds that reason can have no cognition of God."[25]

The greatest evidence of the impact of Protestant theological reflection's overemphasis on the Bible and its 'letter' is to be found in the modern concern over the historicity of the letter of the Bible. However, for Hegel, such zealous concern and scrutiny of the letter of the Bible, in terms of its author, its authors, its languages, and so on, further deflects modern theological reflection into digressions that ultimately are untheological.[26] Indeed, Hegel contended that the type of theological reflection that "wants to adopt *only a historical attitude* toward religion" evaporates the spiritual content of religion leaving only 'historical cognition'.[27] Theologians who embrace this attitude are, to use Hegel's somewhat scathing metaphors, "counting house clerks" who at best experience vicariously the religious experiences of other people, whereas, for Hegel: "In philosophy and religion...the essential thing is that one's own spirit itself should recognize a possession and content, deem itself worthy of cognition, and not keep itself humbly outside."[28] Indeed, those who keep themselves in an external relation by ruminating over the letter of the biblical text formulate works that are, as Hegel said in the Foreword: "Produced in the interest of what is finite, they are not supported by the testimony of the Holy Spirit, but by finite interests."[29] Therefore, to pierce through this 'plague' propagated by the 'theology of our time' and 'regain' a 'fullness, a content, and an import' that is spiritually alive, thinking must recenter itself in thinking about God as pictured in the objective doctrines of God as Trinity, as Spirit:

> If "spirit" is not an empty word, then God must [be grasped] under this characteristic [Spirit], just as in the church theology of former times God was called "triune." This is the key by which the nature of spirit is explicated. God is thus grasped as what he is for himself within himself; God [the Father] made himself an object for himself (the Son); then, in this object, God remains the undivided essence within this differentiation of himself within himself, and in this differentiation of himself loves himself, i.e., remains identical with himself—this is God as Spirit. Hence if we are to speak of God as spirit, we must grasp God with this very definition which exists in the church in this childlike mode of representation as the relationship between father and son—a representation that is not yet a matter of the concept. Thus it is just this definition of God by the church as a Trinity that is the concrete determination and

nature of God as spirit; and spirit is an empty word if it is not grasped in this determination.[30]

Therefore, we can see that over and against the way of the theology of his time, Hegel's path to the enlivening process of the 'witness of spirit' revolves around comprehension of the eternal truth of the doctrine of the Trinity. In this way, human reason will raise itself out of the finite morass of the Understanding (where it squanders itself), to the level of infinite thought and Spirit. Let us now turn our attention to the question of how Hegel's philosophy of theology will construe the relationship of the philosophy of religion to positive religion and its doctrines such that Spirit can come to know itself as Spirit.

The Relationship of the Philosophy of Religion to the Doctrines of Positive Religion

Amid the various theologies of the Understanding with their tendency to stray from the center of theological reflection, God, and oppilate true knowledge of this center, Hegel confirmed that "There is still a theology that has a content—a content consisting of the church's doctrines—which we call the content of a positive religion," that is, the theology of the historically mediated and revealed religion, Christianity.[31] With more than a touch of irony, Hegel mused that his philosophy of religion is "infinitely closer to positive doctrine" than it is to rational theology, which, on the surface, would seem more likely to be Hegel's ally.[32] Indeed, when we move beyond the superficial similarity of rational theology and philosophy of religion, the use of reason by rational theology seems barren. By contrast, the doctrines of the church have "solid content" and, in reality, are the embodiment of reason: "Human reason, human spiritual consciousness, or consciousness of its own essence, is reason generally, is the divine within humanity."[33] For Hegel, a "divine productive process" places the divine, that is "a living God who is effective, active," not in a transcendent realm, "beyond the stars or beyond the world," as it were, but fully within the most rational depths of human consciousness.[34] But the immanent presence of God as consciousness is not to be thought of as an anthropomorphic projection, "an invention of human beings," but as that which "has emerged as religion, and is a product of the divine spirit itself" and which, indeed, "shows itself first as faith."[35] Alluding back to the Foreword's discussion of faith, Hegel said: "So we must have faith that what has emerged in the world is precisely reason, and that the generation of reason is a begetting of the spirit and a product of the divine spirit itself."[36]

It is evident that for Hegel the chief verification of God could not be accomplished by a reason that is not grounded in the subjective conviction that what is presented to us in the doctrines of the church as spiritual is spiritual. Doctrines, like the Trinity, may be perceived as merely contingent and historical human constructions, but this view indicates a lack of due consideration of human religious faith as something that can and does shape reality, a shaping that affects the very fabric of how human beings reason about reality 'in the present time'. This means that instead of limiting the notion of reason to something that lies outside of the sphere of religious consciousness, Hegel recognized the full impact faith has on reason. On the other hand, the philosophy of religion fully appreciates that its activity is not one of faith, but one of reason, of thinking about thinking:

> When we philosophize about religion, we are in fact investigating reason, intelligence, and cognition; only we do so without the supposition that we will get over this first, apart from our [real] object; instead the cognition of reason *is* exactly the object, is what it is all about. Spirit is just this: to be for itself, to be for spirit. This is what finite spirit is; and the relationship of finite spirit or of finite reason [to infinite reason] is engendered within religion itself and must be dealt with there.[37]

Thus, the philosophy of religion reaches out to embrace within its thinking activity all rational activity that takes place within religious consciousness, even though the theologies of the Understanding are not part of this science of Spirit proper: "Also pertinent here is the distinction between a science and conjectures concerning a science. These conjectures are contingent; but insofar as they are thoughts containing viewpoints relating to the matter, they must fall within the treatment itself, though in their proper order and where they are necessary; then they are not [just] contingent bubbles of thought that arise within us."[38] Thus, for Hegel, undertaking the philosophy of theology is necessary; indeed, the conjectures and opining of the theologies of the Understanding are not to be cast aside but to be grasped as "brought up with the content itself," as "viewpoints" that "occur within religion itself."[39]

Thus, we can see that by carrying out this philosophy of theology, the Introduction to the 1824 *Concept of Religion* is conducting itself 'in an internal, thinking fashion', which, as we suggested at the beginning of this chapter, is Hegel's concern in constructing the 1824 *Concept of Religion*. Thus, it is a thinking about thinking that knows all the relations between the determinations of thought in religious consciousness as inner relations of the 'self-consciousness of absolute spirit'. Indeed, it is through this thinking about theological thinking that Spirit witnesses to its own truth.

Feeling and Thinking

As a result of our reflections on Hegel's philosophy of theology, we are led to conclude that the witness of Spirit in the science of Spirit does not stay within the contours of the witness of the Spirit as an hermeneutic for reading a text. Rather, it has taken the thinking of the community of the theologians of the Understanding as its pre-text. Now, with these theologies located and clarified, Hegel unfolded the 1824 *Concept of Religion* in the manner of the 1821 manuscript, that is, in the triadic sequence of feeling, representation, and thought, but with a notable modification in the description of the beginnings of religious consciousness in feeling.[40] In light of the similarities between Hegel's discussion of religious sensibility in the 1821 *Concept of Religion* and Schleiermacher's claim that religion is the immediate self-consciousness of the absolute other, and in light of the differences outlined in the 1824 Introduction's philosophy of theology, Hegel confirmed that feeling is also an important ingredient in religion: "Feeling, too, must show itself in religion. Feeling is the subjective aspect, what pertains to me as this single individual. When I feel I thereby appeal to myself, and thus relate myself back to my singular subjectivity; others can have other feelings and thereby appeal to themselves, too."[41]

Many commentators have suggested that Hegel was not fair in his appraisal of Schleiermacher's theology of "feeling."[42] However, as we have argued throughout Chapter Three and this chapter, the crucial difference for Hegel between his philosophy of religion and the theology of feeling lies in the role of thinking in relation to feeling and not whether feeling has a grounding role in religious consciousness.

Indeed, Hegel acknowledged that *"feeling* achieves the status of a ground, and God's being is given to us in feeling."[43] But, following the Foreword's insight into faith, the 1824 *Concept of Religion* confirms that we are ensconced in thinking right at the beginning of religious consciousness. 'Immediate knowledge of God' "is immediate knowledge of an object that is supposed to have strictly the character of the universal, so that only the product is immediate; this [process] is *thinking.*"[44] Indeed, God is not "a bodily object" but is "the highest personality, the most universal personality itself, singularity in its absolute universality."[45] Therefore, Hegel concluded that feeling and thought have to be thought as interacting codeterminations of immediate knowledge: "We have immediate knowledge of God, and God is in feeling. The third characteristic is that these two [moments] are *mutually determined:* God is not I, but the other of the I; and the knowing subject is in itself the negative, i.e., it is the finite, while God is the nonnegative, what is higher, the infinite in every respect."[46]

As we can see, Hegel still held that there is no true priority of feeling over thinking or thinking over feeling. Indeed, immediate knowledge is to be conceived as a unity that incorporates the moment of difference within itself. This is to say, although thought and feeling are thought as differentiated, they are also to be thought as enunciations of the qualities of immediate knowledge. Thus, Hegel does not change what he has already determined in the 1821 *Concept of Religion* as the primogenial religious relationship between 'abstract universality' and 'absolute singularity'.[47] Rather, thinking through Schleiermacher's theology of feeling as an inner determination of the 1824 *Concept of Religion*, Hegel's conceptualization of religious consciousness is forced to allow Schleiermacher's thinking about feeling to reinforce and enhance the way it understands the process of mutual determination between God and the self. Thus, it is apparent that the theology of feeling has effected a determination of the *Concept of Religion*. Now, the last task before us is to envisage how this enhancement and modification are in fact the result of the mutual determination of thought and feeling on the level of philosophical and theological thinking.

The Mutual Determination of Philosophy and Theology

We have spoken of Schleiermacher's rejection of the possibility of objective and rational knowledge of God. In this belief, Schleiermacher falls in with the long tradition of Christian theology, which asserts that because God is the creator and the human being, the created, there must be an essential ontological difference between God and the human being that does not allow for true rational and objective knowledge of God. As creator, God transcends both our world and our reason; his reality cannot be grasped by the human intellect. The being of God, therefore, is ineffable, and his ways are inscrutable. In the face of reason's humbled silence before God, this tradition chooses to shun 'head knowledge' in favor of the 'knowledge' of the heart. Tertullian, for one, believed "because it is absurd." For many, the conversion experience came to personify the essence of 'heart knowledge'.[48] Common to this way of thinking is that the human religious experience of God is both *personal* and *inward* in character, a theme brought to fruition for post-Kantian religious thinking by Schleiermacher's notion of awareness of God as grounded in the nonrational core of the human being, feeling, and its correlate, the feeling of absolute dependence.

This tradition's way of thinking entails, of course, a type of mutual determination between God and the human being. Paradoxically, it thinks that the determination of self in relation to God takes place only in the 'heart' and not in thinking. Schleiermacher took this sense of mutual determination beyond what this tradition has intended by leaving out the immediate knowledge of God as 'completely universal object'. This means that Schleiermacher reconstructed the Christian doctrine of God only in terms of human subjectivity. Thus, the positive doctrines are reappraised accordingly, with the central doctrine of the Trinity as largely the result of "unconscious echoes of what is pagan."[49] Moreover, Schleiermacher suggested, it is unessential to the particular form of piety that manifests itself in the Christian religion: "Similarly, it is natural that people who cannot reconcile themselves to the difficulties and imperfections that cling to the formulae current in Trinitarian doctrine should say that they repudiate everything connected with it, whereas in point of fact *their piety is by no means lacking in the specifically Christian stamp.*"[50]

Without the Trinity as the superstructure in which all other doctrines find their meaning, the other main orthodox doctrine, the orthodox doctrine of the simultaneity of divine and human natures in the person of Christ falls away. Instead, Schleiermacher proceeded to describe Christ on the basis of what he called *the living influence of Christ,* that is, through what the contemporary Christian individual feels about Christ.[51] In this way, Schleiermacher's main position, the primacy of feeling over thinking, conditions his christology. For Schleiermacher, Jesus Christ was a person who had a unique awareness of God in his God consciousness:

> if it is only through Him that the human God-consciousness becomes an existence of God in human nature, and only through the rational nature that the totality of finite powers can become an existence of God in the world, that in truth He alone mediates all existence of God in the world and all revelation of God through the world, insofar as he bears within Himself the whole new creation which contains and develops the potency of the God-consciousness.[52]

Christ thus appears to self-consciousness to be the pinnacle of God-consciousness, insofar as "to ascribe to Christ an absolutely powerful God-consciousness, and to attribute to Him an existence of God in Him, are exactly the same thing."[53] In this way, Christ is the combination of two natures in one person but not as one person within the doctrine of the Trinity in the way described by orthodox theology and, by extension, the Lutheran notion of the *communicatio idiomatum*:

> If now we carry over into the doctrine of the Trinity the explanations usually given of the word 'Person' in the doctrine of Christ—and there is sufficient reason for this, since it is asserted that Christ did not become a Person only through the union of the two natures, but the Son of God only took up human nature into His Person—then the three Persons must have an independent anterior existence in themselves; and if each Person is also a nature, we come almost inevitably to three divine natures for the three divine Persons in the one Divine Essence.[54]

Rather than acceding to this apparent confusion, Schleiermacher found that "We must conclude, then, that ideality is the only appropriate expression for the exclusive personal dignity of Christ."[55] Thus, Christ is both 'ideality', an archetype, and human, and because of the impact of this archetype on human consciousness in general, an individual other than Christ "attains a religious personality not his before."[56]

Nothing seems further from Hegel's appropriation of the objective doctrines of the Christian faith than this treatment. Indeed, Hegel aligns his thinking with the tradition of Western theological thought that found the apex of its thinking in the Trinity. For Hegel, a common mode of thinking is identifiable in the history of thought which comprehends its own thinking as part of the thinking of God. Hegel perceived that there is a *community of speculative thinkers who have conceived of their thinking as the inner thinking of God's triadic self-manifestation*. For these thinkers, God, as the differentiated unity of the One, has othered himself in and through the *logos*, the word, which enunciates itself in the living dynamic of human thinking. According to this view, human thinking then becomes the vehicle of God's self-objectification and, indeed, returns God's thoughts to him. In essence, they conclude, human thinking is God's thinking of himself. Thus, these two modes of thought mutually determine each other. At the same time, human beings only participate in God's knowledge of himself.

Hegel found this inner dynamic of trinitarian thinking as evolving through a community of thinkers over history. For Hegel, trinitarian thinking is not static thinking, but part and parcel of the ongoing revelation of God to himself, first discernible in the pre-Christian trinities of the Hindu Trimurti, Plato and Aristotle, and then further developed and unfolded in the Neoplatonic trinitarianism of Proclus, the Gnostics, the orthodox conception of the Trinity as Father, Son, and Holy Spirit, Meister Eckhardt, and Jacob Boehme.[57] It is absolutely central for Hegel that this trinitarian thinking has taken place in history and that it is an object for human thinking. But, it is also central to Hegel's thinking that the Trinity, with its inner relation of mutual determination of God and the human being, has to be articulated in and for the living individual subject as that form of thinking which sublates human being in itself. Thus, Hegel takes pains to depict the relation that the individual 'I' takes to its divine object in this way:

> the individual is affirmative only as pure knowledge, knowledge that has consumed its object, has submerged its own particular thisness in it, its natural state. The teachers of the Christian church declare that by giving up this natural state—if this

surrender is grasped in a natural manner in the form of natural death—human beings can be united with God. Related to this view, moreover, are the church doctrines about the grace of God and how it operates in the human heart, about how a Holy Spirit is active in the community, leading the community into truth about its justification of humanity, and so on. If we comprehend all this in the concept, in thought, without changing the content, then the characteristics that we have just adduced in abstract fashion are involved in it. Such doctrines are just speculative throughout, and any theologians incapable of acceding to their concept should leave them alone. Theology is not just religious piety as such in the form of religion, but rather the *comprehension* of religious content.[58]

Looking back on the history of trinitarian thinking, Hegel quoted favorably Meister Eckhardt's comprehension of this essential relationship between God and human:[59] "The eye with which God sees me is the eye with which I see him; my eye and his eye are one and the same. In righteousness I am weighed in God and he in me. If God did not exist nor would I; if I did not exist nor would he."[60] This description of the relationship between God and the human is exemplary of what Hegel has in mind in the quotation prior to this. In Eckhardt's thinking, the finite human subject and the infinite trinitarian God stand not only in a state of mutual dependence as two complementary poles, they stand also in a state of mutual dependence as two distinct poles. Each side of this dialectical relationship would be empty, or nonexistent, without the other; the finite human subject found itself and knows itself as concrete existence through its knowledge of God and God knows himself through the existence of the finite subject. But at the same time this mutual determination takes place, Eckhardt recognized that as a finite human subject he surrenders all concern with his own 'thisness' and deals with God as thought, as an intellect. Thus, with Eckhardt seeing his own 'thisness' subsumed into the existence of the divine intellect he then discovered the divine intellect as the ground of his own existence. Thus, this divine intellect, whose operations give forth all existence as individual things in themselves, is not ontologically different from the human intellect insofar that in its natural state it is nothing and exists only because God thinks it. Hence, the individual human subject can participate and know unity with God through the 'death' of its understanding of its self as the natural self.[61]

We can see why Hegel cited Eckhardt in respect to the relation of human being and God in trinitarian thinking: not only do God and the self mutually determine each other in a dialectical interaction, but the self is absorbed into a third moment. And, in this third moment, the relations of the finite and the infinite, the divine and the human, are encapsulated and reconciled. And thus this moment is, as we have outlined in Chapter Four, that of Spirit in its thinking of itself.

But Hegel recognized that this way of thinking has been and is dizzying as it supersedes the normal boundaries of logical thinking. It is not surprising, then, Hegel saw that human thinking has to struggle both to maintain God's thinking as the center of all knowledge of human existence and to find appropriate ways of expressing how this contradiction is overcome in the third moment of the Trinity. If we look at Hegel's treatment of a speculative thinker like Jacob Boehme in the *Lectures on the History of Philosophy* we can see that Boehme stands as an excellent example of this problem.[62] Indeed, Hegel observed that, for all this talk of and insight into the Trinity, Boehme's formations are "rude and barbarous" and difficult to read.[63] Nevertheless, Hegel commended Boehme for "his arduous struggle both to bring the deep speculative [content], which he holds in his intuition, into [the form of] representation and to so master the element of representational [thinking] that the speculative content might be expressed in it."[64]

If the 'times' were not right for Boehme's thinking as the last great attempt to articulate this speculative or mystical comprehension of the contents of religion, then, retroactively, the times were not right for all those who came before Boehme. This means that for Hegel the conditions of the possibility for attaining a full speculative grasp are slowly realized over a long period of development, a development in which an adequate speculative form of cognition could arise out of revelatory discourse and adequately master representational thinking. In a January 19, 1824 letter to von Baader, Hegel described this form of cognition as a matter of reason being "at home *with itself* or *free*" and that "*thinking* reason is not at home with itself in such content [of religion] insofar as the content is merely represented."[65] In this same letter, Hegel equated this 'being-at-home' of Reason [*Vernunft*]) with itself with the witness of the

Spirit to itself. Consequently, for Hegel, it is a matter of Spirit overcoming limitations imposed on it as it develops (unfolds itself) through history so that it can become for itself what it is in itself, Absolute Spirit, and thus truly 'be at home' in form and content. Thus, it is apparent that Boehme and Eckhardt had the content, which was nurtured in the Christian community by the Scholastics and the Neoplatonists, but not the developed form of cognition. And, to some extent, Plato and Aristotle also had the content, but in pristine form due to the absence of the revelation of God through Jesus Christ.[66] We can conclude that for Hegel something more had to occur between Boehme's time and his own time so that the self-consciousness of God would take on the speculative form of self-consciousness of Absolute Spirit.

The clue to the identity of this last historical occurrence is to be found in Chapter Three's description of Hegel's comprehension of Luther's introduction of the principle of subjectivity.[67] As we saw, Hegel's speculative comprehension of the truth of the Trinity and Christ is realized in the heart of the individual subject, who subjectifies the objectivity of the church's doctrines thereby creating a place 'in which he is at home with himself and at home with God.' Thus, it is of paramount importance to Hegel that the knowledge of God as Trinity is grounded in the human subject as subject.

We have already worked through the importance of the principle of subjectivity in Luther's science of faith for Hegel's science of spirit. What is critical for our present considerations is that although a sui generis science of faith arises through Luther's hermeneutic of the witness of the Spirit, he did not explicitly identify human subjectivity as an "object" for formal, methodological study.[68] But, as we also have seen, Luther did draw attention to the importance of the 'heart' for knowing, and relating to, God. Indeed, most of Luther's references to the 'heart' are from 'within', that is, from inside his own experience of being in relation to God. (For example, "I am not speaking empty words, I have often experienced, and still do every day, how difficult it is to believe, especially amidst struggles of conscience, that Christ was given, not for the holy, righteous, and deserving, or for those who were his friends."[69]) What is important here is that even though Luther put emphasis on God as infinite and an objectively existing entity that stands above us, Luther also stressed that this God directly related to human beings, manifesting awareness of his truth in the 'heart' of the individual subject. In other words, what becomes important in Luther is the relationship between God and human being in which God manifests himself as the content for the human subject's cognition. For Hegel, this is also what is significant about the consummate religion, that human subjective consciousness and its object, God, have become unified: "In this religion, religion has become objective to itself; the object [*Objekt*] or content by means of which religion is fulfilled, what is objective for it, is now its *own* definition, namely that spirit is [present] only *for* spirit. Universal and singular spirit, infinite and finite spirit, are here inseparable; their absolute identity is religion, and absolute religion is the awareness of just this content."[70] As well, for Hegel, this interrelationship between God and the human being signifies an important change in the focus of theology:

> At first sight, what theology is about is the cognition of God as what is solely objective and absolute, what remains purely and simply separate from subjective consciousness. Therefore God is an external object [*Gegenstand*]—like the sun or the sky— but still a thought-object [*Gegenstand*]. An external object [*Gegenstand*] of consciousness exists where the object [*Gegenstand*] permanently retains the character of something other and external. In contrast with this, we can designate the concept of absolute religion as follows: what is involved here, the essence of what is involved, is not this external object [*Gegenstand*] but religion itself, i.e., the unity of this object [*Gegenstand*] with the subject, the way in which it is in the subject.[71]

Therefore we can see that, for Hegel, theology can take one of two standpoints: it can approach God either as "something other and external," as an "external object" [*Gegenstand*] that stands over and against human consciousness and that hence is basically noncognizable by the human subject; or it knows the human subject as in an essential relationship with an objective God whose otherness has been overcome.

As we have seen in Chapter Two, Schleiermacher also took human subjectivity as an object for theological study precisely because he treated God as an entity, to again use Hegel's words from the previous quotation, with "the character of something other and external."[72] Therefore, in the 1824 lectures on consummate religion, Hegel noted that the 'present age', as exemplified by the Schleiermacherian point of view, knows *that* God exists as external object but does not know *what* God, in his determinations or content, is:

> We can regard the present age as concerned with religion, with religiosity, or with piety, in which no regard is had for what is objective. People have had various religions; but—[according to] the present dogmatics, at least—that does not matter, as long as they are pious. We cannot know God as an object, we cannot cognize him, and it is the subjective attitude that is important. This standpoint has been recognized in our earlier discussion, and we have already spoken of its one-sidedness.[73]

But, in the 1824 lectures on consummate religion, Hegel also critically confirmed Schleiermacher's innovative marking off of the subject as object for the subject's study and comprehended its depth and significance for his own philosophy. He said:

> It [Schleiermacher's dogmatics and its assertion that we cannot know God] is the standpoint of the age, and at the same time it is a very important advance, which has validated an infinite moment; for it involves the recognition of the consciousness of subjectivity as the absolute moment. There is the same content on both sides, and this being-in-itself of both sides is religion. The great advance of our time is that subjectivity has been recognized as the absolute moment; thus subjectivity is the essential determination.[74]

But he adds a note of caution: "But everything depends on how we define this subjectivity."[75] Indeed, for Hegel, Schleiermacher's emphasis on subjectivity can be a source of alienation from God if subjectivity sees its self, its 'I', as living inside of and experiencing only itself. This exclusive sense of subjectivity does not provide any impetus for the subject to move through its subjectivity to the fundamental reorientation of its thematic center from itself to God as already given to the subject in the primogenial religious relationship and enunciated in the objective doctrines of faith. But on the other hand, Hegel claimed that Schleiermacher's furthering of the principle of subjectivity constitutes a great advance for it brings into view the centrality of subjectivity for the religious relationship.

> The validating of this subjectivity is the important thing, or
> [the recognition] that this subjectivity is absolutely essential
> for the whole sphere of the religious relationship. Thus this
> standpoint elevates subjectivity into the essential determination
> of the whole range of the religious relationship. There is a
> rather close bond between it and the freedom of spirit, in that
> spirit has reestablished its freedom, and there is no standpoint
> within which it is not at home.[76]

Thus, subjectivity is an infinite moment, it does embrace in itself the divine and human sides of the religious relationship. However, for Hegel, it is not a question of *my subjectivity as over and against God's objectivity*, but rather, it is the case that

> what God reveals is this infinite form that we have called sub-
> jectivity; i.e., it is the act of determining or positing distinc-
> tions, of positing content. What God reveals in this way is that
> he *is* manifestation, i.e., the process of constituting these dis-
> tinctions within himself. It is his nature and his concept eter-
> nally to make these distinctions and at the same time to take
> them back into himself, and thereby to be present to himself.
> The content that becomes manifest [*offenbar*] is what is
> revealed [*geoffenbart*], namely, that God is for an other but
> [also] eternally for *himself*.[77]

Therefore, we can see that Hegel is confirming that God is infinite subjectivity. Indeed, God discloses himself in a continuous process of self-determination that embraces within itself finite human subjectivity as the locus of God's self-revelation. This realization would eventually lead Hegel to say in the 1831 lectures: "Finite consciousness knows God only to the extent that God knows Himself in it; thus God is spirit, indeed the Spirit of His community, i.e., of those who worship."[78]

As we saw at the end of Chapter Three, Schleiermacher's emphasis on the significance of feeling assisted Hegel in solidifying in his philosophy of religion the role feeling plays in faith. But now we can also see that the significance Hegel attached to the inclusivity and two-sided nature of infinite subjectivity would not have happened in the way it did without Schleiermacher's particular stress on the finite individuality of subjectivity. Indeed, at the same time that

Hegel criticized Schleiermacher's theology—"which has withdrawn in its empty inwardness after the loss of absolute content"[79]—he also realizes that this type of theologizing had cleared the way for philosophy to take up the content of religious consciousness "in a manner that is unconstrained as well as auspicious and beneficial."[80] Hegel's point is clear: if the theology of the day would not admit that God had attained self-consciousness through finite human consciousness (e.g., in the Incarnation), then philosophy would. Consequently, philosophy sees that "it is a need of the present day to be cognizant of God through thinking reason, and thereby to obtain a concrete, living representation of the nature of truth....Truth is no empty shell [but] something concrete, a fullness of content."[81]

There can be no doubt that Hegel's recognition of the need 'to be cognizant of God through thinking reason' is the result of the Protestant Reformation and the "cleavage"[82] between philosophy and theology initiated by the principle of subjectivity implicit in Luther's emphasis on the heart. But, only Hegel's philosophy of religion attempted to heal this fissure by confirming that the Incarnation is the revelation of the reconciliation of the infinite and finite and that reconciliation therefore means that the infinite sublates the finite within itself:

> Reconciliation begins with differentiated [entities] standing opposed to each other—God, who confronts a world that is estranged from him, and a world that is estranged from its essence. [They are] in conflict with one another, and [they are] external to one another. Reconciliation is the negation of this separation, this division, and means that each cognizes itself in the other, found itself in its essence. Reconciliation, consequently, is freedom and is not something quiescent; rather it is activity, the movement that made the estrangement disappear.[83]

So we can see that Hegel's philosophy of religion, and not Schleiermacher's theology, takes seriously the notion of reconciliation implicit "in a religion that a representation of the unity of divine and human nature occur."[84] Thus, only philosophy has as its explicit "goal" the reconciliation of philosophy and theology.[85]

Now we can further conclude that Hegel could and did effect the healing reconciliation between philosophy and theology by including Schleiermacher's theology of feeling as a moment in the inner determination of the *Concept of Religion* through, what we called earlier in this chapter, the philosophy of theology. As an inner determination of the philosophy of religion, Schleiermacher's theology of feeling cannot be dismissed out of hand as having no relevance to the philosophy's conceptualization of religion; on the contrary, the theology of feeling must be seen as finite moment within the self-consciousness of Absolute Spirit. Indeed, we can surmise that the self-consciousness of Absolute Spirit requires the internal splitting of inclusive subjectivity into finite and infinite sides so that Spirit can come to know itself through finite human consciousness and so that finite human consciousness can come to know itself as a moment in the self-consciousness of absolute Spirit. Indeed, in Chapter One we saw this internal splitting already in the conflict between the thinking subject and the immediate subject, the infinite consciousness and finite consciousness, which occurs in the primordial religious relationship, as described by Hegel in the 1821 *Concept of Religion*. Because this internal conflict is found as the ground of the religious relationship it should not be surprising to find it reenacted in the conflict between the theology—which advocates the primacy of the immediate, finite self-consciousness as the source of religious consciousness—and Hegel's philosophy of religion—which advocates the unity-in-difference of infinite and finite subjectivity. Moreover, this further suggested that the reconciliation of the finite and the infinite achieved in the Incarnation must be constantly reenacted in the life and thought of the community, not only because of the originary conflict within religious consciousness, but also because of the continual possibility of conflict due to human subjects ignoring, forgetting, or simply choosing not to actualize the reconciliation attained for the community through Christ. Indeed, because of this constant falling away from the truth of reconciliation, we can see that finite subjectivity is continuously in the process of coming to know itself as the self-consciousness of absolute Spirit:

> The subsistence of the community is its continuous, eternal becoming, which is grounded in the fact that spirit is an eternal process of self-cognition, dividing itself into the finite flashes of light of individual consciousness, and then re-collecting and gathering itself up out of this finitude—inasmuch as it is in the finite consciousness that the process of knowing spirit's essence takes place and that the divine self-consciousness thus arises.

Out of the foaming ferment of finitude, spirit rises up fragrantly.[86]

Although reconciliation has been accomplished for all time through the Incarnation and recognized in principle in Hegel's lectures, it has not been recognized by all members of the community. Thus, the speculative reconciliation of philosophy and theology will have to be undertaken once again. Indeed, as we will see in the next chapter, the truth of the reconciliation of God and humankind in Hegel's philosophical conceptualization of religion will be subject to a new disruption from within the religious consciousness of the present day. As we will see, this disruption will be provided by the Pietists. Therefore, in 1827, Hegel modified philosophy's conceptualization of religious cognition once again, re-cognizing its thinking in relation to Pietist thinking, thereby realizing its own inner content as part of the eternal activity of the self-development of God in infinite subjectivity.

Chapter Five

1827: THE CONFLICT WITH PIETISM AND HEGEL'S SUBJECTIFICATION OF THEOLOGICAL REFLECTION

Introduction

At the end of Chapter Four, we concluded that Spirit's own inner activity necessitates self-differentiation. Indeed, we said the self-consciousness of absolute Spirit can arise only out of the opposition of philosophy and theology, a splitting apart of Spirit so that reconciliation can take place. Hence, a new theological presence had to make itself known within the horizon of the self-consciousness of absolute Spirit, a presence that would provide Hegel with the theological pretext to fully integrate philosophy and theology into an intimate union of identity-in-difference.

In the period between the 1824 lectures and the 1827 lectures, the theological consciousness that presented itself as decidedly against philosophy was Pietism. Significantly, Pietism furthers the principle of subjectivity, but not in the sense of deepening it, as we said was the case with Schleiermacher's dogmatics; rather, Pietism turns subjectivity back into itself as self-centered subjectivity, by centering on what it believed to be the exclusively inward emotional domain of devotion to God. However, it has become clear to us that for subjectivity to turn back in on itself in this way, it needs an 'other' from which it can distinguish itself, something seemingly external to its own self-certainty of the immediacy of devotion of God. In the case of the Pietism contemporary to Hegel, we can say that it needed something to which it could *object*. And, the object to which Pietism objected was Hegel's philosophy and the doctrines of Christianity as both generated within and by the Christian community and reflected on by Hegel in the philosophy of religion. But, unlike Schleiermacher[1] in *The Christian Faith*, Pietism took Hegel's philosophy as its specific object, by name, something not permitted by the inner parameters established by the theology of feeling for itself which, as we noted in Chapter Two, only 'borrows' concepts from philosophy. On the other hand, Pietism felt quite free to criticize openly thinking in and about religion as it sets no methodological restrictions on its own thinking. Indeed, Pietism sees its own thinking as the fruition of its passionate inwardness.

As Pietism pulled itself away from thinking in any formal sense, it expressed an antidoctrinal stance that extends back to the beginnings of Pietism with Philipp Jakob Spener's *Pia Desideria*, as we noted in our Introduction. The *Pia Desideria* called for setting aside the authority of dogma and church in favor of a devotional life centered in the truths of the Bible thus, in effect, calling for a renewed reformation. Following Spener's example, the Pietist movement emphasized only piety as the devotion to God found in the individual who subjects his or her self to the will of God. Because of the inward nature of this subjugation, piety itself is interpreted by the Pietists as an entirely personal and private phenomenon. According to Pietism, the personal nature of piety is "centered on the ever-repeated experience of guilt and forgiveness."[2] Indeed, the dialectic of guilt and forgiveness eternally recurs in the heart of the individual, thereby necessitating an 'eternal recurrence' of conversion in which the individual finds consolation in God. Conversion is the pivot around which the life of the individual revolves. For the Pietist to consider oneself a true Christian, conversion is so essential that the Pietist should be able to pinpoint exactly when one first had "a certain violent and mystical kind of conversion," "accompanied in all cases by agonies of repentance."[3]

However, entering into the ongoing renewal of this private and personal conversion experience is not enough for the Pietist. Devotion to God must not be just a bringing of oneself over to God in submission, it must also be an "active faith," a faith put into practice in the concrete material world. Thus, for the Pietist, devotion to God should also be manifest in good works as "the test of justification."[4] By attempting to embody or incarnate what is felt to be true in good works, the individual confirms the authenticity of one's salvation before God here and now in the living present of everyday life.

Indeed, concrete action in the world is to be an outer expression of what is inwardly felt. Action should flow out of devotion to God. But, no matter how much the individual lives a life of holiness, one will always fall—into sin and short of finding rebirth in God.[5] Because of the omnipresence of sin, the Pietist feels that one may slip through the blanket of God's grace that covers the hearts of all pious individuals back into the evil perils of the flesh. Therefore, the initial conversion experience has to be reenacted in passionate inwardness that continuously appropriates the truth of God as found in Jesus Christ and the original Christian community, reestablishing this truth as its one foundation.

Important, for our considerations, Pietist thinking found that its heartfelt emphasis on piety means that dogma no longer fetters the heart in its outward expression of its reverence for God,[6] a position similar to Schleiermacher's *The Christian Faith*. But, unlike Schleiermacher, who moved beyond the authority of the Bible into what he perceived to be the authority of the community, Pietism perceived its authority as arising from the Bible only, an authority not guided by dogma but by the individual's reverence for God. This hermeneutic is aptly demonstrated in the Pietist attack on Hegel and his philosophy of religion.

Appropriately, the Pietist attack came from one individual, Friedrich August Gottreu Tholuck, who confronted Hegel on the nature and content of scientific knowledge of God. In fact, Tholuck, a young Pietist theology professor who had recently moved from the University of Berlin to the University of Halle, charged Hegel with 'pantheism' and criticized pantheism's inability "to differentiate good and evil."[7] As well, Tholuck criticized the doctrine of the Trinity in his book, *Die speculative Trinitätlehre des späteren Orients: Eine religionsphilosophische Monographie aus handschriftlichen Quellen der Leydener, Oxforder und Berliner Bibliothek* (Berlin, 1826), by arguing that "the dogma of the Trinity...had been falsely read into practically motivated biblical texts by later theologians influenced by Aristotelianism and Neoplatonism."[8] Indeed, according to Hegel, for Tholuck, the doctrine of the Trinity is "decorative timbering" [*Fachwerk*], it can never be the foundation of the house of faith"[9] because it can be historically determined as originating prior to Christianity.

By appealing to historical evidence in his dismissal of the Trinity, Tholuck's theologizing shared a common ground with the theologizing of rational theology, especially as found in the thinking of a rational theologian like Johann Salomo Semler, the "father of popular rationalism"[10] and "father of the historical-critical method."[11] It is in fact in the use (and, for Hegel, the abuse) of history where rational and Pietist theology intersect. Indeed, Tholuck entered the path of historical inquiry into originary sources usually charted by rational theologians whereas Pietism usually satisfied itself with producing "ascetical books and hymns."[12] For example, Semler, following Spinoza, was concerned with the sources and construction of the Bible. Similarly, Tholuck, in the case of his *Die speculative Trinitätlehre des späteren Orients*, was concerned with the sources and construction of the doctrine of the Trinity. Both favor the authority of the individual's piety over ecclesiastical and theological authority. Karl Barth provided us with a sense of the tone and thrust of Tholuck's theologizing, "With Tholuck...theological concern is in the most marked way concern with oneself, and theological presentation is self-presentation."[13]

Tholuck's direct challenge to Hegel was obviously one he could not ignore. As we shall see, Hegel would not only disagree with Tholuck's analysis but, in fact, would instill his own thinking about the Trinity with new life by taking up the Trinity as both the superstructure and infrastructure of the 1827 philosophy of religion. However, Hegel's first response was to communicate directly with Tholuck. In July 1826, Hegel wrote a personal letter to Tholuck, the content of which is, not surprisingly for Hegel, directed right at Tholuck's personal grasp of the truth of the Trinity:

> Does not the sublime Christian knowledge of God as Triune merit respect of a wholly different order than comes from ascribing it merely to such an externally historical course? In your entire publication I have not been able to feel or find any traces of a native understanding of this doctrine. I am a Lutheran, and through philosophy have been at once confirmed in Lutheranism. I do not allow myself to be put off such a basic doctrine by externally historical modes of explanation. There is a higher spirit than merely that of such human tradition. I detest seeing such things explained in the same manner as perhaps the descent and dissemination of silk culture, cherries, smallpox, and the like.[14]

As will become apparent in our discussion of the 1827 *The Consummate Religion,* this reproach also foreshadowed the approach that Hegel would take toward both Pietism and the Trinity in the 1827 lectures on the philosophy of religion. But, as we can also surmise, Tholuck was repulsed by the interpretation of the Trinity already present in Hegel's philosophy, an interpretation that, for Hegel, is grounded in the 'Christian fact' and attested to by the witness of the Spirit in the life of the community. In expressing this 'repulsion' in his 1826 work, Tholuck presented himself as drawn into impassionate inwardness, into subjective self-certainty, believing that what he feels as true is true.[15] However, because Tholuck required pious feeling as both the base and consummation of his 'self-presentation', this means that his thinking actually burrowed itself into, and gained its spiritual nutrition from, nothing more and nothing less than continual devotion to God as lived event. Therefore, for Tholuck, speculation is not something that is to be forgiven for suffering the absence of the 'one truth' and pious talk; rather, it is to be both pitied and challenged for infringing on, and distracting and detracting from, the realization of one's heartfelt attachment to God. In other words, Hegel had to be shown the error of his ways. Indeed, the bottom line for Tholuck was that the immediacy of devotion to God is to be nurtured in its immediacy and not 'intellectualized' even in the internal methodological manner of Schleiermacher. Karl Barth made this point well when he compared Tholuck with Schleiermacher:

> It is not meant to be a value judgment if we say that in respect of the central concept of his theology, the much-cited 'feeling', Schleiermacher is related to Tholuck as a painted flower to a real one or a game with matches to a conflagration. In the one place there is careful, perceptive teaching about feeling; in the other the reckless, stormy, one-sided language of feeling itself. In the one place there is the theoretical academic and historical understanding of religious experience, in the other religious experience as event and as circumstance. 'Guido!', calls the one letter-writer in Tholuck: 'Guido, there is one truth, which is not there for speculation but for enjoyment. This you are told by someone who has enjoyed it'.[16]

But, as we can surmise from Hegel's criticism of Schleiermacher, such one-sidedness draws itself into an apparent paradox (but not into the absolute Paradox as does Kierkegaard) by arguing for the importance of the immediacy of feeling in an erudite, intellectual way. As we can also deduce, Tholuck's attack on Hegel and the Trinity had to be perceived by Tholuck as flowing out of piety as an outward expression of what is inwardly felt as true. Hence, we can assume that in writing about the Trinity in this manner, Tholuck was essentially confronting Hegel with the question of the proselytizing Christian: "Do you, Hegel, know God in your heart (as I do)?" And, as a philosopher should, Hegel responded not by displaying his knowledge of God as Trinity in the manner of 'silk culture, cherries, etc.,' but rather by showing that God as Trinity was known by Hegel as the heart of both his philosophy and the Christian religion.

Hegel's Trinitarian Response to Tholuck in the 1827 Concept of Religion

For Hegel, Tholuck's charge of pantheism and his antitrinitarianism was patently absurd. In Hegel's view, pantheism means "that everything, the whole, the universe, this complex of everything existing, these infinitely many individual things—that all this is God."[17] However, Hegel detected the presence of pantheism first in Oriental religion, specifically Hinduism, which, according to Hegel, blurs the difference between finite subjectivity and God.[18] Pantheism is manifest secondly in Parmenides' Eleatism, Hegel noted, because it asserts 'There is only the One'.[19] Most recently, Hegel said, pantheism made its appearance in Spinozism, which holds that God is One and that *omnis determinatio est negatio*, that is, that all determination is negation, which Hegel pointed out means that "no actuality is ascribed to individual things," including human beings.[20] Interestingly, Hegel also noted that Spinozism has also been equated with atheism, suggesting that Hegel was recalling the pantheism controversy [*Pantheismusstreit*] of only forty-two years earlier.[21] Of those who made the charges, Hegel remarked:

> But the accusers of Spinozism are unable to liberate themselves from the finite; hence they declare that for Spinozism everything is God, because it is precisely the aggregate of finitudes (the world) that has there disappeared. If one employs the expression "all is one" and [claims] therefore the unity is the truth of multiplicity, then the "all" simply is no longer. The multiplicity vanishes, for it has its truth in the unity. But those

critics cannot master the "being-vanished" of the many, or the negativity of the finite that is implied.[22]

It is apparent that the standpoint of those who, unable to liberate themselves from the finite, rendered this criticism had a certain resonance in Hegel's ears for his own 'pantheism controversy'. Indeed, a striking parallel is to be found between Tholuck and the 'accusers of Spinoza', over the question of the supposed collapse of the distinction between good and evil in Spinoza's and Hegel's 'pantheism'. But, for Hegel, they simply do not recognize the role that the *negativity of the finite* in relation to the infinite plays in religious consciousness. Spinoza did and this is what made him worthy of great respect and admiration as a philosopher. But, for Hegel, Spinoza's stance is only a beginning of philosophizing.[23] Indeed, Hegel found that Spinoza's assertion about God as the One, absolute substance is correct in terms of beginning to think about God, but then we must go further than this standpoint and see "how this [One] substance is related to subjectivity."[24] Without an account of the relation of subjectivity to the One substance then, indeed, everything finite is absorbed into a pantheistic, abstract One, in which the significance of the world is negated in its determinateness:

> God is the absolute substance. If we cling to this declaration in its abstract form, then it is certainly Spinozism or pantheism. But the fact that God is *substance* does not exclude *subjectivity*, for substance as such is not yet at all distinguished from subjectivity. That God is substance is part of the presupposition we have made that God is *spirit*, *absolute spirit*, eternally simple spirit, being essentially present to itself. Then this ideality or subjectivity of spirit, which is the perspicuity or ideality of every particular, is like this very universality, this pure relation to itself, the absolute being-with-self and abiding-with-self; it is absolute substance. At the same time, when we say "substance" there is then the distinction that that universal is not yet grasped as internally concrete. Only when grasped as concrete is it spirit.[25]

Therefore, "we do not stop at that point [of thinking about God as One substance]"; rather, we have to go on thinking and realize that "A further determination is that the substantiality or unity of absolute actuality with itself is only the foundation, only one moment in the definition of God as spirit."[26] In fact, what is missing in Spinoza's thoughts about God is any sense of God as spirit, as an inclusive subjectivity, whose trinitarian infrastructure only starts with the Oneness of God and then proceeded to other itself into a world that, in its determinations, is a negation of the 'abstract', 'initial simplicity' of God as substance. Without the notion of a tripersonal God, Hegel was observing, we would have to stay with Spinoza and reason along with him that God is not truly differentiated within Himself because all determinations are ultimately absorbed in God's Oneness. However, Hegel noted: "That he is the absolute Person however is a point which the philosophy of Spinoza never reached: and on that side it falls short of the true notion of God which forms the content of religious consciousness in Christianity."[27] Indeed, Christian religious consciousness shows that God has not only created the world, but also entered human form, underwent death, and was resurrected. For philosophy, this theological truth portrays, in representational terms, the divine process through which the finitude of the world is first posited as the negation of the initial unity of God that is then, in turn, negated, lifted up and preserved, or sublated [aufgehoben] into the infinity of Absolute Spirit. Indeed, according to Hegel, the incarnation, death, and resurrection of the divine human, Jesus Christ, is the central determination on which the doctrines of the consummate religion have been based, and thus has to be affirmed by philosophy as both the positive moment when eternal truth was revealed and as the basis of the ongoing revelation of Absolute Spirit. In this way, Tholuck and others of similar conviction would be shown what is the true significance of the negativity of the finite.

The Introduction to the 1827 Consummate Religion

Hegel commenced his consideration of the consummate religion by stating what is for him the most important attribute of it, revelation.

> This absolute religion is the *revelatory* [offenbar] religion, the religion that has itself as its content and fulfillment. But it is also called the *revealed* [geoffenbart] religion—by which is understood, on the one hand, that it is revealed by God, that God has given himself for human beings to know what he is;

and on the other hand, that it is a revealed, *positive* religion in the sense that it has come to humanity from without, has been given to it.[28]

But, that Christianity is both a revealed and revelatory religion is the greatest stumbling block to the theologians like Tholuck. By revealed religion, Hegel means that

> the absolute religion is, of course, a positive religion in the sense that everything that is *for* consciousness is *objective* to consciousness. *Everything must come to us from outside.* The sensible is thus something positive. Initially there is nothing positive other than what we have before us in immediate intuition. Everything spiritual also comes to us in this fashion, whether it be the spiritual in general or the spiritual in finite or historical form.[29]

In other words, it is the case that God revealed his presence to humankind in an immediate, sensible, and historical fashion, that is, as a human being who walked and talked and lived a human life. Moreover, the development of the thinking of the Christian community into the doctrines of the church is also positive insofar as these doctrines were developed by human beings at certain times and in certain places.[30] Thus, positivity always presents a troublesome aspect: "Since historical, externally appearing elements are found in it, there is also present a positive and contingent [feature], which can just as well take one form as another."[31] Therefore, it also follows that these positive truths of Christianity require further verification for those who live centuries after these events. Indeed, the truth of Jesus Christ as the God-man was hard for human beings to grasp, even for those to whom Christ was present. Consequently, those who come after Christ (and after the formation of the doctrines of the church) think their positivity "should bear witness to the truth of a religion, and should be regarded as the ground of its truth."[32] Thus, "Verification may take the form of the positive as such—namely, *miracles* and *testimonies*, which are supposed to verify the fact that this individual has done this or that, has given this or that doctrine."[33]

As we can see, Hegel admitted that the problem of interpretation for the theologian comes from this positive, external, and historical characteristic of Christianity's mode of revelation. Theologians try to substantiate the facticity of Jesus's birth, death, and resurrection to cut through the veil of historical distance between themselves and the God-man. Indeed, they try to determine the historical facticity of the claims of the Christian community about Christ and establish to what degree the historical reports (in the Bible) are true. As Hegel noted, they then focus on Christ's miracles as evidence to prove that he was God. Or, they may then see him only as a thaumaturge. And, if they can find no historical support for his miracles, they may reinterpret him as a moral teacher, political revolutionary, and not as God. Although there is this positive, historical dimension to the Christian religion and its doctrines and history, which one may investigate, the *verification of the truth of the consummate religion must come*, Hegel asserted, *from the revelatory nature of Christianity itself*. Thus, Hegel stated that "the witness of the Spirit is the authentic witness."[34] As we will see presently, Spirit's verification of God's revelation starts with the 'death of God' to which the community witnesses. Indeed, as we will see, Hegel held that the faith of the *cultus* holds within itself its own verification of the life, death, and resurrection of Christ. Faith interprets these events as revelation of divine history and not as external history per se. Through faith, the external characteristics of God's revelation resonate in the heart of human being and thus fall away as external: "In history, all that is noble, lofty, and divine speaks to us internally; to it our spirit bears witness. This witness may remain nothing more than this general resonance, this inner agreement, this empathy and sympathy."[35] But the witness of the Spirit does not stay at this level: "But beyond this, the witness of spirit may also be connected with insight and thought. Insofar as this insight is not sensible in character, it belongs directly to thought; it appears in the form of reasons, distinctions, etc."[36] But it is not yet the last form: "The witness of spirit in its highest [third] form is that of philosophy, according to which the concept develops the truth purely from itself without presuppositions."[37] This last, highest, and third form of the witness of the Spirit then is the standpoint of the philosophy of religion: "In our present consideration of this [the Christian] religion, we are not going to work historically after the fashion of that mindset which starts from what is external, but rather we will proceed from the concept."[38] And, as we have already established, this *is* the case in the philosophy of religion.

As we have seen, this is not the case with the theologians (like Tholuck), who Hegel now likend to "the Englishman who didn't know that he was speaking prose."[39] To use another analogy to reinforce Hegel's point, theologians simply have not crossed Socrates' divided line by recognizing that they are thinking and hence are already across the divided line. In other words, thinking should recognize when it is thinking. But, a theology like Tholuck's represses its own spiritual, thinking character when it denies the witness of the Spirit the chance to witness to its own truth on all levels, including the level of reason. Indeed, when it tries to live by the positive letter of the Bible, it succeeds in only killing the spirit of the truth that is waiting to reveal itself to thought. For Hegel, the lesson that theology, especially Pietism and Schleiermacher, has to learn is that, "In regard to positivity, the main point is that spirit conducts itself in a thinking fashion and its activity occurs within the categories or determinations of thought; here spirit is purely active, sentient, or reasoning. But most people are not conscious of the fact that they are active in this reception."[40] Indeed, Hegel found that they cloak God's revelation in mystery, making the process of revelation itself mysterious and, in the last analysis, ineffable on the rational level. But, as we can see, Hegel was confirming that he thinks that the witness of the Spirit requires the thinking of finite spirits to disclose the truth of God to itself, and, as such, there is no mystery: "The nature of God is not a secret in the ordinary sense, least of all in the Christian religion. In it God has made know what he is; there he is manifest. But he is a secret or mystery for external sense perception and representation, for the sensible mode of consideration and likewise for the understanding."[41]

The First Element: The Idea of God in and for Itself

What we have just seen is Hegel once again employing the second-order criticism of the philosophy of theology to discern what is both accurate and inaccurate in the theological reflection of a theologian contemporary to himself. Indeed, Hegel is very critical of those, like Tholuck, who remain fixated on the positive, historical side of the Christian religion, and thus, seek only historical verification of its truths. Of course, for Tholuck, the discovery of the existence of the notion of the Trinity in pre-Christian religions constitutes sufficient reason to dismiss it as the central truth of Christianity. But Hegel, recognizing the limitations of historical inquiry, proclaimed the speculative truth of the trinitarian God as witnessed to by Spirit as its own truth; a truth that sublates the historical within its eternal embrace: "Specifically, the eternal idea is expressed in terms of the holy *Trinity*; it is God himself, eternally triune. Spirit is this process, movement, life. This life is self-differentiation, self-determination and the first differentiation is that Spirit is as this universal idea itself."[42]

Thus, we can see that, for Hegel, philosophy already knows the Trinity as the universal, eternal Idea before it unfolds the determinations of the consummate religion. In fact, Hegel had already examined God as he is in and for himself as eternal, abstract Idea prior to the 1821 lectures on the philosophy of religion in the *Wissenschaft der Logik* and the 'Lesser Logic' of the *Encyclopaedia*.[43] With this 'preknowledge', he commenced his discussion of consummate religion with a recital of the logical determinations of the *Logic*: "This is always the pattern in scientific knowledge: first the concept; then the particularity of the concept—reality, objectivity; and finally the stage in which the original concept is an object to itself, is for itself, becomes objective to itself, is related to itself. So this is the pattern of philosophy; first the concept of the conceptualizing science—the concept that *we* have. But at the end science itself grasps its concept, so that this concept is for itself."[44]

But this pure thinking about thinking, when the concept is 'for itself', is the result of the phenomenological journey of consciousness through its penultimate form, consummate religion. Therefore, the *Logic* is both beginning of speculative thinking and end of phenomenological thinking. As speculative thinking, the *Logic* mirrors what consummate religion thinks is triune God but in purified form, hence, the scientific pattern of the logic of the concept: concept (or universality), objectivity (or particularity), and the Idea (individuality). Thus, the *Logic* views itself as "the presentation of God...as he is in his eternal essence before the creation of finite nature and spirit."[45] As prior to consummate religion (and, indeed, all religion) God is the Idea that preexists as "the subject-object, the unity of the ideal and the real, of the finite and the infinite, of soul and body, as the possibility which has its actuality in its own self; that of which the nature can be thought only as existent, etc."[46] Moreover, as the unity-in-difference of these oppositions, the Idea is absolute Idea, which is, as one commentator succinctly stated, "the concept or category of self-consciousness, personality, self-thinking Thought which knows itself in its object and its object as itself. It is thus the category of Spirit. In religious language, it is the concept of God in and for himself, knowing himself as the totality."[47] But, what Hegel has to disclose to a theologian skeptic like Tholuck is that the consummate religion not only should, but does, manifest this idea of God as its own truth and thus as intrinsic to its own spiritual consciousness.

As we can see, Hegel has set for himself the task of demonstrating to both the philosophers and the theologians of his time that the Idea is 'at home' in the consummate religion and therefore is not some heresy or pagan religious philosophical Idea. Thus, his thinking has a double thrust: to allow the truth of the Idea to shine through the determinations of consummate religion—as both Idea and in representation as holy Trinity. Corresponding to this double thrust, and to add support to it apodictically, Hegel also has to demonstrate that philosophy is at home in religion, that they do indeed share the same object. Therefore, he claims from the outset of the lectures: "Philosophy is only explicating *itself* when it explicates religion, and when it explicates itself it is explicating religion. For the thinking spirit is what penetrates this object, the truth; it is thinking that enjoys the truth and purifies the subjective consciousness. Thus religion and philosophy coincide in one. In fact, philosophy itself is the service of God, as is religion. But each of them, religion as well as philosophy, is the service of God in a way peculiar to it....They differ in the peculiar character of their concern with God."[48]

As we learned in Chapter One, philosophy and theology are indeed identical in their 'shared object', and the difference between theology and philosophy lies in their mode of cognition. Indeed, philosophy maintains an impartial stance in its conceptual cognition, whereas theology is quite partial in its representational cognition. However, in 1827, Hegel added support to his claim of mutuality of philosophy and theology by observing that philosophy aided theology in its formulation of doctrine: "The church owes to their philosophical instruction the first beginnings of Christian doctrine, the development of a *dogmatics*."[49] In fact, "Even in the Christian religion the Holy Trinity does not appear in the immediate appearance [itself]; rather the idea is first completed only when the Spirit has entered in the community and when the immediate, believing has raised itself to the level of thinking."[50] Indeed, we have noted that the Church Fathers adopted and adapted the philosophical notion of the triune God of Christianity with the church councils of the *fourth* and *fifth* centuries. However, as we also discussed, the idea of a triune deity 'preexisted' in the philosophical thinking of the Pythagoreans, Plato, the Gnostics, and so forth. (There was no need for Tholuck to point this out to Hegel.) But, of course, the church located its doctrine of the triune being of God as already formulated in and through the historical revelation provided by the events recorded in the Bible. At the same time, as Hegel accurately observed, the first formulators of this doctrine, Tertullian and Origen, for example, "had steeped themselves particularly in Neopythagorean, Neoplatonic, and Neoaristotelian philosophy" and had "passed over to Christianity from philosophy" bringing "that philosophical profundity of spirit to the teachings of Christianity."[51]

The idea of a triune deity enunciated in the Christian doctrine is that of an *economic* Trinity, who is active in the world through the inner trinitarian activity of Father, Son, and Holy Spirit. Indeed, the operations of the Trinity are first revealed through the concrete event of the life, death, and resurrection of the Son of God, Jesus Christ. But, it would not make sense that God is only Trinity with the coming into being of the Christian community. Therefore, as early as Tertullian, this Trinity was thought to *preexist* as a *logically necessary prior* Trinity, an *immanent* Trinity, who others himself in the form of the economic Trinity. Consequently, we find belief in this Idea formally expressed, as Hegel noted in his presentation of faith in the Foreword, in creeds: "we worship one God in Trinity, and Trinity in Unity," "uncreated," "incomprehensible," and "eternal" (the Athanasian Creed), and this immanent Trinity is located as the 'Father', "by whom all things were made" (the Nicene Creed).[52] In other words, God is the utterly transcendent absolute, which exists prior to space and time in its own inner self-differentiation as immanent Trinity and which, through the act of Creation, is the ultimate source of all that exists and, consequently, is that on which all existing things depend for their existence. Therefore, we can see that the Church Fathers were moved to speak of the immanent Trinity, of God in himself, prior to existence of creation as the ground of all that is created, on the basis of the historical occurrence of the revelation of the economic Trinity in Jesus Christ.

For Hegel, the Christian notion of the immanent Trinity must be the starting point of philosophy's conceptualization of the consummate religion because "what is universal or abstract must precede everything else in scientific knowledge; scientifically, one must start with it. But in existence it is in fact what comes later."[53] In other words, we must not allow ourselves, like Tholuck, to be overwhelmed by the historicity of such a doctrine. On the contrary, the 'idea of God in and for itself' is the 'first element' to examine in the consideration of the essence of Christianity. Thus, if we proceed scientifically (and not historically), we find:

> In accord with the first element, then, we consider God in his eternal idea, as he is in and for himself, prior to or apart from the creation of the world, so to speak. Insofar as he is thus within himself, it is a matter of the eternal idea, which is not yet posited in its reality but is itself still only the abstract idea. But God is the creator of the world; it belongs to his being, his essence, to be the creator; insofar as he is not the creator, he is grasped inadequately. His creative role is not an *actus* that happened once; [rather,] what takes place in the idea is an *eternal* moment, an eternal determination of the idea.[54]

As we can see, Hegel confirmed and expressed in conceptual language what the creeds taught about the immanent Trinity. But Hegel's concern was not to spend time meditating on this idea of God in and for itself as, he noted: "We already know this pure idea, and there we need only dwell on it briefly."[55] (As we have discussed earlier in this section, the *Logic* has this eternal Idea as its subject matter.) Rather, what is significant for Hegel's present consideration is that this eternal Idea has found its complete expression in the Christian religion. Indeed, that this 'abstract' Idea of God comes fully into its own in Christianity is what marks the Christian religion off from all other world religions, contrary to what Tholuck may think. Indeed, Hegel asserted (contra Tholuck): "although it must be conceded that the Church Fathers studied Greek philosophy, it is still primarily immaterial where that doctrine came from. The question is solely whether it is true in and for itself."[56] Of course, for Hegel, answering this question entails dealing with the Idea of God as an idea, that is, from the level of thinking and not from the basis of immediate, sensible experience, because, as we noted earlier in this section, "the idea is first completed only when the Spirit has entered into the community and when the immediate, believing spirit has raised itself to the level of thinking."[57] Therefore, the linkage of philosophy and theology in the determination of the doctrine of the Trinity (both immanent and economic) by the Church Fathers is nothing to be condemned; rather, Tholuck should take note. Indeed, "We can see the same linkage between theology and philosophy in the Middle Ages, too. Scholastic philosophy is identical with theology; theology is philosophy and philosophy is theology. So far were they from believing that thinking, conceptual knowing, might be injurious to theology that it was regarded as necessary, as essential to theology itself. These great men—Anselm, Abelard, etc.—built up theology out of philosophy."[58]

Therefore, we can see that for Hegel the Idea is 'at home' in the doctrines and the thinking of the consummate religion. Of course, Tholuck, who wanted to get back to the immediacy and feeling tone of the first Christian community, would find all this talk about doctrinal and logical thinking reprehensible. But, as Hegel outlined in the Foreword, the actuality of faith is its dialectic interaction between subjective conviction and objective doctrine. Feeling therefore is only one aspect. Moreover, as the history of Christian thought demonstrates, the actuality of doctrine is the dialectic interaction between theology and philosophy: philosophy is at home in the Christian religion. Indeed, 'philosophy is theology' and 'theology is philosophy' when believing has raised itself to the level of thinking about the Idea of God in and for itself. As we have seen, the construction of the horizon of meaning for both theology and philosophy has not occurred in isolation, but rather in direct interaction with each other when they think about God as Trinity.

However, this relationship has not remained static. Most Protestant theologians contemporary to Hegel neglect or dismiss the doctrine of the Trinity; rather, philosophy maintains interest in and builds theological doctrines such as the Trinity. Indeed, the path to realizing everything "according to the [logical] determinations of the Trinity" comes next from the speculative mysticism of Jacob Boehme and (somewhat obliquely) from the critical philosophy of Kant.[59]

"Although it follows on a period when the antipathy became once more a presupposition," Hegel remarked, "the present day seems again to be more propitious for the linkage of philosophy and theology."[60] It is Hegel himself who sees his way to display "that this idea is what is true as such, and that all categories of thought are this movement of determining is the [task of] logical exposition."[61] In this, "it [philosophy] suffers the reproach of containing within itself too much of the teachings of the church, more than the generally prevailing theology of the time."⁶² In spite of this criticism of the theologians, speculative philosophy would resurrect the unity of theology and philosophy of the Middle Ages and allow the revelatory and scientific modes of thinking to mirror, once again, their identity and their difference.

The Second Element: Representation, Appearance

As we have seen, Hegel's philosophy suffers the reproach (from Tholuck and the Pietists) of 'containing within itself too much of the teaching of the church' when it grasps the immanent Trinity or, in the language of speculative philosophy, the eternal Idea as the object of its cognition. We also saw that Hegel disagreed with the negative tone of this reproach, although he would agree that its observation is essentially correct: philosophy does contain within itself the teachings of the church. Indeed, the eternal Idea is at home in the conceptual cognition of philosophy as well as in the doctrinal thinking of the consummate religion. Moreover, as we have seen, Hegel confirmed that this divine Idea is the point of intersection in the thinking of speculative philosophy and orthodox theology. Indeed, their common cognition of the truth of the 'idea of God' means that, for Hegel, philosophy can and will reflect in conceptual form the content of the theological thinking of the consummate religion. And, Tholuck should note, the truth of this common content of speculative philosophy and orthodox theology will be displayed by philosophy in the form of the dynamic unfolding of the Idea through the three moments or 'elements' of philosophy's conceptual treatment of the consummate religion. Therefore, the trinitarian structure of the Idea becomes the form and structure of the 1827 *The Consummate Religion*. Hence, its first element, as we detailed in the previous section, was that of the immanent Trinity, that is, the Idea of God in and for itself. The second 'element' of the consummate religion, as we will now detail, is "the eternal idea" comprehended "in the form of *consciousness* or of *representation* in general," where philosophy will now "consider this idea insofar as it emerges out of universality and infinitude into the determinacy of finitude."⁶³ And, as we will see in the last section of this chapter, the third 'element' will follow, consisting of the "element of the community" as the concretization of Spirit.

On the basis of the foregoing, we can see that *the Idea indeed inhabits philosophy and theology as their content* and therefore is not mere 'decorative timbering', as we saw Tholuck claim earlier in this chapter; rather, it is very much the foundation of both the orthodox Christian faith and the science of Spirit. Indeed, because the formal trinitarian structure of the 1827 conceptual cognition of the consummate religion is also thought by philosophy as the consequence of the self-development of the Idea into the self-consciousness of absolute Spirit, we can see that, for Hegel, it has become the function of philosophy to witness to this eternal truth.

Accordingly, Hegel continued the unfolding of the self-development of the Idea of God with the contemplation of, as he described it in 1824, "the process of self-differentiation, of diremption"[64] manifest in the creation of the world and the activity of the Trinity in the operations of the world; that is, as economic Trinity. From the point of view of philosophy, the second element—the progression of the Idea into the element of appearance—can be considered from either of the two distinct sides found in the dialectical unity of the self-consciousness of absolute Spirit; that is, from the side of the human subject or from the side of the Idea. Hegel, of course, would discuss both sides. We, however, will start from the side of the Idea to clarify what exactly is appropriated by the human subject in the second element.

Starting from the Idea, Hegel found that externalization of the first moment, the immanent Trinity, into the economic Trinity could not take place without the immanent interaction of the Idea:

> Eternal being-in-and-for-itself is what discloses itself, determines itself, divides itself, posits itself as what is differentiated from itself, but the difference is at the same time constantly sublated. Thereby actual being in and for itself constantly returns into itself—only in this way is it spirit. What is distinguished is defined in such a way that the distinction immediately disappears, and we have a relationship of God, of the idea, merely to Himself. The act of differentiation is only a movement, a play of love with itself, which does not arrive at the seriousness of other-being, of separation and rupture.[65]

This immanent interaction of diremption and return constitutes the relational ground of all reality. It does so by establishing the

Father as the founding person, without origin, who has derived within himself a second moment, which Hegel now called the (eternal) Son. This derivation of the Son is a necessary "primal division of the idea."[66] Indeed, this primal division sets the relational ground of reality precisely because its *internal* self-differentiating renders possible the *external* self-differentiation of creation:

> the primal division of the idea is to be conceived in such a way that the other, which we have also called "Son," obtains the determination of the other as such—that this other exists as a free being for itself, and that it appears as something actual, as something that exists outside of and apart from God. Its ideality, its eternal return into actual being in and for itself, is posited in the first form of identity, the idea, in an immediate and identical way. Otherness is requisite in order that there may be difference; it is necessary that what is distinguished should be the otherness as an entity.[67]

Therefore, in this first step in comprehending the movement of the immanent Trinity into the economic Trinity, we can discern that for Hegel the establishment of otherness, in the sense of a creation of an ontological reality that exists outside of God, requires as its precondition the establishment of a formal other within the immanent interaction of the Idea. Moreover, as Hegel already noted, this internal grounding interaction is a 'play of love'. Hence, the eternal Idea already establishes its inner nature as love. Without this inner dialectic of love between the Father and Son, the movement out of the pure inner dynamism of the Idea into an independent other, that is, into the world, would not be possible. Therefore, the second step in this process is the movement of the Idea's self-othering into an external other. That the Idea takes this second step also signifies for Hegel the Idea's absolute, unlimited freedom in determining itself:

> Only the absolute idea determines itself and is certain of itself as absolutely free within itself because of this self-determination. For this reason its self-determination involves letting this determinate [entity] exist as something free, something independent, or as an independent object. It is only for the being that is free that freedom *is*; it is only for the free human being that an other has freedom too. It belongs to the absolute freedom of the idea

that, in its act of determining and dividing, it releases the other to exist as a free and independent being. This other, released as something free and independent, is *the world* as such.[68]

As the creation of the world is a free act on the part of God the Father, this also means that the world is not its own true reality, subsisting by itself; rather, its true reality is found in the ideality of the free creative act of the Father, who maintains the world as a moment in his inner totality:

> The truth of the world is only its *ideality*—for it is not true that it possesses genuine actuality. Its nature is to *be*, but only in an *ideal* sense; it is not something eternal in itself but rather something created, whose being is only posited. For the world, to be means to have being only for an instant, so to speak, but also to sublate this its separation or estrangement from God. It means to return to its origin, to enter into the relationship of spirit, of love—to *be* this relationship of spirit, of love, which is the third element. The second element is, therefore, the process of the world in love which it passes over from fall and separation into reconciliation.[69]

Therefore, the world in its ideality as part of the totality of God will return to its source in the third element.

Although the preceding notion of differentiation within God may be difficult to grasp, there is no possible way for Tholuck to confuse Hegel's account of the relation of God and world with pantheism. Hegel clearly did not identify God with all things in nature nor with the world in general as would a pantheist. On the contrary, Hegel identified the world as entity separate from, yet involved in, with, and under the action of the divine. Indeed, a pantheist would never suggest, as both orthodox Christianity and Hegel did, that God creates an object that is both independent of and dependent on its creator. In other words, contra Tholuck's charges of pantheism, Hegel was being *panentheistic*, in the full meaning of the term.[70] This is exactly what Hegel was indicating when he rendered his speculative account of the orthodox Christian doctrine of creation. Therefore, we can also conclude that this section of *The Consummate Religion* stands as an effective rebuttal of Tholuck's charge of pantheism.

We can surmise that for a theologian like Tholuck, no amount of clever argumentation about the world as a moment of the eternal

Idea would suffice; on the contrary, we can assume that Tholuck's view would still revolve around what could be discerned through the immediacy of feeling alone.

As we noted near the beginning of this section, Hegel proposed that there is another side or path to the comprehension of this truth of the Idea. This opening is by necessity from the human side, from the side of a finite human subject who will think the Idea and thus become sublated within, but who, first, has to be inwardly certain of its truth through *immediate* knowledge:

> Absolute truth is for thinking. But the idea must not only be the truth for the subject; the subject must also have the [sort of] certainty about the idea that belongs to the subject as such, as a finite, empirically concrete, sentient subject. The idea possesses certainty for the subject only insofar as it is a perceptible idea, insofar as it exists for the subject. If I can say of anything, "it is so" [*das ist*], then it possesses certainty for me; this immediate knowledge, this certainty. To prove "what is so" is also *necessary*, that it is what is true that is certain for me—that is the further process of mediation and is no longer something immediately apprehended; so this mediation is the transition into the universal.[71]

Therefore, the absolute truth of the Idea must appear to the finite subject within the parameters of the natural conditions in which it lives. This would mean that the Idea would have to present itself to humanity in time and in a particular place "as concrete self-consciousness, as an actual subject"[72] so that its truth can be apprehended in immediacy. Then, once the Idea is made perceptible for the finite subject in this way, the finite subject, as it raises itself from sensibility into thinking, will also come to comprehend the truth of the Idea in thinking. As we will see, the Idea will make its appearance in the person of Jesus Christ, but, first, we have to discern how the inner logic of the divine process we have just described in this section produces "the *need* for truth."[73]

Natural Humanity

Because God enters into an eternal self-differentiation by begetting the eternal Son this distinct moment, the Son, remains identical with the Father and, indeed, remains in the original identity of the Father. Moreover, as we have also seen, this self-differentiation is the precondition for the othering of the Idea into the world. Indeed, once this precondition is set then the natural world ushers forth as part of God's self-determination, but as the other, external side of this determination. As independent object (although it is still vitally interconnected with the Father) it is in the furtherest extreme of being other and, as we will now see, this means the world is in opposition to "the side [the eternal Son] that remains in unity."[74] Therefore, for Hegel, this positing of the natural world is then that through which the Idea's self-diremption appears as real separation of unity into the oppositions of the ideal and the real, the infinite and the finite, the spiritual and the natural: "The finite world is the side of distinction as opposed to the side that remains in unity; hence it divides into the *natural world* and the world of *finite spirit*."[75] But, this division also engenders a set of relationships between God, humanity, and nature in which human beings are *in between* God and nature, relating to both nature and God as a spirit, that is, as an entity able to think about its situation:

> On its own account, nature enters into relationship only with humanity, not with God, for nature is not knowledge. God is spirit; nature knows nothing of spirit. It is created by God, but of itself it does not enter into relationship with him—in a sense that it is not possessed of knowledge. It stands in relation only to humanity, and in this relationship it provides what is called the dependent side of humanity. But to the extent that thinking recognizes that nature is created by God, that understanding and reason are within it, nature is known by thinking human beings. To that extent it is posited in relation to the divine, because its truth is recognized.[76]

Therefore, for Hegel, nature and spirit simply fall apart from each other. But, this falling apart is not yet at its furtherest extreme; finite spirit is not yet estranged from the Idea. (In fact, it always subsists in God whether it knows it or not.) As we will see presently, it is the individual finite subject that withdraws itself from God through isolating itself in its particularity, not God who withdraws from the finite subject. Indeed, Hegel seems to be suggesting a view of human being that is not based on a dualism that insists on the existence of two basic and irreducible principles. Instead, Hegel's view is monistic: finite spirit is a concrete entity, invested with a natural body as are all other entities in the natural world, which continues to exist as part of the one divine process. But, the finite spirit, as enclosed within this dynamic unity, is an entity that is already "passing beyond" immersion in the immediacy of the natural world, "because the implicit [natural] being of human being is spirit, humanity in its immediacy is already involved in stepping forth from immediacy, in falling away from it, from its being."[77] Indeed, Hegel proposed, in finite spirit, "there is present…the demand to *know* the absolute truth."[78] Thus, this innate demand of finite spirit to know the absolute truth is what pulls the human being out of its immersion in immediacy and places it into something other than immediacy, into the realm of reflection and thought. Consequently, this inner movement produces within finite spirit, a "separation," a "cleavage."[79] Furthermore, Hegel noted, human being also has a need for overcoming this bifurcation and "its attendant cleavage from the truth" so that both cleavages are "annulled" and "the subject should be reconciled…with the truth."[80] However, as we will see in the next section, this inner rupture within the human subject will be objectified by human beings into expressions about the natural state of being human, even though it is not inherently good or evil. Thus, as we will see, for Hegel, 'natural humanity' has within it the condition for the possibility of knowledge of good and evil.

Because Hegel's account of 'natural humanity' displays humanity as possessing only the potential for the *knowledge* of good and evil, this also means that the world in its unthinking naturalness is also not evil nor good in itself. Hence, he dismissed the whole inquiry into whether humanity is by nature good or humanity is by nature evil as "false."[81] According to Hegel, the first proposition—that humanity is naturally good—is "The more or less predominant notion of our time."[82] Indeed, the Enlightenment period can be seen as a period of Pelagianism inasmuch as Enlightenment thinkers rejected the doctrine of original sin.[83] However, Hegel judged this view to be "one-sided,"[84] as is its opposite. Indeed, both these assertions about the natural state of humanity must be construed as one-sided by Hegel because, as we have just detailed, natural humanity is an internally split human being; thus, it must see itself as having two sides to its nature. Indeed, for Hegel, human beings will see themselves as having a 'good' side in relation to its opposite, the 'evil' side: "both of them, both good and evil, are posited, but essentially in contradiction, in such a way that each of them presupposes the other. It is not that only one of them is [there], but instead we have both of them in this relation of being opposed to each other."[85]

Important, because this knowledge of good and evil is not embedded in immediacy of naturalness *per se*, but arises through reflection in finite spirit, it will be "regarded as something that *happened*."[86] This past event is what Christian theology has described in the doctrine of the fall. And this representation, as we will now see, is how good and evil will appear to consciousness before consciousness recognizes the movement of the Idea in its own consciousness as the eternal activity of the self-development of God in infinite subjectivity.

The Story of the Fall

Because human being found itself already in the intersubjective sphere of the *cultus*, representation is a shared, communal way of articulating and actualizing the implicit presence of the Idea. Indeed, a representation like the story of the fall arises as a story of the origin of not only the religious community but as a story of the first, decisive moment in the past of all humanity (at least according to the religious community). Therefore, for the community of believers, this 'fall' is the prehistorical point from which all humanity fell into history and into sin. From this event, the *cultus* then traces its own evolution as a necessary return from sin into the eternal, sublating all vestiges of temporality in the process. Hence, the story of the fall, as representation, presents itself as the opening act of the eternal drama of the *cultus* on the stage of history.

In the communal religious consciousness of consummate religion, this story is first given and taken up as the literal truth of human being. Indeed, in what we have described as the *literalist* view of scriptural revelation, all the events described in the Bible, from its beginning in Genesis to its anticipation of last things in Revelation, are unfolded in time under the divine auspices of God. But, as we have noted, this literalism is not an invention of the 'present day' of Hegel's time; however, we can now say that it is a necessary first confirmation by the community of its own inner truth as it represents this truth to itself. In fact, this literalism extends back to the New Testament writers who not only treated the Old Testament as literally true but also wrote their accounts and letters as a *witness* to events they experienced; in other words, the Bible was, for the most part, an articulation of what was believed to be literal truth. This means that the philosophy of religion should also retain the content of these representations as the content of its witness to the Spirit.[87] But, philosophy also knows that the religious community discerns its own spirituality in these texts, and witnesses to this spirituality by communally extrapolating doctrines from these texts as formal statements about its spiritual life. In this way, the literalness of the biblical events is annulled, preserved, and transcended by the *cultus* in its collective thinking. Doctrines, therefore, are the medium through which the *cultus* lifts itself into spiritual truth and witnesses to itself as the concretization of Spirit. Moreover, as Hegel pointed out, "The words of the Bible constitute an unsystematic account."[88] But, as human thinking does draw a narrative coherence out of these disparate texts, then, in Hegel's view, what should be understood by the biblical "word" is determined by the way "spirit is disposed."[89]

At this point, we must make a distinction between the derivation of doctrine from these texts and the continuing interpretation of these stories as literally true in and of themselves. For literalist theologians of Hegel's day, such as Tholuck, the direct experiences recorded in the Bible speak for themselves. They are illuminating and authoritative as they stand, requiring no doctrinal interpretation whatsoever. Indeed, the literalists of Hegel's time construe the actual wording of the Bible as divinely dictated and all the texts, although varied in content and style, as together constituting a story of stories. But, for Hegel, this literalism already constitutes an hermeneutic: "Whether the Bible has been made the foundation more for honor's sake alone or in fact with utter seriousness, still the nature of the interpretative explanation involves the fact that thought plays a part in it. Thought explicitly contains definitions, principles, and assumptions, which then make their own claims felt in the activity of interpreting."[90] For Hegel, this means that not only does interpretation of the Bible take place at the most basic exegetical level, but this should be recognized by those who do the interpretation. For Hegel, such interpretation is not only a matter of thinking but what produces faith, in the two-sided sense of the Foreword. As such, communally articulated doctrines are the manifestation of the spirit of the *cultus* and are the vehicle through which the witness of the community to itself as infinite subjectivity takes place. In this sense, the witness of the Spirit is self-revelation, the revelation of the community to its own truth.

By not formally recognizing the creation of doctrine out of the stories of the religious community, a theologian like Tholuck short-circuits the possibility of realizing the intersubjective witness of the Spirit out of the intertwining correspondence of subjective feeling and objective thinking as found in faith. Hence, true interaction with other believers is not possible, and belief remains not only subjective, but also singular.

On the other hand, the spiritual community's thinking about God is central to Hegel's own thinking. Indeed, in Hegel's view, for Spirit to comprehend its own development into infinite subjectivity it must appreciate the validity of both the pictorial forms of its stories about itself and the doctrinal representation of these forms. In essence, then, what we called the philosophy of theology now becomes a *third-order activity*: it clarifies, sorts out, and criticizes the main 'definitions, principles, and assumptions' that theologians bring to their enterprise (second-order theology) and it does the same work as theological reflection; that is, it reflects the faith of the community as it arises from its eternal ground, and found its eternal completion, in the Idea but from the point of view of the Idea. Indeed, the philosophy of theology recognizes that the *cultus's* inner movement from individual immediacy of religious consciousness into representation and positive doctrine is a process of thinking founded in and propelled by the Idea 'incarnating' itself in human being.

Because the inner difference implicit in immediate knowledge is carried over into the religious community's self-representation, the religious community views itself originally as inner difference within the divine interaction of the Trinity, which then suffers an explicit estrangement from God. This means that the story of the fall when written and taken as literally true is "the mode and manner of the shape in which this conceptual determination [of natural humanity] appears representationally as a story and is represented for consciousness in an intuitable or sensible mode, so that it is regarded as something that *happened*."[91]

The beginning of this narrative concerns itself with both the creation of the world (in six days) and the creation of the first human being, Adam (on the sixth day). God called forth the things of creation; but he created Adam in his image, which Hegel took as signifying "the concept of human being."[92] In this way, Adam represented "humanity in itself" or "humanity as such"—not some single, contingent individual, but the absolute first one, "humanity according to its concept."[93] Moreover, humanity, represented by Adam, lived in a "state of innocence" until "human beings disobeyed God's command by eating" of the tree of *knowledge* of good and evil.[94] For the literalist, this origin of sin is a historical fact based on the assumption that the possibility of sin lies in the free will granted to human beings by God. Of course, this means that God was not the author of sin, but rather sin was a possibility actualized by the human being in its failure to exercise its free will according to God's will. Therefore, the immediate result of this first, original sin is that the human being's 'eyes were opened', God evicted Adam and Eve from the garden, nature itself became hostile, and human nature became tainted, corrupt, and unbalanced.

For Hegel, however, "What it really means is that humanity has elevated itself to the knowledge of good and evil."[95] Indeed, the world in itself, as the other of God, is not evil in itself; rather, it is as we said, nothing in its ideality. People, however, have and do speak of 'natural evil' as the type of evil that springs from nature. Earthquakes, tornadoes, and other occurrences within nature are all manifestations of this natural evil. Nevertheless, for Hegel, human consciousness and cognition are the real source of evil, "For cognition or consciousness means in general a judging or dividing, a self-distinguishing within oneself."[96] Thus, consciousness, because of its own bifurcation, is able to distinguish between good and evil, and evil, therefore, arises out of consciousness's knowledge of this distinction: "and this cognition, this distinction, is the source of evil, is evil itself."[97]

Therefore, evil is not the result of a malignant force engaged in an eternal fight with God for the possession of the soul of human beings, as many quasi-Manichaean Christians assume. Rather, the story of the fall confirms that evil is within the thinking of human being as the result of the ability to both make and be aware of distinction, as we discussed in the previous section. Therefore, to be conscious of evil means that evil is to be considered as *solely interior* to consciousness as a determination of consciousness. And this awareness itself creates *anguish*[98] in human being, anguish over the contradiction that it posits and pictures in terms of good and evil as residing in the very heart of human being.

Hence, through consciousness's awareness of the distinction between good and evil, the inner conflict of the religious relationship as we described in Chapter One is now provided a direct representational content. Indeed, anguish over this inner antithesis arises over the ascription of good and evil in relation to either the otherness of God or the otherness of the world both present to the subject in the subject's consciousness. The first ascription that arises is "the *antithesis vis-à-vis God*."[99] Where there is belief in one God as the absolute other, this God becomes the absolutely other personification of the notion of goodness. But, because this absolute goodness is unattainable, the human being knows itself as the opposite of this goodness; as that which fails to reach goodness, which must fall short in its efforts to satisfy the good in and for itself. Hence, "The task and demand is infinite."[100] Therefore, the human being places itself on the opposite side of the negative of this perfectly good God, as estranged from, and incapable of 'corresponding' to, the pure goodness of God. Thus, human being *both feels* and *knows* itself as degraded, 'humiliated' being. In this regard, Hegel said, "I experience anguish because I as a natural being do not correspond to what at the same time I *know* to be my own essence, to what I should be in my own knowing and willing."[101]

The human being then feels and knows itself as unachieved potential goodness, which has to admit that it is never good, and, in a further self-denigration, also never innocent, but somehow always involved in evil through existing as natural human being. Its sin therefore is original sin, sin that permeates its very fiber as conscious being.

The second form of the antithesis is "the *antithesis vis-à-vis the world*."[102] In this form, the human being affirmed the positive side of the distinction it made between good and evil as its own nature. But, the desire to be good, to live a moral life—"for human beings know what is good, and the good is in them"—is hindered and cut off by the facticity of its surroundings, its being in "the external world," with which it clashes.[103] This sense of estrangement from the natural environment causes the human being to sever its natural bond with the world as a sensible being and creates "unhappiness," which further "drives and presses human beings back into themselves," into a renouncement of the world, to find "inner harmony" of "self with itself."[104] Indeed, the human being, as unhappy consciousness, may, in fact, become totally self-centered, divorcing itself from what it is.

In both cases, what was important for Hegel is that these are relations to good and evil conjured and cognized by the human being. The human being, by creating the distinction through its consciousness or knowledge of good or evil, found itself longing for some sort of resolution of this conflict, especially when it measures its present state against the originary state of innocence that it itself posits. Indeed, for Hegel, this is only proper inasmuch as the story of the fall is the outward expression of the Idea embedded in the human being. However, the inner differentiation of the Idea is now the human being's cognition of itself as alienated from God and from the world. But, even more important, this alienation is *self-alienation*: in relation to the absolute goodness of God, the human being estranges itself from God by separating itself from its own goodness; and, in relation to the world, the human being separates itself from the world by accentuating its own goodness in direct juxtaposition to the world. Moreover, the second mode of self-alienation, in which the human being accentuates its own goodness is one-sided self-affirmation, a self-satisfaction, which arises as a compensation for its self-alienation from God:

> The first contains that anguish and abstract humiliation, the crowning feature of which is the utter lack of correspondence between the subject and the universal, the cleavage or rupture that is not bridged, is not healed. This is the standpoint of the most abstract antithesis between the infinite on the one side and a fixed finitude on the other—and this finitude is abstract finitude. Here everything that is reckoned as belonging to me is simply evil. This abstraction found its complement on the other side, namely in the process of internal thought; here we have the correspondence of self with self, [the claim] that I am satisfied, and can be satisfied within myself.[105]

Therefore, humanity has a fundamental need to overcome its own inner disjunction and recognize that it itself resides in the reconciling synthesis of all oppositions. Hence, it needs to cognize its own inner differences as reconciled in a unity-in-difference. However, this reconciliation does not occur first internally, but externally, in the form of a single human being, Jesus Christ.

The Life, Death, and Resurrection of Christ

The central problem of christology for Christian theology can be expressed in one simple question: "How is the divinity of Christ related to the humanity of Christ?"[106] For Hegel, this christological question becomes the central concern of the philosophy of religion as it thinks through the content of the consummate religion.

Hegel reformulated the christological question into two intersecting questions. "The question immediately divides itself into two questions: (a) Is it true *in general* that God has a Son, that he sends him into the world? (b) Was *this Jesus of Nazareth* in Galilee, a carpenter's <son,> the Christ [*der Christ*]?"[107]

As we can see, Hegel's division of this question takes up both sides of the christological problem: the divine side (from the point of view of the self-diremption of the Trinity), and the human side (from the point of the concrete, historical individual). But as Hegel assumed these questions are "so interwoven," everything rests on affirming or denying that this single individual is the incarnation of God.[108] No other viable alternatives are available to Spirit; docetism (the view that the humanity of Christ was only apparent) or ebionism (the view that Christ was only human) and other such christologies are to be rejected out of hand. Rather, for Hegel, the answer was already provided in the doctrinal formulation of the simultaneity of the Son and the carpenter's son as 'Jesus Christ', an objective doctrine that had to be subjectively confirmed within the context of the doctrine of the immanent Trinity: "The reconciliation in Christ, in which one believed, made no sense if God is not known as the triune God, [if it is not recognized] that God *is*, but also is as the other, as self-distinguishing, so that this other is God himself, having implicitly the divine nature in it, and that the sublation of this difference, this otherness, and the return of love, are the Spirit."[109]

As we commented earlier, the appearance of the Idea in a "single individual [who is there] as the soil of certainty"[110] should convince Tholuck that Christianity and Hegel are panentheistic insofar as this Son, Jesus Christ, is real, concrete, separate, and independent from God and not to be confused with the ideal Son of the immanent Trinity. Of course, this point would not persuade Tholuck to give up his atomistic piety for either orthodox doctrines or Hegel's philosophy or both. In fact, Tholuck balked at such presumption of the church and Hegel to claim to *know* the nature of the divine. Nevertheless, Hegel confirmed that Jesus Christ represents the reconciliation of the divine with the human, a reconciliation that is already implicit in humankind as the 'divine idea'. Indeed, Hegel stressed that the human subject must know itself as dwelling within an infinite cleavage and feel, as a consequence, anguish as precondition for the reconciliation available through the 'God-man'. But, with the inner rift thematized in terms of good and evil, all aspects of this infinite cleavage are ready to be revealed to religious consciousness as conjoined: first of all in the human subject who implicitly "is the infinite power of unity" that "can bear this contradiction" as "implicitly and truthfully sublated";[111] and, second, in the subject who knows explicitly that "the antithesis arises eternally and just as eternally sublates itself" in "eternal reconciliation."[112] Moreover, this 'Idea' has to become explicit not only to but *in* humankind through the intuitive certainty of the divine Idea as dwelling in and as a particular human being, that is, "in the form of *certainty*," "*before* us" and "*before* me," that "God *had to appear in the world in the flesh*" as "*just one human being.*"[113] Therefore, Hegel stressed that this is the second moment of the economic Trinity: "This is the presentation of the second [element of the] idea, the idea in appearance, the eternal idea as it has become [present] for the immediate certainty of humanity, i.e., as it has appeared. In order that it should become a certainty for humanity, it has to be a sensible certainty."[114]

Indeed, with the Incarnation as the second moment of the economic Trinity, the abstract precondition of reconciliation now turns into the actual condition for an existential relationship with God, as we discussed in relation to Luther's faith in Chapter Three. One could have walked and talked with this God-man. Therefore, for Hegel, this person, Jesus Christ, brings the idea of the unity of the divine and the human to the forefront of consciousness of the human subject. Because the divine and the human appear consubstantiated in one subject, this Jesus Christ now represents the synthesis, the being together of the divine and human in human subjectivity. Like Luther, Hegel saw that this conjoining also means that God is not an object like any other, but a subject who interacts with another subject. On the speculative level, as we have seen, this means that the subject-subject relationship presents the prototype for philosophy overcoming the epistemological rupture between philosophy and theology by opening up the possibility of true communication between the two modes of knowledge of God.

For the sake of adequately covering both sides of the appearance of the unity of divine and human natures in Jesus Christ, Hegel noted:

> This appearance of the God-man has to be viewed from two different perspectives at once. First, he is a human being according to his external circumstances. This is the nonreligious perspective [dies irreligiöse Betrachtung] in which he appears as an ordinary human being. Second, there is the perspective that occurs in the Spirit or with the Spirit. Spirit presses toward its truth because it has an infinite cleavage and anguish with itself. It wills the truth; the need of the truth and the certainty thereof it will have, and must have. Here for the first time we have the religious view [das Religiöse].[115]

In terms of the nonreligious perspective, Jesus appears "in the same light as Socrates" or "a messenger of God," that is, "as an ordinary human being," subject to "all the temporal exigencies" of being human.[116] Thus, Jesus Christ is an individual whose activity we can both apperceive and empathize as analogous to our own, but with the additional (and, we can assume, disquieting) perception that "he does not share the corruption, the passions, and the evil inclinations" that the human being has come to see in itself before God.[117] Moreover, his teachings are revolutionary—"The most outstanding and at the same time comprehensive teaching of Christ is...*love*" and "breaking away" from all finite attachments[118]—but, to not miss the true import of Christ, his humanness and teachings must also be viewed through the religious perspective: "What is involved here is this intuitive certainty, not a divine teacher—not to mention a mere moral instructor, or even a teacher of the [philosophical] idea; and it is not a matter of representation or persuasion, but rather the *immediate* certainty and presence of divinity."[119]

As we can see, all the perspectives of Enlightenment philosophy of religion and rational theology are to be set aside. Unlike either Spinoza or Kant and their rational christological constructions—Christ as 'frame of mind' (Spinoza) or Christ as 'moral archetype' (Kant)—Hegel asserted that the appearance of the divine Idea in Christ is verified by the witness of the Spirit, by the religious community that concerns itself with the central truth of the death and resurrection of Christ. This 'religious view' therefore, "leads us for the first time into the religious sphere as such, where the divine itself is an essential moment."[120] Indeed, "it is precisely in his [Christ's] death that the transition into the religious sphere occurs," an element not found in either Spinoza or Kant.[121] Thus, Christ's death sublates the merely human relationship of the nonreligious perspective. In this way, Hegel's treatment of the death and resurrection of Christ comes right out of the theological reflection of the Christian community as undergirded by the principle of subjectivity. Hegel, in fact, echoed Luther's christology in which the atoning death of God in the death of this person, Christ, is the most important element for the human subject:

> "God himself is dead," it says in a Lutheran hymn, expressing an awareness that the human, the finite, the fragile, the weak, the negative are themselves a moment of the divine, that they are within God himself, that finitude, negativity, otherness are not outside of God and do not, as otherness, hinder unity with God. Otherness, the negative, is known to be a moment of the divine nature itself. This involves the highest idea of spirit. In this way what is external and negative is converted into the internal. On the one hand, the meaning attached to death is that through death the human element is stripped away and the divine glory comes into view once more—death is a stripping of the human, the negative. But at the same time death itself is this negative, the furthest extreme to which humanity as natural existence [*Dasein*] is exposed; this existence [*Dasein*] is therefore God himself.[122]

Thus Hegel's thinking starts out affirming Spinoza's position on the negativity of the finite (*omnis determinatio est negatio*) in which all things, in their various modifications and relations are ultimately absorbed into an abstract identity, God, the one substance. But, then, contra Spinoza, the negativity of the finite is real difference, concretized by appearance of God in the human world through Christ, the reality of which is maximized by death. Therefore, for Hegel, this negativity cannot simply be asserted as resolved in a Spinoza-like abstract identity but, rather, it has to be attended to through the negation of negation, the death of death found in the resurrection. Indeed, the death and resurrection of Christ signifies for those who believe the overcoming of human alienation from God (and from the world) in "an infinite relationship to God."[123] Moreover, empathetic appropriation of this death of death opens the way for the "outpouring of the Holy Spirit: it is the Spirit that has revealed this."[124] In a strong sense, *the death of God is a moment of atheism on the representa-*

tional level.[125] Indeed, as James Collins suggested, this "*representation of death*" also entails the "*death of representation.*"[126] This means that the death of Christ is the death of the representation of God held by humankind in its state of alienation. But, this death of God as 'absolutely other' would also suggest a death of the representation, 'man', as well.[127] In fact, *both God and human being become spiritualized*, reconciled together in the living process of Spirit: "Thus the community itself is the existing Spirit, the Spirit in its existence [*Existenz*], God existing in his community."[128]

As we will detail in the next section, the community itself is essential to the life of Spirit. Without the community attending to and participating in the witness of Spirit, this spiritualization of human being would not take place. God would still be perceived as beyond humanity's grasp, and Spirit would not realize itself as Spirit.

Indeed, the witness of the Spirit, as we detailed in Chapter Three, is a hermeneutic of self-verification, self-enclosed and self-generating. Thus, if Tholuck, Schleiermacher, and, indeed, all the rationalist theologians and Enlightenment philosophers of religion wanted verification of these claims they have had to enter into and subjectively appropriate this spiritual interpretation already existing in the faith of the community:

> The community begins with the fact that the truth is at hand; it is known, extant truth. And this truth is what God is: he is the triune God; he is life, this process of himself within himself, the determining of himself with himself. The second aspect of this truth, then, is that it has also appeared, it has a relation to the subject, and is [present] for the subject; moreover, the subject is essentially related to it, and is meant to be a citizen of the kingdom of God....The third aspect is the relationship of the subject to this truth, the fact that the subject, to the extent that it is related to this truth, arrives precisely at this conscious unity, deems itself worthy of this known unity, brings this unity forth within itself, and is fulfilled by the divine Spirit.[129]

As we outlined in Chapter Three, this means that faith, as Christian faith itself, has to be appreciated from the inside of the infinite subjectivity of the *cultus* as that modality of being human in which reconciliation is both felt and objectified as the truth *for me* and *for us*. If Tholuck and the others enter into this faith they too will find the truth of the triune God and Christ witnessed to in the objective doctrines of the community as it develops itself into a church. In this way, they will grasp what is: that *we* participate in the eternal interaction of the Trinity.

Assuming that Hegel's critics submit themselves to such a method of verification, there was still one more step for them to take before they would grasp *conceptually what is* in the fashion of Hegel's philosophy of religion. As we will now see, this last step involves realizing what is involved in the third element, "the element of community."[130]

The Third Element:
The Realization of the Spirituality of the Religious Community

We can see from the aforegoing that instead of treating philosophy and theology as disparate, mutually exclusive forms of knowledge of God as did the Enlightenment philosophers, Schleiermacher, and the Pietists, Hegel confirmed Christ as the center—the 'speculative mid-point'—of his thinking which also serves to unite philosophy and theology. Indeed, philosophy and theology come together in agreement over the unity and reconciliation of God and humankind as displayed in the person of Jesus Christ. However, we should not mistake this agreement as an uncritical acceptance of Christian theological reflection. As we will see, for Hegel, the speculative comprehension of the consummate religion does not stop with the doctrine of Christ, but proceeded on to develop the doctrine of Spirit as the actual presence of the divine in human experience. Thus, it is in this section of *The Consummate Religion*, the 'Third Element: Community, Spirit', that Hegel focuses his attention on how Spirit made possible belief in Jesus Christ for the members of the community. But, as we will see, this work of the Spirit in the community is also the self-manifestation of Spirit wherein faith, theological reflection, and the philosophical conceptualization of religion are Spirit's disclosure of its reality to and for itself.

Hegel commences his discussion of the third element by locating the first coming of the witness of Spirit, "the outpouring of the Holy Spirit"[131] (presumably at Pentecost). This outpouring is then the origin of the community. But immediately after using the representation, the Holy Spirit, he adds this speculative insight: "[It is] spirit that comprehends this history spiritually as it is enacted in [the sphere of] appearance, and recognizes the idea of God in it, his life, his movement. The community is made up of those single, empirical subjects who are in the Spirit of God."[132] That this spiritualizing of the individual human subjects, who then coordinate together into community, is carried out by the Spirit further means, Hegel said: "Thus the community itself is the existing Spirit, the Spirit in its existence [*Existenz*], God existing as community."[133]

As we can see, Hegel was saying that the community is the medium through which Spirit witnesses to itself about the reconciliation of God and humankind found in the person of Jesus Christ. Thus, the community is the concretization of Spirit—a realization that extends the notion of the witness of the Spirit beyond the domain of textual hermeneutics as established by Luther, as we noted in Chapter Three. But, as well, as the last passage in the preceding paragraph tells us, God cannot be considered apart from either the Spirit or the community. It is crucial for us to understand from the outset of our discussion of 'The Origin of the Community' that the community as the existing Spirit cannot be construed to mean that God is merely a projection of human consciousness (as in Feuerbach or Freud, for example); on the contrary, it means that human thinking about God, as it arises in and through religion, is also God's thinking of himself. This interdependency of God and humankind then is the ground through which Hegel justifiably said that, within the consummate religion, "Finite consciousness knows God only to the extent that God knows himself in it; thus God is spirit, indeed the Spirit of his community, i.e., of those who worship him."[134] That God is Spirit in the community therefore means that the triadic structure contained in the Christian doctrine of God as Trinity also is the structure of the unfolding of Spirit's consciousness of itself in the life of the community. Hence, we find three moments constituting the third element. These are: "The Origin of the Community," "The Subsistence of the Community," and "The Realization of the Spirituality of the Community." We now turn to the first moment, the origin of the community.

The first moment, the origin of the community, is consequently a result of Spirit generating the faith on which the community will be built. For this reason, Hegel saw the origin of the community as not resting solely on the basis of the sensible, historical appearance of Jesus. As we have already recounted in our discussion of the second element, Hegel held that such a sensible presence is not sufficient in itself to ascertain the truth of the reconciliation of the divine and human that becomes evident in the person of Jesus Christ. Hegel reiterated: "Verification is spiritual, it does not lie in the sensible, and cannot be accomplished in an immediate, sensible fashion."[135] Because the elevation of humankind into the realm of the divine should not be understood as effulging solely from the immediate certainty of the sensible appearance of the person, Jesus, the belief that God has become a sensible human being in the form of Jesus Christ has to come from another source, which, as we already know, is Spirit. Indeed, Spirit transmutes the naturalness of the appearance of Jesus Christ into a spiritual content for the comprehension of the individual subject: "For the origin of faith there is necessary first a human being, a sensible human appearance, and second, spiritual comprehension, consciousness of the spiritual. The content is spiritual, involving the transformation of immediacy into what has spiritual character."[136] Moreover, for Hegel, it is also absolutely pivotal to the formation of the community that Spirit sets an overall spiritual context in which appropriation of the meaning of this appearance can take place. Consequently, faith grasps not just the sensible, historical appearance of Jesus but also the sensible world as transposed into a spiritual reality: "there is also a sensible world, although the truth is not the sensible, not the immediate world of finitude, but is rather the infinite."[137]

We can see that, for Hegel, faith arises out of the witness of the Spirit as the mediated immediacy of immediate knowledge:

> The fact that the single subject is now filled by the divine Spirit is brought about by mediation in the subject itself, and the mediating factor is that the subject has this faith. For faith is the truth, the presupposition, that reconciliation is accomplished with certainty in and for itself. Only by means of this faith that reconciliation is accomplished with certainty and in and for itself is the subject able and indeed in a position to posit itself in this unity. This mediation is absolutely necessary.[138]

Hence through this initial mediated unity of faith the human being also comes to know itself as lifted and united in, with, and under God.

Faith, however, serves only as the inception of the process of the self-manifestation of Spirit. Further development must take place and, therefore, we find in the second moment of the third element, "The Subsistence of the Community," Spirit realizes itself in the positive institution of the Church. "In the subsisting [*bestehende*] community the church is, by and large, the institution whereby [its] subjects come to the truth, appropriate the truth to themselves, so that the Holy Spirit becomes real, actual, and present within them and has its abode in them, whereby the truth can be within them and they can enjoy and give active expression to the truth of the Spirit; it is the means whereby they as subjects *are* the active expression of the Spirit."[139]

As the active expression of Spirit, the Church serves to develop, refine, and consolidate this truth for its members and, hence, for Spirit. In the doctrine elaborated by the Church, "The truth is here presupposed, that it exists as truth already present."[140] Thus, it has 'universality'. In other words, the Church is the truth that it knows and bears in its doctrines, which, as universal, presupposed truth, is not only accessible for all human beings but applicable to all human beings and in all possible aspects of human affairs, both spiritual and temporal. Therefore, the truth to which the Spirit witnesses in the Church's doctrines is presented to the members of the community as accomplished fact. In this way, the reconciliation manifest in the death and resurrection of Jesus Christ is *taught* to the individual as not only objectively true but as something external to the individual subject.[141] Accordingly, this truth is seen to extend not only to those who have subjectively appropriated this truth but also to the individual subject who, by virtue of baptism as an "unconscious" child, has been granted entry into the "fellowship of the church, where evil has been overcome, implicitly and explicitly, and God is reconciled, implicitly and explicitly."[142] In other words, the individual becomes *socialized* into the Christian faith whose truths are sedimented into the very language and customs of one's sociocultural environment through the religious education provided by the Church, a process we described in Chapter Three.[143] In imparting doctrine through teaching, Hegel said: "This means that truth necessarily comes to humanity at first as *authority*."[144]

The Church must also ensure that its members have become conscious of the estrangement and evil of being human—which, as we have seen earlier in this chapter, is represented by the biblical story of the fall—but, as overcome through the truth of reconciliation which has been effected through Christ:

The child, inasmuch as it is born into the church, has been born in freedom and to freedom. For one who has been so born, there is no longer an absolute otherness; this otherness is posited as something overcome, as already conquered. The sole concern of such cultivation is to prevent evil from emerging, and the possibility of this does in general reside in humanity. But insofar as evil does emerge among human beings when they do evil, at the same time it is present as something implicitly null, over which spirit has power: spirit has the power to undo evil.[145]

Consequently, it is the "concern of the church" that this truth is taken up by the individual as his or her own truth.[146] Therefore, the anguish of the utter scission and separation manifest in the death of Jesus Christ also has to be identified by the individual subject as its own initial state. Indeed, when the individual subject encounters Christ through the received doctrines of the Church, it also encounters itself as a sinner. But the individual can realize the sublation of this evil attested to in the doctrine of the redemption available through Christ through repentance: "*Repentance* or *penitence* signifies that, through the elevation of human beings to the truth, which they now will, their transgression is wiped out. Because they acknowledge the truth over against their evil and will the good—through repentance, that is to say—their evil comes to naught."[147] Penitence allows the truth of the resurrection to become the subject's own truth. Thus, the subject becomes like Christ through faith in Christ:

> It [evil] is a question only of contingent subjectivity. Linked with that element of faith consisting in the determination that the subject is not as it ought to be, there is simultaneously the absolute possibility that the subject can fulfill its destiny, can be received into the grace of God. This is the concern of faith. The individual must lay hold of the implicitly subsisting unity of divine and human nature; this truth is laid hold of through faith in Christ. Thus God is no longer a beyond for the individual, and the laying hold of this truth is opposed to the basic determination referred to above, namely, that the subject is not as it ought to be.[148]

The subject's unity with God is not completed until the fullness of the community is accomplished "by sharing the appropriation of God's presence [i.e., the *communion*]."[149] For Hegel, "This unity begins with the host."[150] It is the central sacramental means through which God becomes present to human beings within the life of the Church. Indeed, the spiritual union manifest in the faithful partaking of the host maintains, in the present life of the community, continuity with the unity of God and humankind accomplished in faith. Therefore, for Hegel, the host should not be understood in terms of Catholicism's transubstantiation nor in terms of a psychological reminder as in the Reformed Church, a point we discussed in Chapter Three.[151] Rather, the Lutheran conception of communion as consubstantiation, grounded in the doctrine of *communicatio idiomatum*, displays this unity as a *spiritual union*: "The second view is the Lutheran one, according to which the movement does indeed begin with something external, which is an ordinary, common thing, but the communion, the self-feeling of the presence of God, comes about only insofar as the external thing is consumed—not merely physically but in spirit and faith. God is present only in Spirit and faith."[152] For Hegel, the union of God and humankind *is* the true partaking of the one Jesus Christ, that is, "not merely physically but in spirit and in faith."[153] We can also see that this spiritual union with God, as found in its Lutheran form, constitutes the completion of the second moment of the third element.

We can further see that Hegel's account of the unfolding of Spirit's self-development through the first moment of faith of the individual into the supraindividual entity of the Church and its doctrines and rituals stands in marked contrast to the individualism of Tholuck's Pietism. Indeed, Hegel's view of the formation and explication of doctrines by the Church means that once again, for Hegel, doctrines cannot be easily written off as institutional aberrations artificially imposed on the religious feeling, as Tholuck did in relation to the doctrine of the Trinity.

On the other hand, in the third moment of the third element, "The Realization of the Spirituality of the Community," Hegel further grasped that reconciliation of the divine and human side in the communal partaking of the presence of God with a "pure heart" should not be seen as extinguishing, but as preserving, the actual existence of the human world and its historicity in a 'transformed' state.[154] Therefore, in this section, Hegel portrays the spirituality of the community as reaching its consummation by having "a developed worldliness present in it."[155] In fact, this spiritual-worldly relationship must be comprehended: "In order that reconciliation may be real it is required that it should be known in this development, in this totality; it should be present and brought forth [into actuality]. The principles for this worldly realm are ready to hand in the spirituality of the community; the principle, the truth, of the world *is* the spiritual."[156] Consequently, we can see that the spiritual and the worldly must be 'realized' as conjoined and reconciled in Spirit in the same way that the divine and human are in the *communicatio idiomatum*, that is, sublated into a higher synthetic unity. In this way, the spiritual can be discerned in the worldly and vice versa. Hence, the central task of this third element is to show how the world of human activity is to be affirmed and reclaimed as reconciled as a moment of the one Spirit by Spirit.

Not surprisingly, Hegel grasped the realization of the spirituality of the community as consisting in a threefold inner structure: the real, the ideal, and speculative philosophy, which grasps the unity of the two prior moments as reconciled in Spirit's all-encompassing infinite subjectivity. As well, each of these three inner moments has within it three points or stages that are an integral part of the process of Spirit's self-actualization. Each must be considered in some detail.[157]

In the first inner moment or 'stage', the true spirituality of the worldly realm is initially to be found in an immediate, undeveloped form. This stage of immediacy displays itself in a nay-saying to the world in favor of another, more real, spiritual world, or heaven, in which the subject supposedly dwells.[158] As a result, the worldly is perceived as nothing more than an aspect "in the subject."[159] Therefore, this stage is "more an abstraction than it is reconciliation."[160]

In the second stage, the reality of reconciliation takes on a concrete, actual existence in the institution of the Church. Here, "worldliness and religiosity do indeed remain external to each other, but they have to enter into relation all the same."[161] Indeed, within human history a relation arises between the spiritual and secular in which the Church believed that the spiritual has to rule over and subjugate the secular. (There is little doubt that Hegel, in this stage, is referring to Medieval Christendom, whereas the first stage corresponds to the preinstitutionalized Christian community.) "Accordingly," Hegel said of the relation effected by the Medieval Church, "this is an uniting with a worldly realm that remains unreconciled."[162]

The outcome of this unreconciled union of the spiritual and the worldly in this stage is an outward orientation in which the inwardness and abstractness of the first stage are inverted into a "worldliness devoid of spirit."[163] This outward orientation produces "unfreedom" and a "cleavage" in the life of the community, both of which signify that what appears as "the corruption of the church" is, in actuality, "the absolute contradiction of the spiritual within itself."[164] However, the rupture and contradiction of the second stage is not a static state of affairs. The domination of the Church over worldly affairs comes to an end when its external authority is surmounted and resolved in the internal authority of the ethical realm which follows the Protestant Reformation. After the collapse of the hegemony of the Medieval Church, "The institutions of ethical life [*Sittlichkeit*]" become realized as "divine institutions" insofar as the individual members of the community willingly subject themselves to the dictates of the institutions of ethical life.[165] In other words, the ethical is no longer perceived as being imposed from outside the human world through the agency of the Church but is appreciated as arising from the free and rational choice of the members of the community. Consequently, this inward realization of ethical in and through the life of community also produces the community's recognition of civil organizations like the state as the outward expression of its reconciliation of the divine and human: "It is in the organization of the state that the divine has broken through into the sphere of actuality; the latter is permeated by the former, and the worldly realm is now justified in and for itself, for its foundation is the divine will, the law of right and freedom. The true reconciliation, whereby the divine realizes itself in the domain of actuality, consists in the ethical and juridical life of the state: this is the authentic discipline of worldliness."[166]

The second inner moment of "The Realization of the Spirituality of the Community" occurs in the ideal side, that is, in the element of thinking that "emerges explicitly in religious consciousness."[167] In this stage, "Inwardness knows itself as subsisting with itself precisely in this reconciliation of spirit with itself; and this knowledge of being at home within itself is precisely thinking."[168] In short, reconciliation has to be cognized and appreciated in thought. But the cognition of inwardness has also to be developed through three stages, as we mentioned earlier. Accordingly, the first stage in the inner development of thinking is "abstract universality,"[169] which places itself in a negative relation to "the concrete in general."[170] Historically, this way of thinking is the *Enlightenment* which treats the finite as illusory or, at best, as a manifestation of its own version of reason. For Hegel, Enlightenment thinking exemplifies "the freedom of reason that has been acquired in religion and now knows itself to be for itself in spirit";[171] however, even more important for our present concern, Hegel found that Enlightenment exercised this freedom gained from religion to turn around and deny the rational, objective content of religion. It follows then that the knowledge of reconciliation of the Enlightenment stays at the level of "abstraction."[172] Thus, it still exists, as Hegel concluded, in "unfreedom and servitude of spirit in the absolute region of freedom."[173]

The second stage in the development of the ideal side occurs when thinking lowers itself to envisage itself as only one aspect of its own religious consciousness, feeling. This mode of thinking is Pietism, which, as we have seen in our discussion of Tholuck at the beginning of this chapter, also denies the objective and rational truth of religion. For Hegel, Pietism's flight from reason into the isolation of abstract subjectivity is also a general tendency of the theology of the time, as we have seen in our discussion of Schleiermacher and Tholuck. Therefore, Hegel appraised Pietism in this way: "Pietism acknowledges no objective truth and opposes itself to dogmas and the content of religion, while still preserving an element of mediation, a connection with Christ, but this is a connection that is supposed to remain one of mere feeling and inner sensibility."[174] As such, Hegel held, it is still "devoid of content."[175]

Unlike Enlightenment and Pietistic modes of abstract subjectivity, the third stage of the ideal is where thinking explicitly comprehends all the content of religion as the inner content of itself as true subjectivity; that is, as Spirit. "The third [moment], then, consists in the fact that subjectivity develops the content from itself, to be sure, but in accord with necessity. It knows and acknowledges that a content is necessary, and that this necessary content is objective, having being in and for itself. This is the standpoint of *philosophy*, according to which the content takes refuge in the concept and obtains its justification by thinking."[176]

As Hegel indicated in this passage, when this third moment is reached thinking ceases to regard the objective content of the consummate religion as something foreign to it and thus in need of being 'volatized', as did Enlightenment and Pietism.[177] Indeed, religion is now comprehended as having transformed itself into philosophy, which then turns around and conceptualizes the consummate religion as its own content. Philosophy sees its conceptualization of religion as "the justification of religion, especially of the Christian religion, the *true* religion."[178] This means that religion is "sustained by philosophy"[179] and that the task of upholding the truth of God has now passed from religion to speculative philosophy, although the assumption of this task in no way negates religion and its inherent right to articulate the truth of God.

We should further note that at the same time that philosophy reaches this standpoint it also extends its grasp back to include everything that had preceded it within the horizon of religion. Thus, the prior two moments of the Idea, Enlightenment and Pietism, are also to be comprehended as part of the development of consummate religion. As moments of the thinking found within consummate religion, they can also be understood as modes of theological thinking, albeit as "two extremes opposing each other,"[180] and, of course, as two modes that also oppose the content of religion, as we have already observed. In this respect, we can assume that Hegel is reminding us that, although these modes of thinking have ceased to serve religion and its doctrine, they have not ceased to think about religion. Hence, even the community's *disagreement* over how to understand religion is part of what present philosophy has to cognize in its conceptualization of religion.

This is the first time in the Berlin lectures on consummate religion that Hegel has included Pietism at this point in the development of consummate religion. Previously, in the 1824 *Consummate Religion*, Hegel had explicitly located only Enlightenment as the prior moment to the realization of the truth of religion in philosophy.[181] And, in 1821, Hegel implied that only Enlightenment should be situated in this manner.[182] In granting Pietism this formal recognition in 1827, we can see that Hegel was confirming that Pietism had become a formidable force within the religious life of consummate religion. This deliberate inclusion also means that, for Hegel, the thinking of the post-Reformation stage of consummate religion had developed further than he had earlier appreciated. Of course, Pietism had been considered in other locales in both the 1821 and the 1824 lectures on the philosophy of religion; indeed, all we have to do is recall Hegel's debate with Schleiermacher to confirm that this is the case. As we detailed in Chapter Four, Hegel had seen fit to criticize Schleiermacher in the 1824 lectures through what we called *the philosophy of theology*. We should further note that Schleiermacher's theology of feeling was indirectly addressed at the end of the 1824 lectures on consummate religion in a manner not unlike the way Hegel conceived of Pietism at the end of the 1827 lectures.[183] But, for all of Hegel's pre-1827 concern with the Pietistic orientation, we do not find Pietism elevated to the status equal to that of the Enlightenment, that is, as part of the penultimate moment of the process of the development of philosophical thinking out of the consummate religion. Now, in 1827, philosophy knows that it has to resolve what was inaugurated by *both* Enlightenment and Pietism: "But insofar as thinking begins to posit an antithesis to the concrete and places itself in opposition to the concrete, the process of thinking consists in carrying through this opposition until it arrives at reconciliation."[184] In this way, the inner fissure between Enlightenment and Pietism and, in turn, their mutual opposition to the content of religion, has allowed philosophy to see all the ways thinking can relate to religion. For philosophy, Pietism has taken the form of individual, finite subjectivity to its limit as self-centered subjectivity. Although this atomistic form of subjectivity maintains a link with the objective content of the consummate religion through its inchoate allegiance to Christ, as Hegel mentioned earlier, it shows the extent to which subjectivity can be drawn in the direction of feeling before it becomes vacuous and incoherent. Now, philosophy knows that: "The form of the subject as one who feels, etc., concerns the subject as a single individual; but feeling as such is not eliminated by philosophy. The question is only whether the *content* of feeling is the truth and can prove itself in thought. Philosophy *thinks* what the subject as such *feels*, and leaves it to the latter to come to terms with its feeling."[185] As well, we can see that, in fact, this form of subjectivity also constitutes a type of limitation within thinking itself; once philosophy has appreciated the Pietistic form of subjectivity it comprehends that there are only *three* possible ways thought can form itself in relation to the true content of religion and only one is capable of "bearing witness to, and expressing the witness of, spirit in a developed thoughtful fashion."[186] "This thinking is not merely the process of abstraction and definition according to the law of identity; it does not have the concrete 'over there', but is itself essentially concrete, and thus it is comprehension, meaning that the concept determines itself in its totality and as idea. It is free reason, which has being on its own account, that develops the content in accord with its necessity, and justifies the content of its truth."[187] Philosophy, thus, displays to Pietism how they too fit into the rational development of the content of religion. Indeed, as a third-order philosophy of theology, philosophy now views all relations within religion *pneumatologically*, that is, as oppositions reconciled in, with, and through Spirit. Spirit *is* the unity of the divine and human. Therefore, it is clear that God (as Trinity) has achieved full self-consciousness in the self-consciousness of humanity that now is realized as the self-consciousness of absolute Spirit. Moreover, we can see the truth of this self-consciousness displayed in the very form and content of the 1827 philosophy of religion. First, the philosophy of religion is triadically divided into *Concept of Religion*, *Determinate Religion*, and *The Consummate Religion*; then, the *Concept of Religion* is triadically divided into The Concept of God, The Knowledge of God, and The *Cultus*. Next, *Determinate Religion* is sectioned into three parts: Immediate Religion or Natural Religion, The Elevation of the Spiritual Above the Natural: The Religion of the Greeks and the Jews, and The Religion of Expediency: Roman Religion. Last, *The Consummate Religion* has been divided in the threefold manner we explicated in this chapter. As well, the omnipresence of trinitarian structure in the 1827 lectures means that, for Hegel, philosophical form and theological content have been reconciled, a reconciliation that required the consummate religion for its realization in and for the present life of the community. Hegel concluded,

> This reconciliation is philosophy. Philosophy is to this extent theology. It presents the reconciliation of God with himself and with nature, showing that nature, otherness, is implicitly divine, and that the raising of itself to reconciliation is on the one hand what finite spirit implicitly is, while on the other hand it arrives at this reconciliation, or brings it forth, in world history. This reconciliation is the peace of God, which does not "surpass all reason," but is rather the peace that *through* reason is first known and thought and is recognized as truth.[188]

In conclusion, this explicit recognition of the reconciliation of philosophy and theology should lead our own thought to circle back to the Preface of the 1821 Concept of Religion to see that what had been presupposed there—"philosophy *is* theology, and [one's] occupation with philosophy—or rather *in* philosophy—is of itself the service of God"[189]—has now been brought to its fruition.

Conclusion

THE RECONCILIATION OF
PHILOSOPHY AND THEOLOGY

I n the 1827 *The Consummate Religion,* we saw philosophy totally at home with the content of religion. Moreover, we noted that this being-at-home of philosophy and religion is
a matter of philosophy and theology reflecting each other in the
form and content of the entire philosophy of religion. This mutual
mirroring of philosophy and theology shows that no longer is the
God-human relationship a question of finite subjectivity standing
over and against the objective, infinite subjectivity. Rather, the consciousness of God and human consciousness are blended together in
the self-consciousness of absolute Spirit. Hegel gives us a glimpse of
how this plays out in an individual human life in his review of
Göschel's *Aphorismen über Nichtwissen und absolutes Wissen im Verhältnisse zur christlichen Glaubenserkenntnis,* written two years after
the 1827 lectures on the philosophy of religion:

> The rare excellence of this work—which (if one wants to put it
> so) made it into a so-called significant sign of the times—con-
> sists in the fact that the author's pious mind proves itself to be
> thoroughly imbued both with the truth of the old, i.e., of the
> authentic doctrines of the Christian faith and with the need for
> the thinking reason and (what is more) in its diligently prac-
> tised formation. The concern here found itself therefore imme-
> diately in the very center of the speculative philosophy, with
> regard to the content as well as with regard to the form. The

distinction between Christianity and philosophical thinking which is wont to be falsely presented as an infinite existence and a gap that cannot be filled, is at once put aside; at this depth this pretended distance is not present at all.[1]

As we can see, Hegel thought that the author to whom he was referring, Karl Friedrich Göschel, has found himself at home in and thoroughly 'imbued' with both speculative philosophy and the doctrines of Christianity. There is no "gap" between philosophical form and theological content in Göschel's thinking. Indeed, we can surmise that for an individual like Göschel the interstice in which the divided self is situated by the religious relationship (as we saw in Chapter One) is now filled in and *healed* insofar as Göschel knows himself as lifted up into the eternal embrace of God *and* as existing in the present life of the community. Moreover, Göschel's 'pious mind' does not go against the intersubjective level of religious consciousness implicit in the objective doctrines; instead, they fill his heart with the objective knowledge that he dwells in the community that is the concretization of Spirit.

However much Göschel may be exemplary of the reconciliation of philosophy and theology, we cannot overlook that for Hegel the activity of the philosophy of religion must continuously aim at comprehending the whole of the relationship between God and human beings as it develops through the religious consciousness of *all* the members of the community. Therefore, no matter how much Hegel recognized Tholuck's spiritual depth (and vice versa) the philosophy of religion has to reformulate itself in response to the appearance of new modes of thinking within the theological sphere that may appear to be opposed to philosophy. Indeed, because the community is the concretization of Spirit, the self-revelation of Spirit does not disappear once reconciliation has been achieved. As an eternal process of reconciliation, Spirit's self-manifestation is always taking place in the community. In other words, and in terms of the philosophy of religion, the role of philosophy is to mirror in its thinking all the elements that make up the religion of its time. Hence, speculative philosophy reflects in thought not only what has taken place in the development of religion in the past but also what is taking place in the present situation as a continuation of the process of Spirit's self-comprehension.

As we have seen, this view of Spirit is itself a result of Luther's science of faith transforming itself into the science of Spirit which unfolds itself through Hegel's Berlin lectures on the philosophy of religion. Where the 'old' science of faith and the 'new' science of Spirit differ is over what it ultimately means for finite consciousness to be part of the witness of Spirit. For Luther, as we have seen, God remained hidden although he had revealed himself in Christ and the Word. Therefore, Luther's theology remains christocentric: through the Word we discover God himself becoming human in the person of Jesus Christ in conjunction with the action of the economic Trinity and, by implication, the inner divine life of the immanent Trinity.

On the other hand, Hegel found that the implications of Luther's notion of the witness of the Spirit is that we now are to think of God totally in terms of Spirit. In other words, Luther had not seen that all the relations of God and humankind must be seen 'pneumatologically'; that is, as engaged in Spirit's eternal process of self-differentiation. Although Luther's (and Christianity's) emphasis on christology has lead into thought about God as Trinity, theological thinking has stayed too firmly attached to the sensible appearance of God in Christ, therefore not fully appreciating that the opposition between the divine and human, the infinite and finite, had become overcome and reconciled in Spirit.

Hegel's philosophy of religion recognizes that the revelation of reconciliation in Christ is the inspiration for his own accent on Spirit. But, rather than keeping the notions of 'faith' and the 'witness of the Spirit' revolving solely around Christ and the Bible, Hegel reversed Luther's understanding of the relation of philosophy and the Bible, and of faith and the Bible: "philosophy arises not from the Bible; so too faith, it also does not arise from the Bible, but goes to the Bible in which it grasps its truth."[2] Indeed, as we detailed in Chapter Four, for Hegel, faith is the witness of Spirit concerning absolute Spirit. As well, philosophy overcomes Luther's separation of faith and reason by showing that the thinking through of consummate religion allows for the conceptualization of religion and the realization of the Idea. Following this realization, philosophy then views the Idea of God (the immanent Trinity) as the precondition for faith and theological reflection and their conceptualization in philosophy.

We can see that for Hegel the mediation of philosophy and theology in the philosophy of religion also entails the mediation of philosophy and faith in the science of Spirit. Louis Dupré noted: "The development of the mind never leads *beyond* Christian faith: that faith *continues* to provide the content of philosophical thought. That philosophy presents a very different position does not mean that it replaces religion or that its own concerns are non-religious. In a well-known passage Hegel credits the very notion of Spirit to Christian faith as interpreted by the theology of Reformation: 'The idea which represents the Absolute as Spirit—the grandest conception of all, and one which is due to modern times and its religion.'"[3] But, as well, this mediation requires the thinking of their unity in Spirit in a manner hitherto not found in theology, Lutheran or otherwise. What we have called the *second-order philosophy of theology* in Chapter Four does accomplish this for the science of Spirit; it analyzes and criticizes theology to see if it displays any real spiritual substance, cutting away those forms that conceal the truth of faith. In this way, philosophy clears the way for its development of the science of faith into the science of Spirit.[4] In so doing, the second-order philosophy of theology reveals that the very existence of Pietism and its counterpoint, Enlightenment, is the result of an inevitable tension within religious consciousness that philosophy cannot overlook or reject. Indeed, it is the task of Spirit to overcome all tensions and comprehend them as reconciled through its witness to itself. Therefore, as we have seen in Chapter Four, the resolution of the tension between philosophy and Schleiermacher's 'theology of feeling' and, in Chapter Five, between philosophy and the Pietistic thinking of Tholuck requires philosophy coming to grips with what constitutes the *proper relationship* between philosophy and theology.

This task is even more difficult because the philosophy of theology, as a second-order activity, necessitates philosophy of religion to differentiate itself from all forms of theology and, at the same time, think the same content as does orthodox theology. However, the problem in establishing philosophy's identity with the content of orthodox theology lies not in theology's misappropriation of doctrine, but in the difference between representational and conceptual thinking: "The language of representation differs from the langauge of the concept. Further, man not only to begin with knows Truth by the name of representation. He is also, as a living man, at home with it alone. The task of philosophical science, however, is not to write its figurations into...abstract realms only. It is also to show...their existence in actual Spirit. But that existence is representation."[5]

As this passage confirms, Hegel found that religion knows truth but only in the mode of 'representations', which, as we have seen in Chapter One, are elevated into objective doctrines of the *cul-*

tus. Of course, what philosophy has to do is extract the truth in philosophical form from the representations in doctrine, all the while preserving these representations. In fact, the relationship of philosophy and religious representation is one of a dynamic fluctuation of thinking between representation and concept and between concept and representation,[6] much as we found in the mirroring of theological content in the philosophical form in 1827.

This intermovement of representation and philosophical thinking poses a significant challenge to philosophy, as Hegel acknowledged: "When philosophy transposes what is in the form of representation into the form of the concept, there does certainly emerge the difficulty of separating, in a content, what is content as such or thought from what belongs to representation as such."[7]

As we proposed in Chapter Five, the way in which Hegel surmounted this difficulty is through a *third-order philosophy of theology* that clarifies, sorts out, and criticizes the work of theologians and then accomplishes what the orthodox theologians accomplish, that is, reflect the content of faith of the community in thought, but in the form of philosophy.[8] Through separating and unifying, the third-order philosophy of theology turns the science of faith over into the science of Spirit in a manner similar to the 'flipping over' of the phenomenology of Spirit into speculative philosophy as we noted in the Introduction. Indeed, through this philosophy of theology's thinking through of the truth of reconciliation found in the doctrines of consummate religion, philosophy knows that the finite subject has been lifted up into the inclusive subjectivity of Spirit. As a result of this knowledge gained through the philosophy of theology, philosophy also knows that this elevation of the finite subject to infinite subjectivity is also the return of Spirit's witness to itself in the self-consciousness of absolute Spirit. Indeed, all the forms of theologizing as now seen by philosophy as integral to the mediation of the finite subject and infinite subjectivity in the process of reconciliation undertaken by Spirit. Consequently, the development of Hegel's philosophy of religion from 1821 to 1827 is to be understood as an inner development that parallels Spirit's trinitarian self-development from initial identity to difference and identity-in-difference. This correspondence between the inner self-development of Spirit and the development of the Berlin lectures on the philosophy of religion is significant insofar as the philosophy of religion was the last aspect of Hegel's philosophy of Spirit to be worked out in detail.

As we have seen at the end of Chapter Five, the healing reconciliation in Spirit means that philosophical form and theological content should mirror each other throughout the philosophy of religion as the self-consciousness of absolute Spirit. Therefore, we can conclude that the difference of form between philosophy and theology is itself a self-differentiation necessitated by Spirit's own inner activity. Indeed, we simply have to remember that in the early life of the consummate religion philosophy and theology were together in the differentiated unity initially implied in the speculative statement 'philosophy is theology'. (However, the predicate was recognized as the superior term, with the subject, philosophy, subordinated to theology as its 'handmaiden'.) With the post-Reformation Enlightenment philosophy of religion, human thinking shifted to emphasize philosophy over theology, which caused theology either to submit to the dictates of the Understanding or to recoil into a private journey into the inner vacuum of finite subjectivity. Thus, the unity implied in the statement 'philosophy is theology' broke into what seemed to be irreconcilable extremes: Enlightenment and Pietism.

With Hegel's opening lecture on the philosophy of religion, philosophy and theology were brought together once again but in a way that did not destroy their difference but brings them into a new identity. Indeed, under the rubric of the philosophy of religion, philosophy attempts to cognize conceptually the reconciliation of all oppositions, not just that of philosophy and theology. However, as we have seen, this reconciliation is never static; on the contrary, it has to be continuously realized. Hence, when the theology of feeling and Pietistic theology arose to oppose philosophy, the reconciliation of philosophy and theology achieved in principle in the 1821 and 1824 lectures was torn asunder. Nevertheless, the pulling apart and gathering in of philosophy and theology implied in the speculative statement 'philosophy is theology' was realized in its fullest reciprocity in the 1827 lectures when the form of philosophy and the content of theology were conjoined in the self-consciousness of absolute Spirit. But, that this reconciliation took place after a seemingly irretrievable fissure between philosophy and Pietism initiated by Pietism should make us realize that reconciliation requires opposition. And, as we observed in Chapter One, the greater the opposition, the greater is the need for reconciliation. Therefore, Hegel's proclamation of reconciliation—"Philosophy is to this extent theology"—at the end of the 1827 *The Consummate Religion* shows us that philosophy and theology will always inform and conflict with each other. However, this relation will always be sublated in philosophy if and only if philosophy, as the self-consciousness of absolute Spirit, appreciates that: "It wins its truth only when, in utter dismemberment, it finds itself."[9]

N O T E S

Introduction. Relation of the Philosophy of Religion to Theology

1. G. W. F. Hegel, *Lectures on the Philosophy of Religion, vol. 1*, ed. Peter C. Hodgson (Berkeley: University of California Press, 1984), p. 83. Hereafter we will abbreviate this edition as LPR1 and the subsequent editions on Determinate Religion and The Consummate Religion as LPR11 and LPR111 (respectively). The lecture year will follow the volume number to help clarify the context. If the quotation is from a student transcript then reference to student transcripts will use the abbreviations established by Hodgson in his editorial introduction, LPR1, pp. 15–32 and will follow the year of lecture. We will also follow the system of bracketing used in the English translation and outlined by Hodgson in the editorial introduction, LPR1, pp. 40–42. Thus, <...> indicates a marginal annotation which has been woven into the text by the editor. Brackets, [...], indicate editorial additions designed to complete the syntax of the sentence and are used most extensively in the translation of the 1821 lecture manuscripts because of the somewhat fragmentary nature of the manuscript. Because this translation is a parallel publication to *Vorlesungen: Ausgewählte Nachschriften und Manuskripte*, by G. W. F. Hegel, Band 3–5, *Vorlesungen über die Philosophie der Religion*, ed. Walter Jaeschke (Hamburg: Felix Meiner, 1983–1985)—hereafter abbreviated as VPR (with part [*Teil*] number following, e.g., VPR111)—the German pagination will follow the English in the footnote. For example, the preceding quotation is referenced as LPR1, 1821, p. 83; VPR11, p. 3. Also, I worked mainly on the basis of translation, amending the text when necessary.

2. Paul Tillich defines revelation as "a special and extraordinary manifestation which removes the veil from something which is hidden in a special and extraordinary way." *Systematic Theology*, vol. 1 (Chicago: University of Chicago Press, 1951), p. 108. Thus, when we apply the term *revelatory* to the term *theology* we mean the knowledge of God in which God is purported to have removed the veil of mystery that cloaked or hid his Being and thereby disclosed to human beings the eternal truth of God, especially as it pertains to the salvation of humankind. Of course, Jesus Christ as the incarnation of God in human form has been customarily considered the primary medium of revelation by this type of theology. As well, revealed theology posits that this initial revelation is then further disclosed through

the Holy Spirit in its 'witness to itself' in the word of God, the Bible, and in the Church and its doctrinal traditions. Revelatory discourse, then, is what is found within the Bible as God's self-revelation and in the Church's conversation and doctrinal thinking about the content of revelation over the centuries. But at all times, revelatory discourse must stay within the theological form (or the theologic) set out by the Church in its doctrines. As such, revelatory discourse is thought to transcend the limitations of human thought, and therefore does not need to express itself according to human laws of thought like the laws of identity, contradiction, and excluded middle, but rather according to the inner logic of its own theologic. Tertullian (ca. 160–230) and Søren Kierkegaard (1813–1855) are excellent examples of this point of view when they emphasize the 'absurdity' of belief in Jesus Christ. Proponents of revelatory theology have been hostile to philosophy (see I Corinthians 1:18–21 for the origins of this position in St. Paul) unless philosophy is grounded first in faith in revelation.

Perhaps the most famous statement about philosophical thinking arising out of faith and revelation in the history of Christian thought is St. Anselm's 'faith seeking understanding'. In the twentieth century this notion still holds for some theologians in varying degrees; for example, when discussing St. Anselm, Karl Barth wrote: "It is my faith that summons me to knowledge." *Anselm: Fides Quaerens Intellectum*, trans. I. W. Robinson (Richmond, Va.: John Knox Press, 1960), p. 18.

3. By *natural theology*, we mean knowledge of God obtained through the human intellect unaided by revelation. Thus, reason and experience become the sole sources of knowledge of God. Natural theology can be traced back to Plato. (See, for example, *Euthyphro*, sections 10a–d on the relation between God and morality; *Timaeus*, sections 34a–35b on the nature of God as trinitarian; and *Phaedo*, in general, for a discussion of the immortality of the soul.) As well, the term *natural theology* is applied to the philosophical knowledge of God that complements the Christian tradition of revealed theology, with St. Anselm (see the previous footnote) and St. Thomas Aquinas as the best examples. In the Enlightenment, Christian Wolff, popularizer of Leibnizian philosophy, developed natural theology as the "third and final part of *metaphysica specialis*" in *Theologia naturalis methodo scientifica pertractata* (LPR1, 1821, p. 83, n. 3). Also, see n. 5 for further discussion of Wolff.

The term *rational theology* has often been used as a synonym for natural theology but the term *rational theology* has also been used to describe the works of theologians of rationalism, such as J. S. Semler and J. A. Ernesti, who subjected the Bible to historical criticism and about whom Hegel would have been aware from his seminary days. (See Otto W. Heick, *A History of Christian Thought*, Philadelphia: Fortress Press, 1966.) We will use the term *natural theology* for the attempts at knowledge of God undertaken by philosophers and reserve use of the term *rational theology* for the attempts at knowledge of God undertaken by theologians influenced by the Enlightenment, as this is the way Hegel uses these terms. (See LPR1, 1824, pp. 115–116, pp. 121–128; VPR1, pp. 33, 38–45.)

4. Benedict de Spinoza, *Theologico-Political Treatise* (New York: Dover Publications, 1951), p. 42.

5. Wolff asserted that "Everything must be proved by reason, as on the philosopher's stone." Thus, Wolff "methodically delineated the conditions which any true revelation must fulfill." Simply stated, these conditions are "its necessity," it does not "reveal anything which contradicts these [God's] perfections," it does not "obligate man to deeds which run counter to the laws of nature," and (decidedly, the most stringent of them all) "the entire arrangement of words must agree with the general rules of grammar and rhetoric." Henry Allison, *Lessing and the Enlightenment* (Ann Arbor: University of Michigan Press, 1966), p. 37.

6. Gadamer captures the irony implicit in the Enlightenment's rejection of all previous knowledge when he suggested that "the fundamental prejudice of the enlightenment is the prejudice against prejudice, which deprives tradition of its power." *Truth and Method* (New York: Continuum Publishing Corporation, 1975), pp. 239–240. Descartes best expresses this 'prejudice against prejudice' in *Discourse on Method,* Part Four: "Because I wish to give myself entirely to search after truth, I thought it was necessary for me to adopt an apparently opposite course and to reject as absolutely false everything concerning which I could imagine the least ground of doubt, in order to see whether afterwards there remained anything in my beliefs which was entirely certain."

7. Immanuel Kant, *Critique of Pure Reason*, trans. Norman Kemp-Smith (New York: St. Martin's Press, 1965), A12.

8. Ibid., Bxxx. The full text reads: "This discussion as to the positive advantage of critical principles of pure reason can be similarly developed in regard to the concept of *God* and of the *simple nature* of our *soul*; but for the sake of brevity such further discussion may be omitted. [From what has been said, it is evident that] even the *assumption*—as made on behalf of the necessary practical employment of my reason—of *God, freedom,* and *immortality* is not permissible unless at the same time speculative reason be deprived of its pretensions to transcendent insight. For in order to arrive at such insight it must make use of principles which, in fact, extend only to objects of possible experience, and which, if also applied to what cannot be an object of experience, always really change this into an appearance, thus rendering all *practical extension* of pure reason impossible. I have therefore found it necessary to deny *knowledge*, in order to make room for *faith*."

9. LPR1, 1821, p. 82; VPR1, p. 3.

10. John Hick, *Philosophy of Religion* (Englewood Cliffs, N.J.: Prentice-Hall, 1963), p. 2.

11. Hegel stated this unequivocally in the 1824 lectures on consummate religion: "religion is *human* religion"; LPR111, 1824, p. 189; VPR111, p. 123. As we will see, this means that all knowledge of God must be grasped as *human knowledge* of God and not as objective, transcendent knowledge of God as he exists in himself.

12. LPR1, 1821, p. 83; VPR1, p. 3. This description remains essentially the same in the 1824 and 1827 lectures.

13. LPR1, 1821, p. 84; VPR1, p.3.

14. LPR111, 1821, p. 161; VPR111, p. 96.

15. LPR111, 1821, pp. 161–162; VPR111, p. 96.

16. Lewis White Beck, *Early German Philosophy. Kant and His Predecessors* (Cambridge, Mass.: Belknap Press of Harvard University Press, 1969), p. 9.

17. See n. 3.

18. This term is usually used to refer to the "doctrines of the Schoolmen" who utilize a method perfected by St. Thomas Aquinas. However, by *scholasticism* we mean any type of thinking that insists on espousing the traditional doctrines of a school of thought according to already well-delineated forms. Thus, the term *scholasticism* can be applied to any group falling outside of the medieval Catholic period, and in this case, we are applying it to developments in late seventeenth-century Lutheranism. In fact, Philip Jacob Spener (1635–1705) founded Lutheran pietism (with the publication of his *Pia Desideria* in 1675) in protest against what he perceived as scholasticism among the theologians and clerics of the Lutheran church.

19. Pietism, especially as propounded by F. A. Tholuck (1799–1877), will have a significant effect on Hegel's reformulation of the 1827 lectures.

20. The publication of F. Schleiermacher's work of dogmatics, *The Christian Faith*, in 1821–1822 is one such event. Pietism's criticism of Hegel prior to the 1827 lectures is the other. See the previous note.

21. LPR111, 1827, pp. 343–347; VPR111, pp. 266–270.

22. LPR1, 1821, p. 84; VPR111, p. 4. By way of anticipation it should be pointed out that Hegel uses the term *theology* in at least three ways: first, to refer equally with philosophy, as the science of God (here, philosophy is theology); second, as the discipline of theological reflection as such; third, to refer to the efforts of Schleiermacher, Tholuck, and so forth (theologies). In the second and third usages, *theology* remains characterized by otherness and representational thinking. Hegel of course maintains throughout the Berlin lectures an overall identification of philosophy and theology (in the first sense indicated previously) so it is against the background of this overall project of Hegel's that we will argue that a dialectical integration of philosophy and theology takes place.

23. For an excellent description of the development of Hegelian schools of thought both during and after Hegel's life, see John Toews, *Hegelianism. The Path Toward Dialectical Humanism*, 1805–1841 (Cambridge: Cambridge University Press, 1980). Also see Johann Eduard Erdmann, *A History of Philosophy*, trans. W. S. Hough, 3 vols (London, 1890–1892), for an account from a participant in the debates of the 1830s.

24. J. Toews, *Hegelianism*, p. 148. To wit: "Marheineke was convinced that the Hegelian transformation of representation into concept, faith into knowledge, did not threaten the viability of the Christian faith or the existing church, but provided the basis for their revitalization."

25. H. S. Harris, "The Hegel Renaissance in the Anglo-Saxon World Since 1945," *The Owl of Minerva* 15, no. 1 (Fall 1983): 86: "the new orthodoxy...according to which Robert C. Whittemore was right to call Hegel a 'panentheist'."

26. Kem Luther and Jeff L. Hoover, "Hegel's Phenomenology of Religion," *Journal of Religion* 61 (July 1981): 229–241.

27. For an interesting comparison of Hegel and Husserl, see Frank M. Kirkland, "Husserl and Hegel: A Historical and Religious Encounter," *Journal of the British Society for Phenomenology* 16, no. 1 (January 1985). Recently a number of books comparing Hegel and Heidegger have been published. Among these are Michael Allen Gillespie, *Hegel, Heidegger and the Ground of History* (Chicago: University of Chicago Press, 1984); Edith Wyschogrod, *Spirit in Ashes: Hegel, Heidegger, and Man-Made Mass Death* (New Haven, Conn.: Yale University Press, 1985); David Kolb, *The Critique of Modernity. Hegel, Heidegger and After* (Chicago: University of Chicago Press, 1986). Of these three, I found Wyschogrod's *Spirit in Ashes* the most stimulating as she looks at the notions of death in Hegel and Heidegger and utilizes them to illuminate the creation of what she calls a "deathworld"—a play on Husserl's notion of *Lebenswelt* in *The Crisis of European Sciences*—in the Nazi extermination camps.

28. Martin Heidegger, *Being and Time* (New York: Harper and Brothers, 1962), section four, pp. 32–35.

29. For example, Roger Schmidt, *Exploring Religion* (Belmont, Calif.: Wadsworth, 1980).

30. Martin Heidegger, *The Basic Writings of Martin Heidegger* (New York: Harper and Row, 1977), p. 39.

31. LPR11, 1824, p. 271 (see also n. 107, same page); VPR11 (4a) p. 176. These terms arise in connection with Hegel's discussion of the ability of philosophy to grasp the inner essence of 'nature religion' and give us the sense of Hegel's phenomenological method as it applies to forms of religious consciousness not his own: "Certainly we can *understand* nature religion therefore but we cannot *represent* it *from within*, we cannot have the *sense* or *feeling* of it *from within*....Only spirit fully comprehends spirit, and here, where we are not dealing with free spirit, we may be able to understand it *from within*." The German reads: "*Verstehen können wir deswegen die Naturreligion wohl, aber wir können uns nicht hineinvorstellen, uns nicht hineinempfinden, nicht hineinfühlen....Der Geist fasst ganz nur den Geist, und hier, wo wir es zu tun haben nicht mit dem freien Geist, ist wohl, dass wir uns hineinverstehen können.*"

32. G. W. F. Hegel, *Phenomenology of Spirit*, trans. A. V. Miller (Oxford: Oxford University Press, 1977), p. 412, hereafter referred to as PS; G. W. F. Hegel, *Phänomenologie des Geistes* (Hamburg: Felix Meiner, 1952), pp. 475–476, hereafter referred to as PG.

33. Mark C. Taylor, *Journeys to Selfhood, Hegel and Kierkegaard* (Berkeley: University of California Press, 1980).

34. LPR11, 1824, p. 251; VPR11, p. 155–156.

35. LPR11, 1824, p. 251; VPR11, p. 156.

36. PS, section 5, p. 3; PG, p. 12: "To help bring philosophy closer to the form of Science, to the goal where it can lay aside the title '*love* of knowing' and be *actual* knowing—that is what I have set myself to do. The inner necessity that knowing should be Science lies in its nature and only the systematic exposition of philosophy itself provides it. But the *external* necessity, so far as it is grasped in a general way, setting aside accidental matters of person and motivation, is the same as the inner, or in other words, it lies in the shape in which time sets forth the sequential existence of its moments. To show that now is the time for philosophy to be raised to the status of a Science would therefore be the only true justification of any effort that has this aim, for to do so would demonstrate the necessity of the aim, indeed at the same time be the accomplishing of it."

37. Heidegger captures the sense of the *Phenomenology* as Spirit's own existence very well in *Hegel's Phenomenology of Spirit,* trans. Pravis Emad and Kenneth Maly (Bloomington: Indiana University Press, 1988), p. 24: "phenomenology is not one way among many but the manner in which spirit exists. The phenomenology of spirit is the genuine and the total coming-out of spirit. But before whom does it come out? Before spirit itself."

38. PS, sections 59–67, pp. 36–41; PG, pp. 48–55. For the best accounts of Hegel's theory of the speculative sentence see J. P. Surber, 'Hegel's Speculative Sentence,' *Hegel-Studien* 10 (1975): 221–230; Stephen Houlgate, *Hegel, Nietzsche and the Criticism of Metaphysics* (Cambridge: Cambridge University Press, 1986).

39. PS, section 62, pp. 38–29; PG, pp. 51–52.

40. PS, section 61, p. 38; PG, p. 51.

41. To do so would be like perpetuating the mistake of Schelling and positing an identity from the outset in which all distinctions disappear and which "the night in which...all cows are black." As Hegel noted, "this is cognition naively reduced to vacuity." (PS, section 16, p. 9; PG, p. 19.)

42. Houlgate, *Hegel, Nietzsche and the Criticism of Metaphysics*, pp. 267–268, n. 103.

43. It should be noted that we will locate Hegel's debate with Schleiermacher within the context of Hegel's conceptualization of religion and its development. Our purpose, therefore, is not to adjudicate as to the correctness of either position, but to show the relevance of Schleiermacher's dogmatics for Hegel's philosophy of religion.

Chapter One. The 1821 Concept of Religion

1. LPR1, 1821, p. 89; VPR1, p. 8.

2. Hegel's emphasis on the importance of religious experience for the philo-

sophical investigation of religion itself is taken up in the twentieth century by phenomenologists such as Rudolph Otto, who, in his 1917 study of the experience of
holiness, *The Idea of the Holy* (Oxford: Oxford University Press, 1969), wrote: "The
reader is invited to direct his mind to a moment of deeply felt religious experience,
as little as possible qualified by other forms of consciousness. Whoever cannot do
this, whoever knows no such moments in his experience, is requested to read no
further" (p. 8). We will have occasion to compare Otto with Hegel at several points
in this chapter.

3. G. W. F. Hegel, *Vorlesungen über die Aesthetik.* vol. 1 (Frankfurt-am-
Main: Suhrkamp, 1971), p. 143. Quoted in Quentin Lauer, *Hegel's Concept of God*,
pp. 36–37. Hegel is also reported to have said to his housekeeper in reference to her
query about his not attending church: *"Meine liebe Frau, das Denken ist auch Gottes-
dienst."* (My dear woman, thinking is also the service of God.) Quoted in W. R. Inge,
Mysticism in Religion (Chicago: University of Chicago Press, 1948), p. 145. A similar
thought is expressed by Hegel in a letter to Niethammer: "Our universities and
schools are our church." G. W. F. Hegel, *Hegel's Letters*, p. 327; *Briefe*, letter 272.

4. Paul Tillich, *Systematic Theology*, vol. 1, p. 3.

5. LPR1, 1821, pp. 89–90; VPR1, pp. 8–9.

6. LPR1, p. 85; VPR1, p. 5.

7. Otto, *The Idea of Holy*, p. 12.

8. LPR1, p. 186; VPR1, p. 95.

9. LPR1, p. 186; VPR1, p. 95.

10. LPR1, p. 191; VPR1, p. 100.

11. Ibid.

12. LPR1, p. 204; VPR1, p. 113.

13. LPR1, p. 204, n. 57.

14. LPR1, 1824, p. 318; VPR1, p. 222.

15. Ibid.

16. LPR1, p. 318, n. 120, 'Ho'; VPR1, p. 221–222, 'Ho'.

17. VPR1, p. 199.

18. LPR1, 1821, p. 201; VPR1, p. 110.

19. Ibid.

20. Ibid.

21. LPR1, p. 202; VPR1, p. 111.

22. LPR1, p. 199; VPR1, p. 108. Translation amended.

23. LPR1, p. 221; VPR1, p. 130.

24. LPR1, p. 207; VPR1, p.115.

25. Ibid.

26. LPR1, p. 207; VPR1, p. 116. My emphasis.

27. LPR1, pp. 207–208; VPR1, p. 116.

28. LPR1, p. 208, 'W$_2$'; VPR1, p. 116, 'W$_2$'.

29. LPR1, p. 208; VPR1, p. 117.

30. Ibid.

31. Hodgson noted that *Andacht* and *Denken* are "related etymologically": "The root of *Andacht* is from the imperfect of the verb *denken*, namely, *dachte*." LPR1, p. 208, n. 66. We should also note that *denken* is also etymologically related to the Old English verb *thencan*, meaning "to think," which itself is etymologically tied to the Old English verb, *thancan* or *thankan*, which means "to thank" whose "primary sense was therefore thought" and thus signifies "thought," "favorable thought," "the expression of gratitude," and so forth. Thus, the shared sense of both thinking and thanking is to be grateful, to appreciate something. *Appreciate*, although a word of Latin origin, is the most suitable word that we can use to point to what is meant by *thancan* and *thencan* as *appreciate* signifies "to make or form an estimate of worth," "to perceive the full force of," "to esteem adequately or highly," and "to raise in value," all attributes ascribable to both thinking and thanking. *Thinking* and *thanking* then are to appreciate what has been given. In terms of our discussion of the primary modality of religious consciousness, this etymology of *thinking* ties in quite nicely with Hegel's play on *Andacht* and *Denken*. (Definitions and etymologies are taken from the *Oxford English Dictionary*.) See also Martin Heidegger, *Was heisst Denken?* (Tübingen, Niemeyer, 1954).

32. LPR1, p. 211; VPR1, p. 119.

33. LPR1, p. 212; VPR1, p. 120.

34. LPR1, p. 213; VPR1, p. 121.

35. We use the word *embryonic* because it is not until Christianity, as the consummate or absolute religion, that the notion of reconciliation becomes fully known. In keeping with the paradoxical structure of reconciliation emerging at this primordial level, the reconciliation Christianity offers comes through Jesus Christ, who, as the 'God-man', is the union of the divine and human and therefore is the fullest expression of this paradoxical reconciliation. It is appropriate that Kierkegaard will call Christ the "Absolute Paradox."

36. LPR1, p. 211; VPR1, p. 118. The divided self is the 'interstice' or 'space' between the two extremes because the self sees the union and nonunion of subject

and object within itself. Following what Plato has Socrates and Diotima say in the *Symposium* (200C–202B), this 'space' is the realm of the spiritual: "for all the spiritual is between the divine and the mortal." It is spiritual for insofar as the self sees this union and nonunion within itself, this union and nonunion become an object for this subject, an object unlike any to be found in natural, empirical consciousness. This is the beginning of the reflective mode that arises within religious consciousness. Indeed, this new, spiritual object becomes objectified by reflection, for example, in the form of Christ. This object and its objectification is then the core structure of theology. As we will see in Chapter Five, speculative reflection will take as its object not only this spiritual object (i.e., the initial union and nonunion objectified by reflection), but also the union of this initial union and nonunion that has taken place in theological reflection. In fact, this multileveled speculative reflection is what is presupposed in the thinking of the concept of religion. In Chapter Five, we will characterize this multileveled reflection as *third-order philosophy of theology*.

37. LPR1, p. 210, 'W₂'; VPR1, pp. 116–117, 'W₂'.

38. LPR1, 1821, p. 210; VPR1, pp. 118–119.

39. G. W. F. Hegel, *Hegel's Philosophy of Mind*, trans. William Wallace (Oxford: Clarendon Press, 1971), section 402; hereafter cited as PM. The 'Zusätze' will be cited as Z. *Encyclopädie der Philosophischen Wissenschaften Im Grundrisse*, ed. Johannes Hoffmeister (Leipzig: Felix Meiner, 1949). Because the English and German editions number the sections the same, we will include only Enc. and section number in our citations.

40. Enc. 402Z.

41. Enc. 402. Note that Hegel is playing on the notion of *finding* implicit in the root of *Empfindung, Finden*.

42. Enc. 403.

43. Enc. 403. Translation amended.

44. LPR1, 1821, p. 209; VPR1, p. 118.

45. Ibid.

46. LPR1, p. 219; VPR1, p. 128. Translation amended.

47. For a detailed exposition of the mechanics of representation and its three components, recollection (*Erinnerung*), imagination (*Einbildungskraft*), and memory (*Gedächtnis*), see PM, sections 451–463. For an excellent discussion of representation in relation to philosophy, see James Yerkes, *The Christology of Hegel*, pp. 71–89.

48. LPR1, 1821, p. 208, 'W₂'; VPR1, p. 117. 'W₂'. My emphasis.

49. LPR1, p. 219; VPR1, p. 128. My emphasis.

50. LPR1, p. 218; VPR1, p. 127.

51. LPR1, p. 220; VPR1, pp. 128–129.

52. Hegel discusses 'fear' (and its dialectical complement, 'trust') in detail in his discussion of the biblical passage 'The fear of the Lord is the beginning of all wisdom' in relation to the Jewish conception of God (LPR11, 1824, pp. 442–44; VPR11, p. 345). It is significant for us to note that for Hegel 'fear' arises only when the cleavage between God and human being has become explicit, as it does in a 'spiritual religion' like Judaism. The cleavage was only implicit in the earlier, 'nature religions', Buddhism and Hinduism. These 'immediate' religions are "the lowest level...the spiritual still joined with the natural in their first undisturbed, untroubled unity" (LPR11, 1824, p. 239; VPR11, p. 144). Although 'fear' is not present, they are still 'spiritual' insofar as they are the world-historical determinations parallel to the 'differentiated unity' of absolute universality and absolute singularity we discussed earlier.

53. Inasmuch as Otto does not make 'thinking' an issue in his account of the genesis of religious consciousness.

54. This grounding of thinking in the body and its sensible being in the world will also help us comprehend the importance of the Incarnation for consummate religion.

55. LPR1, 1821, pp. 221–222; VPR1, p. 130.

56. LPR1, p. 233; VPR, p. 142.

57. LPR1, p. 241, 'W$_2$'; VPR1, p. 150, 'W$_2$'. Translation amended. My emphasis.

58. Quoted from Enc. 24Z (Sämtliche Werke: Jubiläumsgabe in zwanzig Banden, ed. Herman Glockner, Stuttgart: Friedrich Frommann, 1927–1930, Band 8) in Yerkes, The Christology of Hegel, p. 76. Also: Hegel's Logic, trans. William Wallace (Oxford: Clarendon Press, 1975), pp. 38–39.

59. LPR1, p. 232; VPR1, pp. 141–142.

60. LPR111, 1827, p. 283; VPR111, p. 209.

61. Luther, for example, said in Lectures on Genesis Chapter 1–5: "Now these are functions of the Second Person, that is, of Christ, the Son of God: to adorn and separate the crude mass which was brought forth out of nothing." Martin Luther, Luther's Works, vol. I, ed. and trans. Jaroslav Pelikan (St. Louis: Concordia Publishing House, 1958), p. 9.

62. LPR1, p. 284, 'W$_2$'; VPR111, p. 209, 'W$_2$'.

63. LPR1, 1821, pp. 233–234; VPR1, pp. 142–143.

64. LPR1, p. 234; VPR1, p. 143.

65. LPR1, p. 235; VPR1, p. 144.

66. LPR1, p. 238; VPR1, p. 147.

67. Ibid.

68. Ibid.

69. LPR1, p. 238; VPR1, p. 148.

70. Ibid.

71. LPR1, p. 239; VPR1, p. 148.

72. LPR1, p. 240; VPR1, pp. 149–150.

73. Hegel defines the *cultus* in this way: "However, we shall conceive of *cultus* as that activity which, encompassing both inwardness and outward appearance, in general brings about restoration of unity with the absolute, and which in so doing is also essentially an inner conversion of mind and heart. Thus the Christian *cultus*, for example, contains not only the sacraments and ecclesiastical actions and duties but also the so-called 'plan of salvation' as an absolutely inner history and as the successive stages of the activity of the disposition—generally speaking, a movement that transpires and rightly transpires in the soul" (LPR1, 1821, p. 190, 'W$_2$'; VPR1, pp. 98–99, 'W$_2$'). Hegel thus uses the term, *cultus*, to signify "an organized system of religious worship in reference to its external rites and ceremonies" (OED) but, with the added nuance that this external worship has as its internal complement, an 'inner' disposition. He further noted: "The term *cultus* is usually taken only in the more limited sense of referring to external, public action, while the inner action of disposition is not given much prominence" (LPR1; VPR1, pp. 97–98, 'W$_2$'). But, for Hegel's use of the term, the outer and the inner are to be coequal.

74. LPR1, p. 241; VPR1, p. 151.

75. LPR1, pp. 241–242; VPR1, pp. 151–152.

76. LPR1, p. 243; VPR1, p. 152. Translation amended.

77. LPR1, pp. 243–244; VPR1, pp. 152–153. Translation amended.

78. LPR1, p. 245; VPR1, p. 153. Of course, within the Christian tradition there are a variety of definitions of faith. A number include thinking as an important part of faith, as our discussion indicates is the case for Hegel. St. Thomas Aquinas, for example, in *Summa Theologica*, 1111, Qu. 4, Art 5, says faith is "an act of the intellect assenting to the truth at the command of the will." *Basic Writings of St. Thomas Aquinas*, ed. Anton C. Pegis (New York: Random House, 1945), p. 11. An example of this inclusion of thinking as a part of faith from the twentieth century, although more vague, is from Paul Tillich: "Faith as the ultimate concern is an act of the total personality." *Dynamics of Faith* (San Francisco: Harper and Row, 1957), p. 4. Examples of those who do not include thinking as a component of faith

are Blaise Pascal and Søren Kierkegaard. Pascal: "It is the heart which experiences God, and not the reason. This, then, is faith: God felt by the heart, not by reason." *Pensées*, trans. W. F. Trotter (London: Dent, 1908), no. 278. Kierkegaard: "An objective uncertainty held fast in an appropriation-process of the most passionate inwardness." *Concluding Unscientific Postscript*, trans. David F. Swenson and Walter Lowrie (Princeton, N.J.: Princeton University Press, 1941), p. 182.

79. LPR1, p. 245; VPR1, p. 154.

80. LPR1, p. 246; VPR1, p. 155.

81. LPR1, p. 244; VPR1, p. 153.

82. LPR1, p. 247; VPR1, p. 156. Translation amended.

83. LPR1, p. 252; VPR1, p. 161.

84. LPR1, p. 255; VPR1, pp. 162–163.

Chapter Two. Religion Within the Limits of Feeling Alone: Schleiermacher's The Christian Faith

1. LPR1, p. 256; VPR1, p. 163.

2. LPR1, p. 116; VPR1, p. 33.

3. LPR1, p. 119; VPR1, p. 36.

4. By *orthodox theology* we do not mean the theology of the Eastern Orthodox Church, but official doctrines of "Western" Christianity, such as the doctrine of the Trinity and the doctrine of the two natures of Christ, established by church councils in the fourth and fifth centuries and maintained in their essential character by the mainstream Roman Catholic and Protestant denominations.

5. Friedrich Schleiermacher's *The Christian Faith* was first published in June 1821 as *Der christliche Glaube nach den Grundsätzen der evangelischen Kirche im Zusammenhange dargestellt*, Vol. I (Berlin: G. Reimer, 1821). The second volume was published the next year. We will be using two translations. The first is *The Christian Faith*, ed. and trans. H. R. MacIntosh and J. S. Stewart (Edinburgh: T. & T. Clarke, 1928), which is based on the second German edition, published in 1830–1831; hereafter cited as CF. The second translation we will use are selections from the first edition included in *Hegel, Hinrichs and Schleiermacher On Feeling and Reason in Religion: The Texts of Their 1821–22 Debate*, trans. Eric von der Luft (Lewiston, New York: Edwin Mellen Press, 1987); hereafter cited as Texts. An interesting discussion of the differences between the 1821–22 and the 1830–31 editions is by Richard Crouter, "Rhetoric and Substance in Schleiermacher's Revision of *The Christian Faith* (1821–1822)," *Journal of Religion* 60 (July 1980): 285–306. Crouter says: "We may briefly characterize the most obvious difference by saying that in the first version the scientific-intellectual (one is inclined to say methodological) dimension is brought forth implicitly from within the exposition of Chris-

tian piety, whereas in the more mature edition this relationship is reversed" (p. 295). We, therefore, will keep to the 1821–22 version by depicting Schleiermacher's descriptions in *The Christian Faith* as *arising from within* piety.

6. Duncan Forbes, in his introduction to *Hegel's Lectures on the Philosophy of World-History*, trans. H. B. Nishet (Cambridge: Cambridge University Press, 1975), made a similar point: "The present edition of the introductory lectures on the philosophy of history has the advantage of bringing home the fact that so much of Hegel's philosophy was talked, not without humour and anecdote and personalities and contemporary references...and also constant tacking and changes of course" (p. xiv).

7. Hermann Friedrich Wilhem Hinrichs (1794–1861), *Die Religion im inneren Verhältnis zur Wissenschaft: Nebst Darstellung und Beurtheilung der von Jacobi, Fichte und Schelling gemachten Versuche, dieselbe wissenschaftlich zu erfassen, und nach ihrem Hauptinhalte zu entwickeln, mit einem Vorworte von Georg Wilhelm Friedrich Hegel* (Heidelberg: Groos, 1822; reprint, Brussels: Culture et Civilisation, 1970); translated as *Religion in its Internal Relationship to Systematic Knowledge* in Texts, pp. 239–486.

8. LPR1, 1827, p. 152; VPR1, p. 63.

9. See our discussion of Hegel's notion of the relations between philosophy and religion in the Introduction.

10. Again, Duncan Forbes puts it nicely in *Introduction to Hegel's Lectures on the Philosophy of World-History*, when he observed that "Hegel insisted that 'Science' was *public* and a discipline of thinking" (p. xiv. My emphasis).

11. In German Protestantism, this would have been traditionally thought to be the case ever since Philip Melanchthon, Luther's colleague and collaborator, established Lutheran universities whose educational mission was to further knowledge of God as witnessed in *The Book of Concord*.

12. For an excellent, thorough discussion of Schleiermacher, see Martin Redeker, *Schleiermacher: His Life and Thought*, trans. John Wallhausser (Philadelphia: Fortress Press, 1973).

13. Schleiermacher's political views and activities are most clearly articulated in Jerry F. Dawson's *Schleiermacher. The Evolution of a Nationalist* (Austin: University of Texas Press, 1966).

14. For a detailed account of Schleiermacher's role in the formation of the United Evangelical Church, see Redeker's *Schleiermacher. Life and Thought*, pp. 187–208.

15. For a contemporary discussion of the impact of Schleiermacher's hermeneutics on philosophy, see Gadamer's *Truth and Method*, pp. 58ff. A number of works are available that depict Schleiermacher's influence on theology. From the vantage point of twentieth-century theology, two works stand out: Karl Barth's

Protestant Theology In the Nineteenth Century. Its Background and History, trans. Brian Cozens and John Bowden (London: SCM Press, 1972); and Paul Tillich's *Perspectives on Nineteenth and Twentieth Century Protestant Theology*, ed. Carl E. Braaten (New York: Harper, 1967).

16. For accounts of the relations between Hegel and Schleiermacher, see Richard Crouter, "Hegel and Schleiermacher at Berlin: A Many-Sided Debate." *Journal of the American Academy of Religion* 48 (March 1980): 19–43; Jeffrey Hoover, "The Origin of the Conflict between Hegel and Schleiermacher at Berlin," *The Owl of Minerva* 20, no. 1 (Fall 1988): 69–79; John E. Toews, *Hegelianism. The Path Towards Dialectical Humanism, 1805–1841* (Cambridge: Cambridge University Press, 1980), pp. 49–67. Our account draws from all three sources.

17. Wilhelm Martin Leberecht de Wette (1780–1849) was a student of Johann Gottfried Herder (1744–1803) and a member of the theological faculty at the University of Berlin from its inception. For a detailed study of his theology, see K. Barth's *Protestant Theology in the Nineteenth Century*, pp. 482–491.

18. Jakob Friedrich Fries (1773–1843) was Hegel's predecessor at the University of Heidelberg (1805–1816). "In 1819 he was suspended by the government for his participation in the Wartburg Festival [of the German Students Societies *(Burschenschaften)*] and for his ultra-liberal views" G. W. F. Hegel, *Philosophy of Right*, trans. T. M. Knox (London: Oxford University Press, 1967), n. 12, p. 299.

19. Ibid., pp. 5–6.

20. See O. Pfleiderer, *The Development of Theology in Germany Since Kant*, trans. J. Frederick Smith (New York: Macmillan Press, 1896); B. Pünjer, *History of the Philosophy of Religion*, trans. W. Harte (Edinburgh, 1887), p. 523.

21. Friedrich Heinrich Jacobi (1743–1819). For a recent detailed study of the development of philosophy in this time period, see Frederick C. Beisler, *The Fate of Reason. German Philosophy from Kant to Fichte* (Cambridge, Mass.: Harvard University Press, 1987).

22. Rudolph Otto, Introduction to Friedrich Schleiermacher's *On Religion. Speeches to Its Cultured Despisers*, trans. John Oman (New York: Harper and Row, 1958), p. vii; hereafter, cited as OR.

23. Ibid., p. 1.

24. Ibid., p. 2.

25. Ibid., p. 14.

26. Ibid., p. 3.

27. As does Hegel's *Phenomenology of Spirit* written eight years after *On Religion*.

28. OR, p. 11.

29. Ibid., p. 13.

30. Ibid.

31. Ibid., p. 27.

32. Ibid., p. 34.

33. Terrence N. Tice, in his excellent article, "Schleiermacher's Conception of Religion: 1799 to 1831," *Archivio di Filosofia*, T11, vols. 1–3 (1984): 334–356, summarizes this point quite nicely: "It is that the whole of human existence found its ground, unity, and goal in that 'fundamental feeling for infinite and vital nature' (*Grundgefühl der unendlichen und lebendigen Natur*) which constitutes religion—or, to put it in another way, in the overall 'perceptive on the universe' (*Anschauung des Univerums*) which is its immediate fundament of religion" (p. 339).

34. Ibid., pp. 38–39.

35. Ibid., p. 36.

36. Ibid.

37. Ibid.

38. Redeker, in *Schleiermacher. Life and Thought*, observed: "To the shock of his contemporaries, Schleiermacher extolled Spinoza as a man of piety because he agreed with Spinoza's rejection of deistic and supernaturalistic interpretations of God" (p. 43). What we are calling Spinoza's *generic monotheism* crystallizes a set of basic and very general precepts about God: (1) God exists (2) God is one (3) God is omnipresent (4) God has supreme dominion over everything (5) loving thy neighbor is equal to worship of God. *Theologico-Political Treatise*, pp. 186–187. As we can see, any sense of personality of subject is absent from Spinoza's conception of God.

39. OR, p. 241.

40. Ibid., pp. 246–247.

41. Paul Tillich, *A History of Christian Thought. A Stenographic Transcription of Lectures Delivered During the Spring Term, 1953*, p. 3. Also published as *A History of Christian Thought* (Philadelphia: Fortress Press, 1968).

42. CF, p. 390.

43. This is the main thesis of Robert Williams in his stimulating study, *Schleiermacher the Theologian. The Construction of the Doctrine of God* (Philadelphia: Fortress Press, 1978).

44. Found on the title page of the first edition.

45. CF, p. 3.

46. Ibid., pp. 3–4.

47. In Chapter Four, we will see how Hegel's philosophy of religion is essentially a *science of Spirit* arising out of theology's *science of faith*, with his distinction

between faith and feeling constituting the essential point of difference between the methodologies of his philosophy of religion and Schleiermacher's dogmatics. The term *science [Wissenschaft]* is used by Hegel and Schleiermacher, and, consequently, by us in its broadest sense, that is, as a systematic body of knowledge. Indeed, neither Hegel nor Schleiermacher equate *science* with the type of "deduction" found in the empirical methods in the natural sciences. See OR, p. 132 and LPR1, 1824, pp. 257–259; VPR1, pp. 165–167.

48. CF, p. 2. Quentin Lauer expressed the same point about the act of defining and its relation to science in his essay "The Phenomenon of Reason," in *Essays in Hegelian Dialectic* (New York: Fordham University Press, 1977): "In the pedagogy of the physical sciences it has become relatively easy in modern times to define, prior to scientific investigation, the particular science with which one is concerned" (p. 18). But Lauer continues to move past Schleiermacher's acknowledgment of this limitation of science by making what is essentially Hegel's point about the scientific character of philosophy: "In regard to philosophy, however, this is not the case. Here, we might say, we cannot be told ahead of time what philosophy is because the very doing of philosophy is a prerequisite for understanding what one is doing, and defining philosophy itself is a philosophical task, in a way in which defining science or mathematics is not a scientific or mathematical task" (p. 18). This ability of philosophy to define itself will become the main point of our discussion of Hegel's philosophy of religion as a 'science of Spirit' with its hermeneutic of 'the witness of the Spirit' in Chapter Four.

49. CF, p. 5.

50. For Schleiermacher, the church is possible only through the prior ethical relationship of the family. Ibid., p. 29.

51. Ibid., p. 3.

52. Ibid., p. 29.

53. This stands in marked contrast with Hegel's concern with *cultus* as that which encompasses both the inner and outer aspects of religion (see Chapter One, n. 73).

54. CF, p. 4. Hegel would agree with this description of the philosophy of religion insofar as it does cover all the various religions in the scope of its description, but not as a history of religion. See his comments on the history of religion, LPR1, 1821, pp. 198–199; VPR1, pp. 107–108.

55. CF, p. 24.

56. Ibid., p. 4.

57. As we have seen, Hegel made a similar point; see the Introduction, n. 31.

58. CF, p. 30.

59. Ibid.

60. Ibid., p. 44.

61. Ibid., p. 33.

62. Ibid., p. 8.

63. Ibid., p. 5.

64. Ibid., p. 8.

65. Ibid.

66. Spinoza, for example, in *Theologico-Political Treatise*, defines *piety* in this manner: "a man is pious or impious in his beliefs only insofar as he is thereby incited to obedience, or derives from them license to sin and rebel" (pp. 180–181).

67. Texts, p. 219.

68. Ibid., p. 220.

69. Ibid., p. 219.

70. Ibid.

71. CF, pp. 6–7.

72. Texts, p. 220.

73. CF, p. 16.

74. Texts, p. 215.

75. Ibid., p. 222.

76. CF, pp. 22–23.

77. Ibid., pp. 23–24.

78. Ibid.

79. Ibid., p. 18.

80. Ibid., p. 26.

81. As we will see in Chapter Four, the 1824 lectures will define religion, not just from the viewpoint of the finite subject but from the viewpoint of absolute spirit. Therefore, Hegel would say, religion is "the self-consciousness of absolute spirit." Indeed, "religion is not the affair of the single human being," in fact, "finite consciousness is a moment of absolute spirit itself. Absolute Spirit is what differentiates and determines itself, i.e., it posits itself as finite consciousness. Consequently it is not from the standpoint of finite consciousness that we consider religion" (LPR1, 1824, pp. 318–319; VPRI, p. 222). We can see that *self* in this sense means the self-knowing of Spirit through the medium of human consciousness. We can therefore see that Schleiermacher's notion of self-consciousness differs from Hegel's

in two significant ways: (1) Schleiermacher's notion of *self* implied in the term *self-consciousness* refers to a single human self; Hegel clearly refers to and includes both God and human consciousness as part of Spirit's "self"; (2) Schleiermacher's notion of *self* also means, as Terence N. Tice puts it: "religion involves an immediate relation to God—or, more broadly stated, to 'the deity.'" As a relatedness of the whole *undivided* self, it is an act of *immediate* self-consciousness ("Schleiermacher's Conception of Religion: 1899 to 1831," p. 351. My emphasis). As we have seen in Chapter One, Hegel depicts the self at this level as *already* divided—"I am the conflict." At the same time, the self knows itself as an unity in and through its thought of God. Therefore, this finite self-consciousness is a *mediated immediate* self-consciousness. (See Chapter One, pp. 24–28. See also Hegel's comments on the relation between immediate and mediated knowledge: LPR1, 1827, p. 173; VPR1, pp. 82–83; LPR1, 1824, p. 305; VPR1, p. 209; LPR1, 1827, pp. 407–413; VPR1, pp. 301–308.) Even though Schleiermacher is also talking of an inner bifurcation of the self, which, at the same time, is an immediate unity, he does not seem to allow that the mediating activity of thought is present, as does Hegel.

82. Ibid., p. 47.

83. Texts, pp. 227–228. For some reason, von der Luft translates *wissenschaftliche* as "systematic" and *systematischen* as "methodical" throughout his translations. Although these renderings do not violate the sense of what Schleiermacher is saying, it would be more appropriate to translate *wissenschaftliche* as "scientific" and *systematischen* as "systematic," in keeping with our understanding of "science"; see this chapter, n. 44.

84. Ibid., p. 228.

85. José Huertas-Jourda, Lectures on *Being and Time*, Winter Term, 1979, Wilfrid Laurier University.

86. CF, p. 67.

87. Texts, p. 238.

88. Ibid.

89. CF, p. 532. Indeed, Schleiermacher said that this mediated knowledge of Christ is an "essential element": "The religious self-consciousness, like every essential element in human nature, *leads necessarily in its development to fellowship or communion*," CF, p. 26. My emphasis. But, this mediated knowledge is in no way a mediated immediate knowledge of God, as Hegel described. (See Chapter One, pp. 24–28, and Chapter Two, n. 81.) On the contrary, for Schleiermacher the individual subject's immediate self-consciousness is *prior* to the mediation involved in fellowship.

90. CF, p. 27.

91. Ibid., p. 68.

Chapter Three. Unveiling Faith and Spirit: Hegel's Criticism of Schleiermacher in the Foreword

1.   *Das nackten Wahrheit Schleier machen,*
            Ist kluger Theologen Amt,
            Und Schleiermacher sind bei so bewandten Sachen,
            Die Meister der Dogmatik insgesamt.

A. W. Schlegel, *Sämmtliche Werke,* ed. E. Böcking (Leipzig, 1846/4), vol. 11, p. 233. Quoted in Karl Barth, *The Theology of Schleiermacher,* ed. Dietrich Ritschl and trans. Geoffrey W. Bromily (Grand Rapids, Mich.: William B. Eerdmans Publishing Co., 1982) p. 186. ("To make veils for the naked truth is the office of shrewd theologians, and all the masters of dogmatics, skilled in these things, are Schleiermachers [veil-makers].") My translation.

2. There are three such references in the 1821 manuscript, *Determinate Religion.* The first reference is to be found in the *"Cultus.* The Religion of Sublimity" [Judaism]: "God's people is the one that he has accepted that they shall fear him, and have the basic *feeling of their dependence,* i.e., of their servitude" LPR11, 1821, p. 158; VPR11, p. 64. My emphasis. The second reference is in the section, "The Religion of Expediency or Understanding [Roman religion]. c. The More Specific Nature of These Powers and Deities in General": "Human self-seeking <(α) is inwardly determined, human beings in their particularity being infinite purpose for themselves; (β)> has *the feeling of its dependence,* precisely because it is finite, and this feeling is peculiar to it" LPR11, p. 209; VPR11, p. 115. The third and last reference comes later in the same section: "in the limitation or shortcoming consisting of the fact that this mode of being lies within the power of an other, in the negative of this positive being, therein lies *dependence*—and therein they *feel* it" p. 218; VPR11, p. 123. As well, Hegel alludes to *The Christian Faith* in the 1821 *Consummate Religion:* first, in relation to the attributes of God, LPR111, 1821, p. 75; VPR111, p. 14; second, in relation to the doctrine of the Trinity, LPR111, pp. 80–81; VPR111, p. 19; third, in relation to the feeling of dependence as "dependence on nature," LPR111, pp. 93–94; VPR111, pp. 30–31; and, last, in relation to the feeling of dependence as denying "the genuine objectivity of truth," LPR111, pp. 156–157; VPR111, p. 92. All these points will be taken up in the 1824 lectures.

3. In *Hegel, Hinrichs and Schleiermacher: On Feeling and Reason in Religion,* trans. von der Luft, there is a German critical edition of Hegel's Foreword. Because von der Luft's translation of the Foreword is based on this critical edition, I will simply refer to the pagination of the German right after the English text. For example, this quotation is referenced as: Texts, p. 260; p. 509. I think Hegel is being unfair to Schleiermacher in the extremely negative tone of this criticism. If we set aside questions of method, it is clear that Hegel and Schleiermacher agree on the fundament of religious consciousness; that is, that religious consciousness is marked, from its inception, by an inner splitting of human consciousness and, at the same time, by a sense of unity (of self with God and of self with self). However, Hegel's disagreement with Schleiermacher on any other fundamental aspects of the

religious relationship (e.g., the *place of thinking* in this fundamental religious relationship and the significance of this location for the objectivity of knowledge of God), is well taken and *does* have serious implications for the relation of philosophy to religion.

4. See, for example, Richard E. Brandt, *The Philosophy of Schleiermacher* (New York: Greenwood Press, 1968), p. 325; Richard Crouter, "Hegel and Schleiermacher at Berlin," p. 36; John E. Toews, *Hegelianism*, p. 63.

5. It is possible to construe Hegel's criticism of Schleiermacher as due to Hegel's supposed "reactionary," "right wing" tendencies. Among those who portray Hegel in this light, are Karl Popper, *The Open Society and Its Enemies* (Princeton, N.J.: Princeton University Press, 1950), and Rudolph Haym, *Hegel und seine Zeit* (Berlin, 1857; reprinted at Hildesheim, 1962). For those who would defend Hegel against such charges, see *Hegel's Political Philosophy*, ed. Walter Kaufman (New York: Atherton, 1970); Schlomo Avineri, *Hegel's Theory of the Modern State* (Cambridge: Cambridge University Press, 1972); and Jacques d'Hondt, *Hegel en son temps.* (Berlin, 1818–1831) (Paris: Editions Sociales Series: Problèmes), 1968, recently translated by John Burbridge as *Hegel in His Time (Berlin 1818–1831)* (Peterborough, Ontario: Broadview Press, 1988). D'Hondt aptly demonstrates that interpreting Hegel as would Popper is simply not in keeping with the facts of Hegel's life.

6. Texts, p. 262; p. 513.

7. *Platons Werke*, trans. F. Schleiermacher (Berlin, 1817–1828). Introduction translated into English by W. Dobson (Cambridge, 1836).

8. Texts, p. 267; pp. 518–519.

9. CF, p. 88.

10. See the Introduction, pp. 4–6.

11. Brandt, *The Philosophy of Schleiermacher*, p. 323.

12. "Tübingen Fragment (1793)," trans. H. S. Harris, in *Hegel's Development. Toward the Sunlight* (Oxford: Oxford University Press, 1972), pp. 511–512.

13. Hegel reiterates this point in 1824, but in relation to truth: "only when the thought is true are one's feelings truthful too" LPR11, 1824, p. 263; VPR11, p. 168. This phrase captures Hegel's main thesis against Schleiermacher.

14. Texts, p. 245; p. 490.

15. Ibid. pp. 490–491.

16. Ibid. p. 491. Although von der Luft consistently translates *Glaube* as "belief," we will transcribe it as "faith" when Hegel is referring to "subjective feeling" and "objective content" together as one "undifferentiated unity." We will use the word *belief* as the translation of *Glaube* when Hegel is referring to the subjective side only.

17. Merold Westphal, Introduction to "Reason and Religious Truth: Hegel's Foreword to H. W. Hinrichs's *Die Religion im inneren Verhältnisse zur Wissenschaft* (1822)," trans. A. V. Miller, in *Beyond Epistemology: New Studies in the Philosophy of Hegel* (The Hague: Martinus Nijhoff, 1974), p. 223.

18. In this, Hegel is very close to Aristotle's thinking insofar as Aristotle said that God is "pure form" and "pure form" means that "thought thinks itself as object in virtue of its participation in what is thought." Thus, as pure form, God "thinks itself...and its thinking is a thinking of thinking...throughout all eternity" (*Metaphysics*, 1072b 19). This similarity has implications for Hegel's philosophy in general and its claims to absolute knowledge. As Errol E. Harris observed in *An Interpretation of the Logic of Hegel* (New York: University Press of America, 1983): "Nor is Hegel's professed knowledge of the Absolute anything exorbitant or inordinately presumptuous. So the highest claim that he made, both here and at the end of the *Geistesphilosophie*, is no more than that made by Aristotle in the *Metaphysics*, whom Hegel explicitly quotes. It is the assurance that God, the infinite and absolute being, is the pure form of the world, pure activity, the realization of all that, in the world and in us, is merely potential—He is absolute self-knowledge" (p. 288). For an interpretation of Hegel as continuing Aristotle's philosophy, see W. T. Stace, *The Philosophy of Hegel. A Systematic Exposition* (Toronto: Dover Publication, 1955), pp. 18–31. For an interpretation of Hegel as continuing Platonic philosophy, see John N. Findlay, "Hegelianism and Platonism" in *Hegel and the History of Philosophy*, ed. Joseph O'Malley, K. W. Algozin, and Frederick G. Weiss (The Hague: Martinus Nijhoff, 1974): "Socrates is seen by Hegel as a world-historical thinker who first brought conscious subjectivity to its own notice. The pre-Socratics thought deeply, but never thought of their thoughts as thoughts, the Sophists thought of thoughts as thoughts, but only as belonging to the arbitrary variable subjectivity of the individual—Hegel again gets his conceptions from Plato" (p. 63). There are, of course, many ways to approach and interpret Hegel, all of which shed light on nuances in Hegel's thinking. Although we are concerned with the intersection of theology and philosophy in Hegel's philosophy of religion and have used twentieth-century phenomenology as our entry point, we essentially agree with W. T. Stace when he wrote (somewhat melodramatically): "The philosophy of Hegel...is not something simply invented out of nothing by himself and flung at random into an astonished world....The true author of it is, not so much Hegel, as the toiling and thinking human spirit, the universal spirit of humanity getting itself uttered through this individual. It has its roots deep in the past. It is the accumulated wisdom of the years, the last phase of the one 'universal philosophy.'...It recognizes all past truth, absorbs it into itself, *and advances*" (p. 31).

19. Texts, p. 245; p. 491. Translation amended.

20. LPR1, 1824, p. 130; VPR1, p. 46.

21. Texts, p. 249; p. 498.

22. Ibid., p. 264; p. 513.

23. Ibid., pp. 266–267; pp. 517–518.

24. Ibid., p. 248; p. 495.

25. Ibid., p. 246; pp. 491–492. Translation amended.

26. Ibid.; p. 492.

27. Ibid.; p. 493.

28. Ibid.

29. Ibid., pp. 246–247; p. 493.

30. Ibid., p. 247; pp. 493–494.

31. Kierkegaard provided an excellent description of the 'pathos of approximation' that can take place both in the acceptance of objective content and in subjective appropriation of this content in "Conclusion," *Concluding Unscientific Postscript,* pp. 537–544.

32. By implication, Hegel's criticism was also applicable to Schleiermacher, *but only* to the extent that Schleiermacher covered over the centrality of thinking in all the levels of religious consciousness. Other than this—extremely crucial *flaw,* according to Hegel—Schleiermacher also sidesteps the "pathos of approximation."

33. Texts, p. 247; p. 494.

34. Ibid.

35. Ibid.; p. 495.

36. Ibid., p. 248; p. 496.

37. Ibid.

38. LPR1, 1824, p. 363; VPR1, p. 263.

39. Martin Luther, *Works*, p. 9.

40. Ibid., p. 10.

41. Ibid., vol. 1, p. 22.

42. Ibid., vol. 22, pp. 19–20.

43. Ibid., p. 8.

44. Merold Westphal, *Kierkegaard's Critique of Reason and Society* (Macon, Ga: Mercer University Press, 1987), pp. 107–108.

45. Martin Luther, *Works*, vol. 22, p. 9.

46. Ibid., p. 17.

47. Ibid., vol. 26, p. 29.

48. Ibid., vol. 22, p. 8.

49. Ibid.

50. Ibid., vol. 26, p. 64.

51. Martin Chemnitz (1522–1586): 'If Martin [Chemnitz] had not come, Martin [Luther] would hardly have stood,' a seventeenth-century adage, from "Translator's Preface" to Chemnitz, *On The Two Natures of Christ*, trans. Jacob O. Preus (St. Louis: Concordia Publishing House, 1971), p. 9.

52. Ibid., pp. 267–285.

53. Ibid., pp. 105–106.

54. Since Jesus asked, "Who do men say that I am?" (St. Matthew 16:13), a variegated series of responses has made up the history of Christian doctrine and heresy. As early as Tertullian, the formula *una substantia, tres personae* was used to explain this synonymity of Christ and God. This formulation was accepted by the Church Fathers in the Council of Nicea (325) and, at Chalcedon (451), in a logic peculiar to Christianity, proclaimed that Jesus Christ is not only the second person of the Trinity, but, also, the unity of divine and human natures in the form of a single person. The Church Fathers defined the personality of Christ in this way: "Therefore, following the holy fathers, we all with one accord teach men to acknowledge one and the same Son, our Lord Jesus Christ, at once complete in Godhead and complete in manhood, truly God and truly man, consisting also of a reasonable soul and body; of one substance with the Father as regards his Godhead, and at the same time of one substance with us as regards his manhood; like us in all respects, apart from sin; as regards his Godhead, begotten, for us men and for our salvation, of Mary the Virgin, the God-bearer; one and the same Christ, Son, Lord, Only-begotten, recognized in two natures, without confusion, without change, without division, without separation; the distinction of natures being in no way annulled by the union, but rather the characteristics of each nature being preserved and coming together to form one person and subsistence, not as parted or separated in two persons, but one and the same Son and Only-begotten God the Word, Lord Jesus Christ; even as the prophets from earlier times spoke of him, and our Lord Jesus Christ himself taught us, and the creed of the Fathers has handed down to us," quoted in Walter Ritter, *Class Manual for Early Church Fathers and Councils* (Camrose, Alta.: Camrose Lutheran College, 1988), p. 5.

55. Chemnitz, *Two Natures*, p. 107: "Christ...consists of two complete, perfect and intact natures, the divine and the human. Therefore, because of this difference they speak of the hypostatic union of Christ."

56. Martin Luther, *The Bondage of the Will* (Grand Rapids, Mich.: Baker Book House, 1976), p. 69. Hegel, however, mentioned 'God himself is dead' coming from a Lutheran hymn (LPR111, 1827, p. 326; VPR111, p. 249). Indeed, it is to be found in the passion hymn, *"O Traurigkeit, O Herzeleid"* by Johannes Rist (1607–1667) in *Wuerzburger Gesangbuch*, 1628. The English translation, "O Darkest Woe," can be found in *The Lutheran Hymnal*, trans. Catharine Winkworth

(1863) (St. Louis: Concordia Publishing House, 1941). This dirgelike hymn is still sung on Good Friday.

57. Martin Luther, *Large Catechism*, trans. Robert H. Fischer (Philadelphia: Muhlenberg Press, 1959), 2.3.65.

58. Hugh T. Kerr, ed., *A Compendium of Luther's Theology* (Philadelphia: Westminster Press, 1956), p. 4.

59. Luther spoke of three forms of reason: "natural reason, ruling within its own domain (the Earthly Kingdom); presumptuous reason, encroaching on the domain of faith; and regenerate reason, serving faith in subjection to the Word of God." *The Encyclopedia of Philosophy* (New York: Macmillan Publishing Co., 1972), vols. 5 and 6, p. 111.

60. Luther, *Works*, vol. 1, p. 13.

61. Ibid., vol. 51, pp. 243–244.

62. G. W. F. Hegel. *Introduction to the Lectures on the History of Philosophy*, trans. T. M. Knox and A. V. Miller (Oxford: Clarendon Press, 1985), p. 133.

63. Letters, p. 531; *Briefe*, Letter 572–574.

64. Letters, p. 532.

65. Letters, p. 520; *Briefe*, Letter 514a. We will have reason to return to this letter in Chapter Five.

66. Lou-Andreas Salomé, *Nietzsche* (Redding Ridge, Conn.: Black Swans Books, 1988), p. 3.

67. LPR111, 'W(1831),' p. 346; VPR111, p. 268.

68. Ibid.

69. LPR111, 'W(1831),' p. 337; VPR111, 'W(1831),' p. 260.

70. G. W. F. Hegel. *Philosophy of History*, trans. J. Sibree (New York: Dover Publications, 1956), p. 415; idem, *Vorlesungen über die Philosophie der Weltsgeschichte*. vol. 4 *Die Germanische Welt*, ed. Georg Lasson (Leipzig: Felix Meiner, 1944), p. 880. Hereafter, the English translation will be cited as PH and the German edition as VPW.

71. PH, p. 415; VPW, p. 878.

72. G. W. F. Hegel, *Hegel's Lectures on the History of Philosophy*, vol. 3, trans. E. S. Haldane and F. H. Simpson (New York: Humanities Press, 1963), p. 149. Hereafter cited as LHP111. Except for *Einleitung in die Geschichte der Philosophie*, ed. J. Hoffmeister (Hamburg: Felix Meiner, 1959), there is no critical edition of these lectures.

73. PH, p. 416; VPW, p. 880.

74. PH, p. 415; VPW, p. 880.

75. LHP111, p. 150.

76. Ibid., p. 149. For Hegel, the Lutheran practice of communion in terms of consubstantiation displays the reconciliation of human being and God more effectively than other denominational renditions. Indeed, the doctrine of *communicatio idiomatum* was devised to ground consubstantiation. In comparison to the one-sided Catholic emphasis on the veneration of the external features of communion (i.e., transubstantiation) and the Reformed emphasis on the psychological side of communion, Lutheranism "regards the host [as actual] only in faith and the partaking. This [is] its consecration in the faith and the spirit of each individual" LPR111, 1821, p. 155; VPR111, p. 91. (See also LPR111, 1824, p. 236; VPR111, p. 166; LPR111, 1827, p. 338; VPR111, pp. 260–261.) Over and against the Catholic and Reformed, Hegel depicts the Lutheran form of communion as putting into practice the sublation of external substance into internal, spiritual substance, an important point for Hegel's own realization that "subject is substance" in the *Phenomenology*. Basically, in Lutheranism, this transfiguration can take place in faith only in what Hegel designates as the *mystical element* of Lutheranism, the individual perceives the wine and wafer as *both* the blood and body of Christ *and* as empirical objects. We will discuss Hegel's relation to the "mystical" in Chapter Four. But, what is important for our present concern, we can see how the whole contents of the entire world are subjectified by the subject in faith.

77. For this and what follows, see HP, p. 412–418; VPW, pp. 877–884.

78. But, Hegel definitely did not agree with Luther on this point. For Hegel, "philosophy goes out not from the Bible; so too faith, it also does not go out from the Bible but goes to the Bible in which it grasps its truth" G. W. F. Hegel, "*Über: 'Aphorismen über Nichtwissen und Absolutes Wissen im Verhältnisse zur christlichen Glaubenserkenntnis*,'" in *Sämtliche Werke*, vol. 20, ed. Herman Glockner (Stuttgart: Fromman, 1968), p. 310. My translation. Thus, as we will detail in Chapter Four, this means that Hegel found no need to limit his use of the witness of Spirit to the hermeneutics of reading a text like the Bible.

79. Carl E. Braaten, *Principles of Lutheran Theology*, p. 10.

80. Ibid., p. 93. See also Werner Elert, *The Structure of Lutheranism*, trans. Walter A. Hansen (St. Louis: Concordia Publishing House, 1962), pp. 441–447.

81. In the *Theologico-Political Treatise*, Spinoza formulated a method of interpreting the Bible on the basis of "reason only" (p. 98). Simply stated, he said that Scripture should be interpreted by Scripture thus necessitating comparison of passages that further necessitates inquiry into their history, their authors, the language, background of the author, and so on. See Chapter 7 "Of the Interpretation of Scripture."

82. Edward Schillebeeckx, *Jesus. An Experiment in Christology* (New York: The Seabury Press, 1979), p. 665.

83. LPR111, 1827, pp. 285–286; VPR111, p. 211. Dale M. Schlitt, in his

splendid *Hegel's Trinitarian Claim. A Critical Reflection* (Leiden: E. J. Brill, 1984), noted: "His [Hegel's] understanding of personhood and its concretization in Person could, where used in Hegel's reconstructed sense of self-donation or becoming, further gather together in one the various affirmations concerning totality, triadicity, method, and identity of form and content....Though Person in its later actualization beyond logic for Hegel tends to be a richer notion than Subject, what is of concern here is the underlying structure common to subjectivity and to personhood, that of inclusive subjectivity. Both personhood and subjectivity are structurally a movement of 'going over into' (*Übergehen*) or 'giving to' (*Hingabe*), a realizing of the Self in the other" (p. 43). Schlitt's main thesis is that, for Hegel, inclusive subjectivity is Spirit, that is, it is "triadically structured inclusive context" (p. 275). Our use of the term *inclusive subjectivity* derives from Schlitt's discussion.

84. LPR111, 1821, p. 140; VPR111, pp. 75–76.

85. Martin Luther, *Selected Political Writings*, ed. J. M. Porter (Philadelphia: Fortress Press, 1974), p. 41.

86. LPR111, 1821, p. 138; VPR111, p. 74.

87. LPR111, p. 139; VPR111, p. 74.

88. LPR1, 1821, p. 189; VPR1, p. 98. Translation amended. Note the similarity between this description and Hegel's discussion of 'subject as substance' in the Preface to the *Phenomenology*.

89. LPR111, 1821, p. 140; VPR111, p. 76. Translation amended.

90. We borrow the term *science of faith* from Martin Heidegger's "Phenomenology and Theology" in *The Piety of Thinking* (Bloomington: Indiana University Press, 1976), pp. 5–21. Of course, *theology,* in terms of its etymology, means the knowledge or science of God. But, with the insight gained from Hegel's discussion of faith, faith, as the unity of subjective feeling and objective doctrine, is the essential constitutive element of what it means to be a Christian. Thus, "that which is primarily revealed to faith and only to it, and which, as revelation, first gives rise to faith, is Christ, the crucified God....One 'knows' about this fact only *by believing*." (Heidegger, Ibid., p. 9.) Because this understanding *arises out of faith for faith,* the faithfilled subject can thematize into a body of knowledge what is already within faith as revealed to faith. In this sense, theology is the objectification and, hence, science or knowledge of faith insofar as it also is an ingredient of faith. As such, this self-enclosed body of knowledge does not require any input from thinking not grounded in faith. This is also Stephen N. Dunning's argument in *The Tongues of Men. Hegel and Hamann on Religious Language and History* (Missoula, Mont.: Scholars Press, 1979): "My argument...is that biblical language cannot be successfully secularized if it is to retain its religious value and meaning for Christian faith" (p. 29). Although Dunning would disagree, this is Hegel's point inasmuch as his "science of Spirit" is the consummation of the science of faith.

91. LHP111, pp. 150–151.

92. Ibid., p. 151.

93. Ibid., p. 152.

94. LPR1, 1821, pp. 192–193; VPR1, p. 101. For other discussions of Hegel and Luther, see Merold Westphal's "Hegel and the Reformation" in *History and System: Hegel's Philosophy of History*, ed. Robert L. Perkins (Albany: State University of New York Press, 1984); Robert Pattman, "Commitments to Time in Reformation Protestant Theology, Hegelian Idealism, and Marxism," in *Hegel Today*, ed. Bernard Cullen (Brookfield, Vt.: Gower Publishing Company, 1988).

95. LHP111, p. 153.

96. Ibid.

97. LPR111, 1821, p. 157; VPR111, p. 92.

98. LPR1, 1824, pp. 341–342; VPR1, pp. 241–242.

99. LPR1, 1821, p. 245; VPR1, p. 154.

100. James Yerkes, *The Christology of Hegel* (Albany: State University of New York Press, 1983), p. 207. Yerkes did an admirable job of showing how this christological understanding runs through Hegel's philosophy. However, we must note that in this passage, Yerkes's use of the term *normed* should be understood only in a historical sense, that is, inasmuch as Luther's theology and Christianity in general preceded Hegel's philosophy of religion by a number of centuries, we can say that the 'Christian fact' 'normed' Hegel's philosophy of religion. But, we also must remember that in our discussion of Hegel's philosophical confirmation of Luther's theology we saw that philosophy is not beholden to any other way of thinking in its determination of truth and, technically then, is *normed* only by itself. However, as we also observed, philosophy, in its autonomy, does confirm the truth of the Incarnation as the revelation of the overcoming of the opposition between God and humankind. Therefore, Hegel has no problem with employing the Christian confession of the event of Jesus as the Christ as a way of conveying (in representational language) what is known conceptually by philosophy.

101. Indeed, Karl Barth wondered in *Protestant Theology in the Nineteenth Century*, "Why did Hegel not become for the Protestant world something similar to what Thomas Aquinas was for Roman Catholicism?", p. 384.

Chapter Four. Philosophy, Theology, and the Introduction to the 1824 Philosophy of Religion

1. LPR1, 1824, p. 318; VPR1, p. 222. As we noted in Chapter Two, this is the definition of the concept of religion in 1824.

2. LPR1, p. 113; VPR1, p. 31.

3. LPR1, pp. 114–115; VPR1, pp. 32–33.

222 PHILOSOPHY, THEOLOGY, AND HEGEL'S BERLIN PHILOSOPHY OF RELIGION

4. LPR1, p. 116; VPR1, p. 33. Translation amended.

5. Ibid.

6. Ibid.

7. LPR1, p. 119; VPR1, p. 35. Translation amended.

8. LPR1, p. 121; VPR1, p. 38. Translation amended.

9. LPR1, pp. 121–122; VPR1, p. 38. Translation amended.

10. LPR1, p. 122; VPR1, p. 38.

11. Texts, p. 265, p. 515. Translation amended.

12. Ibid., p. 266, p. 516.

13. LPR1, 1824, p. 122; VPR1, p. 39. My emphasis.

14. See pp. 104–106.

15. LPR1, 1824, p. 122; VPR1, p. 39.

16. Ibid.

17. LPR1, pp. 122–123; VPR1, p. 39.

18. Ibid.

19. LPR1, p. 123; VPR1, p. 40.

20. LPR1, p. 123; VPR1, p. 39.

21. An excellent example of the new hermeneutics is Spinoza's *Theologico-Political Treatise*. Like Luther, Spinoza used 'Scripture to interpret Scripture', but contradiction between passages in the Bible requires inquiry into the seams of the text: the author, his history, language, education, etc., the history of the book itself, who has owned it, tampered with it, authorized it, etc. (See Chapter Seven, "Of the Interpretation of Scripture.")

22. LPR1, p. 124, VPR1, pp. 40–41.

23. LPR1, pp. 125–126; VPR1, p. 42. Translation amended.

24. LPR1, p. 126; VPR1, p. 42.

25. Ibid.

26. John N. Findlay suggested that Hegel thought that such study of a text is also unphilosophical: "Hegel, however, thinks it better that we should be largely dissatisfied with Plato's writings, than that we should read into them too close an approximation to contemporary truth, and he also deprecates the text of the Dialogues, to the exclusion of any attempt to fathom their deeper drift, which was at the time starting its sinister career in the researches of Hegel's Berlin colleague, Schleiermacher." J. N. Findlay, "Hegelianism and Platonism," pp. 64–65.

27. LPR1, p. 128; VPR1, p. 44.

28. Ibid.

29. Texts, p. 247, p. 494.

30. LPR1, 1824, pp. 126–127; VPR1, p. 43.

31. LPR1, p. 129; VPR1, p. 45.

32. Ibid.

33. LPR1, p. 130; VPR1, p. 46.

34. Ibid.

35. Ibid.

36. Ibid.

37. LPR1, p. 139; VPR1, p. 53.

38. Ibid.

39. LPR1, p. 139; VPR1, p. 54.

40. Hegel also added a long section on faith and its relation to the *cultus* that made the same points as the Foreword's discussion of faith.

41. LPR1, p. 140; VPR1, p. 54.

42. For example, Peter Hodgson, main editor of the English critical edition of LPR, suggested that Hegel "never properly understood what Schleiermacher meant by the feeling of absolute dependence" (LPR1, 1824, p. 444). See my comments on the 'fairness' of Hegel's criticism of Schleiermacher, Chapter Three, n. 3.

43. LPR1, 1821, p. 260; VPR1, p. 167.

44. LPR1, p. 263; VPR1, p. 170.

45. Ibid.

46. LPR1, p. 260; VPR1, p. 167.

47. See pp. 25–28 for our discussion of the primordial religious relationship.

48. For example, the centrality of the conversion experience is already in St. Paul's "Road to Damascus" experience (Acts 9:1–20). See also Saint Augustine, *Confessions*, trans. R. S. Pine-Coffin (New York: Penguin Books, 1961), pp. 177–178. And, as we detailed in Chapter Three, 'heart knowledge' undergirds much of Luther's theology.

49. CF, p. 747.

50. Ibid., p. 749. My emphasis. An expositor of Schleiermacher, Robert

224 • PHILOSOPHY, THEOLOGY, AND HEGEL'S BERLIN PHILOSOPHY OF RELIGION

Williams, tried to show that the Trinity is still 'of central importance' for Schleiermacher. But Williams heavily qualified this claim in terms of Schleiermacher's treatment of the Trinity in *The Christian Faith*. Williams admitted that this account of the Trinity is "problematic," "incomplete," and "fragmentary." See Robert Williams, *Schleiermacher the Theologian*, Chapter Six.

51. CF, p. 476.

52. Ibid., p. 388.

53. Ibid., p. 387.

54. Ibid., p. 395. Schleiermacher treats the *communicatio idiomatum* directly on pp. 411–412.

55. Ibid., p. 379.

56. Ibid., p. 476. Schleiermacher used the word *Urbild* when referring to Christ. This could be translated as "prototype" as well as "archetype." In this conception, Schleiermacher followed Spinoza who located as engaging in an ideal 'mind-to-mind' relation with God (*Theologico-Political Treatise*, pp. 18–19), and Kant, who directly called Christ an *archetype* [*Urbild*] (*Religion within the Limits of Reason Alone*, trans. T. M. Greene and H. Hudson [New York: Harper, 1960], pp. 54–55). But, Schleiermacher's christology 'improved' on Spinoza's and Kant's by treating this archetype ontologically—that is, for Schleiermacher, the 'archetype of humanity' became concretized in the living human being, Jesus Christ. Moreover, Schleiermacher proceeded to discuss this concrete archetype in terms of self-consciousness and the facticity of lived experience. (See his *The Life of Jesus*, trans. S. Maclean Gilmour [Philadelphia: Fortress Press, 1975], which describes its explication of Jesus in these aforementioned terms: "*The task is to grasp what is inward in the man with such certainty that it can be said: I can say with a measure of assurance how what is outward with respect to the man would have been if what affected him and also what he affected had been different than was actually the case*, for only then do I have an actual knowledge of what is inward in him" [p. 8].) Therefore, the inward (self-consciousness) and the outward (the facticity of his life) are the two sides to grasping his ontological nature. In other words, Jesus, as human archetype, must be understood as an existing, historical individual whose own feeling of dependency was so constituted as to permit us to see his religious self-consciousness as a model for our own.

57. For Hegel's discussion of the history of the development of the doctrine of Trinity, see LPR111, 1821, pp. 79–81; VPR111, p. 18–19; LPR1, pp. 193–194; VPR111, pp. 126–128; LPR1, pp. 286–288; VPR111, pp. 211–214.

58. LPR1, 1824, pp. 346–347; VPR1, p. 247.

59. Meister Eckhardt (1260–1327), German mystic.

60. LPR1, pp. 347–348; VPR1, p. 248.

61. Meister Eckhardt, *Meister Eckhardt. Mystic and Philosopher*, trans. Reiner

Schürman (Bloomington: Indiana University Press, 1978): "God made us know himself, and he made us know himself by his act of knowing, and his being is his knowledge. For him to make me know and for me to know are one and the same thing. Hence his knowledge is mine, quite as it is one and the same in the master who teaches and in the disciple who is taught. Since his knowledge is mine, and since his substance is his knowledge, his nature, and his being, it follows that his being, his substance, and his nature are mine....Since, then, it is of the nature of God not to be like anyone, we are compelled to conclude that we are nothing so that we may be transported into the identical being of himself" (pp. 133–134). For a thorough description of Eckhardt's thinking, see Rudolph Otto, *Mysticism East and West* (New York: Macmillan, 1932).

62. Jacob Boehme (1575–1624), German mystic. For Hegel's full treatment of Boehme's thought, see *Hegel's Lectures on the History of Philosophy*, pp. 188–216. For an account of the influence of German mystical thinking on Hegel, Schelling, Fichte, and von Baader, see Ernst Benz, *The Mystical Sources of German Romantic Philosophy*, trans. Blair R. Reynolds and Eunice M. Paul (Allison Park, Pa.: Pickwick Publications, 1983).

63. LHP111, p. 193.

64. G. W. F. Hegel, *Hegel: The Letters*, pp. 573–574; G. W. F. Hegel, *Briefe von und an Hegel*, ed. J. Hoffmeister, vol. 4 in two parts [1977, 1981] ed. Friedhelm Nicolin, letter 192. Nevertheless, Boehme's thinking is thoroughly speculative inasmuch as "his only thought...is that of perceiving the holy Trinity in everything" (LHP111, p. 196).

65. Hegel, *Letters*, p. 572; *Briefe*, letter 466a.

66. Texts, p. 266; p. 517. "Plato and Aristotle teach that *God* is *not jealous*, and that He does not withhold the cognition of Himself and of truth from human beings. It would be nothing other than *jealousy* if God denied the knowledge of God to consciousness; by so doing God would have denied all truth to consciousness, for God alone is what is true; whatever else is true and appears to be something without divine content is true only insofar as it is grounded in God and is cognized through God; all the rest is temporal appearance. The cognition of God and of truth is the only thing that raises man up above the beasts, sets man apart, made man happy, or rather, according to Plato and Aristotle, as well as Christian doctrine—made man blessed." Also, LPR1, 1827, pp. 382–383; VPR1, p. 279: "When the name of God is taken seriously, it is already the case for Plato and Aristotle that God is not jealous to the point of not communicating himself. Among the Athenians the death penalty was exacted if one did not allow another person to light his lamp from one's own, for one lost nothing by doing so. In the same way God loses nothing when he communicates himself." Indeed, both Plato and Aristotle had "traces of the Trinity" (LPR111, 1824, p. 193; VPR, 1824, p. 127.) in their thinking.

67. Hegel also credited Boehme with realizing the "Protestant principle" of subjectivity: "The matter of Jacob Boehme's philosophy is genuinely German; for

what marks him out and made him noteworthy is the Protestant principle already mentioned of placing the intellectual world within one's own mind and heart, and of experiencing and knowing and feeling in one's own self-consciousness all that formerly was conceived as a Beyond" (LHP111, p. 191).

68. Boehme also did not formally objectify subjectivity. Rather, for Hegel, the first inkling of this mode of thinking arises with Descartes, see LHP111, pp. 220–252.

69. Martin Luther, *Works*, vol. 26, p. 36.

70. LPR111, 1824, p. 165; VPR111, p. 100. It is important for us to note that Hegel is employing two terms, *Objekt* and *Gegenstand* in this section (LPR111, pp. 165–170; VPR111, pp. 101–105), both of which are translated as "object" in the English critical edition. *Objekt*, as this passage suggested, is the *end* or *goal* in which religion attains ('fulfills') its *purpose*, which, as we know, is the totality of the self-consciousness of absolute spirit. *Gegenstand* literally means "stands against" and, as we will see in the next quotation, refers to any thing that is understood as *external to* the subject, although the subject's attention is directed to it.

71. LPR111, pp. 165–166; VPR111, p. 101.

72. LPR111, p. 166; VPR111, p. 102. F. Schleiermacher, CF, p. 194: "All attributes which we ascribe to God are to be taken as denoting not something in God, but only something special in the manner in which the feeling of absolute dependence is to be related to Him."

73. LPR111, p. 166; VPR111, p. 101.

74. LPR111, p. 166; VPR111, p. 101. Translation amended.

75. Ibid.

76. LPR111, p. 167; VPR111, p. 103. Translation amended.

77. LPR111, pp. 170–171; VPR111, p. 106.

78. LPR111, 'W(1831)', p. 250; VPR111, 'W(1831)', p. 178.

79. LPR1, 1824, p. 131, 'W₁'; VPR1, 'W₁', p. 47.

80. Ibid.

81. LPR1, p. 128; VPR1, pp. 44–45.

82. LPR1, p. 132; VPR1, p. 48.

83. LPR111, 1824, pp. 171–172; VPR111, p. 107.

84. LPR111, p. 172; VPR111, p. 107.

85. LPR1, 1824, p. 132, 'G,Ho'; VPR1, 'G,Ho', p. 48.

86. LPR111, 1824, p. 233, 'G with D; W₂'; VPR111, p. 163.

Chapter Five. The Conflict with Pietism and
Hegel's Subjectification of Theological Reflection

1. Schleiermacher was brought up in the Pietist environment of Herrn-hutism. Herrnhutism "was based on the Augsburg Confession" and stressed "the emotional *experience* of Christ's suffering." (Bengt Hägglund, *History of Theology*, trans. Gene J. Lund [St. Louis: Concordia Publishing House, 1968], pp. 332–333.) Schleiermacher broke with Herrnhutism at the age of 19. Hägglund also remarked: "The difference between him [Hegel] and Schleiermacher can be accounted for in part on the basis of their diverse religious backgrounds: for whereas the latter came out of the Herrnhut milieu, Hegel was brought up in an 'old Protestant' environment in Swabia" (p. 360). For an exhaustive study of Hegel's "old Protestant" environment, see Lawrence Dickey, *Hegel. Religion, Economics, and the Politics of Spirit, 1770–1807* (Cambridge: Cambridge University Press, 1987).

2. B. A. Gerrish, "The Secret Religion of Germany: Christian Piety and the Pantheism Controversy," *Journal of Religion* 67, no. 4 (October 1987): 454.

3. Thomas M. Greene and John R. Silber, Introduction to Immanuel Kant's *Religion Within the Limits of Reason Alone*, p. xiii.

4. Albrecht Ritschl, "Prolegomena To *The History of Pietism*," in *Three Essays*, trans. Philip Hefner (Philadelphia: Fortress Press, 1972), p. 55. This essay is perhaps the best introduction to Pietism. Ritschl's *Geschichte des Pietismus*, 3 vols (Bonn, 1880–1886) is the first extensive study of Pietism in both the Lutheran and Reformed Churches.

5. Otto W. Heick, *A History of Christian Thought*, pp. 23–24.

6. Hägglund, *History of Theology*, pp. 329–331.

7. G. W. F. Hegel, *Letters*, pp. 517–518. These charges were made in Tholuck's *Die Lehre von der Sünde und vom Versöhner; oder, Die wahre Weihe des Zweiflers.*, 2d ed. (Hamburg, 1825).

8. Letters, p. 518.

9. LPR1, 1827, p. 157, n. 17.

10. Heick, *A History of Christian Thought*, p. 128.

11. G. Maier, *The End of the Historico-Critical Method* (St. Louis: Concordia Publishing Co., 1974), p. 8.

12. Ritschl, *Three Essays*, p. 54.

13. Karl Barth, *Protestant Theology in the Nineteenth Century*, p. 510.

14. G. W. F. Hegel, *Letters*, pp. 520–521; *Briefe*, letter 514a.

15. Colin Brown, in *Jesus in European Protestant Thought, 1778–1860*

(Durham, N.C.: Labyrinth Press, 1985), observed that Tholuck's "chief theological significance lay in his influence as a check to rationalism and his summons to personal commitment and holiness" (p. 241).

16. Karl Barth, *Protestant Theology in the Nineteenth Century*, p. 511. Indeed, Barth further noted that Tholuck's writing's are not "about religion but... *from* religion" (ibid.).

17. LPR1, 1827, p. 375; VPR1, p. 273.

18. LPR111, 1827, p. 315, 'W$_2$'; VPR111, p. 237, 'W$_2$': "In Hindu pantheism a countless number of incarnations occur; it is only a mask that substance adopts and exchanges in contingent fashion." For similar remarks, see also LPR1, 1827, pp. 375–376; VPR1, pp. 273–274; LPR11, 1831, pp. 727–729; VPR11, pp. 617–618.

19. LPR1, 1827, p. 376; VPR1, p. 274.

20. LPR1, pp. 376–377; VPR1, p. 274.

21. In *Ueber die Lehre des Spinoza* (1785), Friedrich Jacobi related a conversation that he had with Lessing in 1780 about Goethe's poem, "Prometheus." Lessing shocked Jacobi by approving of its somewhat pantheistic theme, thus leading Jacobi to think that Lessing was a 'Spinozist', and, therefore, a pantheist. For accounts of this controversy, see *The Encyclopedia of Philosophy*, vol. 5 and 6 and L. W. Beck, *Early German Philosophy*. For Hegel's own account of this controversy, LHP111, pp. 411–413.

22. LPR1, 1827, pp. 377–378; VPR1, pp. 274–275.

23. Hegel interpreted Spinoza as an "acosmist" (LPR1, p. 377; VPR1, p. 274), as Hodgson noted: "because he does not deny the existence of God but of the world" (LPR11, p. 574, n. 172). Acosmism is the "denial of the existence of the universe or a universe distinct from God" (OED). Hegel said of Spinoza's "acosmism": "This idea of Spinoza's we must allow to be in the main true and well-grounded; absolute substance is the truth, but it is not the whole truth; in order to be this it must also be thought of as in itself active and living, and by that very means it must determine itself as mind. But substance with Spinoza is only the universal and consequently the abstract determination of mind; it may undoubtedly be said that this thought is the foundation of all true views—not, however, as their absolutely fixed and permanent basis, but as the abstract unity which mind is in itself. It is therefore worthy of note that thought must begin by placing itself at the standpoint of Spinozism; to be a follower of Spinoza is the essential commencement of all philosophy" (LHP111, p. 257). For an illuminating discussion of Hegel as "acosmist," see Raymond Keith Williamson, *Introduction to Hegel's Philosophy of Religion* (Albany: State University of New York Press, 1984). Williamson concluded that Hegel is not an acosmist pantheist, but a panentheist, a position we will also defend.

24. LPR1, 1827, p. 369; VPR1, p. 269.

25. LPR1, p. 370; VPR1, p. 269.

26. LPR1, p. 371; VPR1, p. 269.

27. E section 151Z. G. W. F. Hegel, *Hegel's Logic*, p. 214; *Enzyklopädie der philosophischen Wissenschaften (1830)*, ed. F. Nicolin and O. Pöggeler (Hamburg: Felix Meiner, 1959), section 151Z.

28. LPR111, 1827, p. 252; VPR111, p. 179.

29. LPR111, p. 252; VPR111, pp. 179–180.

30. LPR111, p. 254; VPR111, p. 181.

31. LPR111, p. 253; VPR111, p. 181.

32. LPR111, p. 254; VPR111, p. 181.

33. LPR111, p. 254; VPR111, p. 182. Tholuck, for one, put great stock in miracles. Albert Schweitzer, in *The Quest of the Historical Jesus* (London: Adam & Charles Black, 1948), quoted Tholuck's *Die Glaubwürdigkeit der evangelischen Geschichte, zugleich eine Kritik des Lebens Jesu von Strauss* (Hamburg, 1837) as 'presenting' a "historical argument for the credibility of the miracle stories of the Gospels. Even if we admit the scientific position that no act can have proceeded from Christ which transcends the laws of nature, there is still room for the mediating view of Christ's miracle-working activity. This leads us to think of mysterious powers of nature as operating in the history of Christ" (p. 101). Hegel, however, argued against the value of miracles for verification by using Christ's words: "'After my death many will come who perform miracles in my name, but I have not recognized them.' Here Christ himself rejects miracles, and we must hold fast to it. Verification by miracles, as well as the attack on miracles, belong to a lower sphere that concerns us not at all" (LPR111, p. 255; VPR111, p. 182).

34. Ibid.

35. LPR111, p. 255; VPR111, pp. 182–183.

36. LPR111, pp. 255–256; VPR111, p. 183.

37. LPR111, p. 256; VPR111, p. 183.

38. LPR111, p. 262; VPR111, p. 188. Translation amended.

39. LPR111, p. 261; VPR111, p. 188.

40. Ibid.

41. LPR111, p. 280; VPR111, p. 205.

42. LPR111, pp. 275–276; VPR111, p. 201.

43. For the sake of convenience, we will use the term *Logic* to signify both the *Science of Logic* and the 'Lesser Logic'.

44. LPR111, p. 249; VPR111, p. 177.

45. G. W. F. Hegel, *Hegel's Science of Logic*, trans. A. V. Miller (New York: Humanities Press, 1969), p. 50; *Wissenschaft der Logic*, Introduction (Frankfurt-am-Main: Suhrkamp Verlag, 1969), p. 44; *Encyclopädie Der Philosophischen Wissenschaften im Grundnisse*, section 214, pp. 187–188.

46. G. W. F. Hegel, *Hegel's Logic*, p. 44.

47. Frederick Copleston, *A History of Philosophy*, vol. 7, *Fichte to Nietzsche* (Westminster, Md.: Newman Press, 1963), p. 194.

48. LPR1, 1827, pp. 152–153; VPR1, pp. 63–64.

49. LPR1, p. 153; VPR1, p. 65.

50. LPR111, 1827, p. 287; VPR111, p. 212.

51. LPR1, 1827, p. 153; VPR1, p. 65.

52. Philip Schaff, *The Creeds of Christendom*, vol. 2 (New York: Harper and Brothers, 1877), pp. 52–71.

53. LPR111, 1827, p. 290; VPR111, p. 215.

54. LPR111, p. 275; VPR111, pp. 199–200.

55. LPR111, p. 275; VPR111, p. 201.

56. LPR1, 1827, p. 157, 'W_2'; VPR1, p. 67, "W_2."

57. LPR111, 1827, p. 287; VPR111, p. 213.

58. LPR1, 1827, p. 154; VPR1, p. 65. At times, it seems as if Hegel was deliberately echoing the thinking of early Christian thinkers. For example, in continuing his discussion of the idea of God in and for itself, Hegel noted: "That this is so is the Holy Spirit itself, or, expressed in the mode of sensibility, it is eternal love: *the Holy Spirit is eternal love*" (LPR111, 1827, p. 276; VPR111, p. 201). This is quite reminiscent of St. Augustine's statement: "We presuppose, however, that the truth itself has persuaded us that, as no Christian doubts, the Son is the Word of God, so the Holy Spirit is love" (St. Augustine. *On the Trinity*, IX, 12, no. 17). We will have occasion to discuss this notion of love later in this chapter; however, we must note that it is odd that Hegel does not refer to St. Augustine in any detail in any of his writings on Christianity, thus we cannot ascertain if it was, indeed, St. Augustine Hegel was echoing.

Hegel, however, did directly allude to St. Anselm when he cited the ontological proof, in summary form, as containing "the same content" as what he has found "within the idea": that is, the "transition from concept to reality" (LPR111, 1827, p. 279; VPR111, p. 204). Indeed, St. Anselm's ontological argument argues for God's existence solely on the basis of a reasoned analysis of the implications of the idea of God. As an *a priori* argument, the ontological argument has no need for sense experience in its demonstration of God's existence; rather, its movement of thought starts with the idea of God as "that than which nothing greater can be conceived" to

His necessary existence as contained within the idea. A generic version of Anselm's argument can be expressed in a simple syllogism:

> God is the greatest (or most perfect) being.
> A being which exists is greater (or more perfect) than a being
>   which does not exist.
> Therefore, God exists.

What was significant for Hegel is not that Anselm actually demonstrated God's existence, but that thinking was now looking at the inner determinations of the Idea of God. In this, thinking does not keep itself bound to the sensible but now conceives within itself a horizon in which the Idea itself determines what is true and real: "We observed the logical aspect of this transition [from concept to being] earlier. [See LPR1, 1827, pp.: 432–441; VPR1, pp. 323–330.] It is contained in those so-called proofs by means of which the transition ought to be made, in, from, and through the concept, into objectivity and being (all within the element of thought). What appears as a subjective need and demand is the content, is one moment of the divine idea itself" (LPR111, 1827, pp. 278–279; VPR111, p. 204). Therefore, what a proof like that of St. Anselm demonstrates is not that God exists, but that existence has to be thought as a moment within the divine Idea itself and that, by thinking in this manner, the finite subject elevates itself to the infinite as part of the self-development of the concept. William Wallace summed this up quite nicely in his Foreword to *Hegel's Logic*: "Hegel further points out, very interestingly, that the so-called proofs of the Divine Existence are not what they are ordinarily thought to be: purely affirmative reasonings in which what we start from furnishes a fixed, solid basis from which we pass on to something which has the same solidity as its premises. The action of thought is to *negate* the basis from which it starts, to show it up as not being self-subsistent, and so to have in it a springboard from which it can ascend to what is truly self-subsistent and self-explanatory" (p. xii).

59. LPR111, 1827, p. 289; VPR111, p. 214. In the *Critique of Pure Reason*, Kant said: "in view of the fact that all *a priori* division of concepts must be by dichotomy, it is significant that in each class the number of categories is always the same, namely, three. Further, it may be observed that the third category in each class always arises from the combination of the second category with the first" (B110).

60. LPR1, 1827, pp. 154–155; VPR1, p. 66.

61. LPR111, 1827, p. 290; VPR111, p. 215.

62. LPR1, 1827, p. 159; VPR1, p. 69.

63. LPR111, p. 290; VPR111, p. 216.

64. LPR111, 1824, pp. 186–187; VPR111, p. 120.

65. LPR111, 1827, pp. 291–292; VPR111, p. 216.

66. LPR111, p. 292; VPR111, p. 217.

67. Ibid.

68. Ibid.

69. LPR111, p. 293; VPR111, p. 217.

70. Basically, *panentheism* entails that "God has all of finite being as part of his being and experience but transcends it" (Van A. Harvey, *A Handbook of Theological Terms* [New York: The Macmillan Company, 1964], p. 172). This seems to be identical to the views of many Classical philosophers of religion. As Hodgson noted: "Hegel's position can best be understood if it is recognized that he shares with Augustine, Aquinas, and the medieval and German mystics the great Neo-Platonic schema of *exitus et reditus*, emanation and return. In such a schema, nature and the created order may be understood as *genuinely* different from the creative ground of being but not *radically* or *wholly* different. For Hegel the difference is to be understood dialectically, because the truth and the telos of the world remains the divine idea" (Peter C. Hodgson, "Georg Wilhelm Friedrich Hegel," in *Nineteenth Century Religious Thought in the West,* ed. Ninian Smart [Cambridge: Cambridge University Press, 1985], p. 102). Raymond K. Williamson, in *Introduction to Hegel's Philosophy of Religion,* argued this as well, see Chapter 12: "A Medial View: Hegel as a Panentheist," pp. 251–294. This position was first espoused by Robert C. Whittemore in "Hegel as Panentheist," *Tulane Studies in Philosophy* 9 (1960): 134–164. This interpretation has become what H. S. Harris called the *new orthodoxy* in Hegelianism, see H. S. Harris, "The Hegel Renaissance in the Anglo-Saxon World Since 1945," p. 86.

71. LPR111, p. 291; VPR111, p. 216.

72. Ibid.

73. LPR111, p. 295; VPR111, p. 220.

74. LPR111, p. 293; VPR111, p. 218.

75. LPR111, pp. 293–294; VPR111, p. 218.

76. LPR111, p. 294; VPR111, pp. 218–219.

77. LPR111, p. 298; VPR111, p. 222.

78. LPR111, p. 295; VPR111, p. 220. My emphasis.

79. LPR111, p. 297; VPR111, p. 222.

80. LPR111, p. 295; VPR111, p. 220.

81. LPR111, p. 299; VPR111, p. 224.

82. LPR111, p. 296; VPR111, p. 221.

83. Pelagianism is the denial of the doctrine of original sin and the assertion that human beings can do good, first propagated by Pelagius, a contemporary of St.

Augustine. For concise descriptions of Pelagius's teachings, see Paul Tillich, *A History of Christian Thought*, pp. 106–108; and Bengt Hägglund, *History of Theology*. Lawrence Dickey applied the term to the Enlightenment in *Hegel. Religion, Economics, and the Politics of Spirit, 1770–1807*, pp. 25–32. For an influential eighteenth-century thinker like G. E. Lessing, this goodness is implicit in humankind; it needs only to be brought forth explicitly through a process of education. See G. E. Lessing, "The Education of the Human Race," *Harvard Classics*, vol. 32 (New York: Collier, 1910).

84. LPR111, p. 296; VPR111, p. 221.

85. LPR111, p. 300; VPR111, p. 224.

86. Ibid.

87. LPR1, 1824, p. 333; VPR1, p. 235: "It is the distinctive task of philosophy to transmute the *content* that is in the representation of religion into the *form* of thought; the content [itself] cannot be distinguished. Religion is the self-consciousness of absolute spirit: there are not two kinds of self-consciousness—not both a conceptualizing self-consciousness and a representing self-consciousness, which could be distinguished according to their content. There can only be a diversity in form, or a distinction between *representation* and *thought*."

88. LPR1, 1827, p. 168; VPR1, p. 77.

89. LPR111, p. 168; VPR1, p. 78.

90. LPR111, 'W(1831)'; VPR1, pp. 77–78, 'W(1831)'.

91. LPR111, 1827, p. 300; VPR111, p. 224.

92. Ibid.

93. 'W(1831)', p. 301; VPR111, p. 225.

94. LPR111, pp. 300–301; VPR111, p. 224.

95. LPR111, p. 301; VPR111, p. 225.

96. Ibid.

97. Ibid.

98. LPR111, p. 304; VPR111, p. 228.

99. LPR111, p. 305; VPR111, p. 229.

100. LPR111, p. 306; VPR111, p. 230.

101. LPR111, p. 307; VPR111, pp. 230–231.

102. LPR111, p. 305; VPR111, p. 229.

103. LPR111, p. 307; VPR111, p. 231.

104. LPR111, pp. 307–308; VPR111, p. 231.

105. LPR111, p. 309; VPR111, p. 233.

106. Hägglund, *History of Theology*, p. 89.

107. LPR111, 1821, p. 143; VPR111, pp. 78–79.

108. LPR111, 1821, p. 143; VPR111, p. 79.

109. LPR111, p. 327; VPR111, p. 251.

110. LPR111, p. 324; VPR111, p. 238.

111. LPR111, p. 310; VPR111, p. 233.

112. LPR111, p. 311; VPR111, p. 234.

113. LPR111, pp. 312–313; VPR111, pp. 237–238.

114. LPR111, p. 328; VPR111, p. 251.

115. LPR111, p. 316; VPR111, p. 239.

116. LPR111, p. 316; VPR111, p. 240.

117. LPR111, p. 317; VPR111, p. 240. Hegel's reference to Jesus as compara-
ble to Socrates can be read as a thinly veiled allusion to those eighteenth-century
thinkers who analyzed the life of Christ only in terms of his ethical teachings, e.g.,
Jean-Jacques Rousseau (*Emile ou De l'education*), Joseph Priestly (*Socrates and Jesus
Compared*), and others. Johann Georg Hamann's satiric *Sokratische Denkwür-
digkeiten* is an example of an eighteenth-century thinker who, like Hegel, saw such
a comparison as inappropriate.

118. LPR111, 1821, p. 118–119; VPR111, p. 53–54.

119. LPR111, p. 110; VPR111, p. 47.

120. LPR111, p. 322; VPR111, p. 245.

121. Ibid.

122. LPR111, p. 326; VPR111, pp. 249–250. Translation amended.

123. LPR111, p. 322; VPR111, p. 245.

124. LPR111, pp. 324–325; VPR111, pp. 247–248.

125. Hans Küng in *Does God Exist? An Answer for Today*, trans. Edward
Quinn (New York: Doubleday and Company, 1980), brought out this point quite
nicely but in relation to the atheism found in both Hegel's and our time (pp.
138–139). We, however, want to keep our discussion centered on Hegel's description of the appropriation of the death of God as a moment of atheism *within* Christian religious consciousness in general. As a moment within religious conscious-

ness, as we will see, atheism then can *not* be read into Hegel's philosophy of religion as its overall orientation or 'secret' as does Robert C. Solomon in *From Hegel to Existentialism* (Oxford: Oxford University Press, 1987), pp. 56–71.

126. James Collins, *The Emergence of the Philosophy of Religion* (New Haven, Conn.: Yale University Press, 1967), p. 341.

127. This point is brought out most dramatically in Max Stirner, *Der Einzige und sein Eigentum*, trans. Steven Byington as *The Ego and Its Own* (London: Rebel Press, 1982): "At the entrance of the modern time stands the 'God-man'. At its exit will only the God in the God-man evaporate? And can the God-man really die if only the God in him dies?...How can you believe that the God-man is dead before the man in him, besides the God, is dead?" (p. 154). Stirner, a young Hegelian, was saying this in relation to the 'killing-off' of God undertaken in the religious criticism of his contemporaries, e.g., David Friedrich Strauss, Bruno Bauer, Ludwig Feuerbach, but the point applies to the death of God in Christian religious consciousness as well. Stirner's book stands as an intriguing description of what subjectivity as all-embracing totality would look like without a center, intersubjectivity or trinitarian infra- or superstructure; i.e., without a metaphysic. An interesting project would be to compare Stirner's description of subjectivity with Kierkegaard's insofar as Kierkegaard retains a center, the God-man, in the form of the Absolute Paradox.

128. LPR111, 1827, p. 331; VPR111, p. 254.

129. LPR111, pp. 331–332; VPR111, p. 254.

130. LPR111, p. 328; VPR111, p. 251.

131. LPR111, p. 328; VPR111, p. 252.

132. LPR111, pp. 328–329; VPR111, p. 252.

133. LPR111, p. 331; VPR111, p. 254.

134. LPR111, 'W(1831)', p. 250; VPR111, 'W(1831)', p. 178. See also Enc. 564Z: "God is God only so far as he knows himself: his self-knowledge is further a self-consciousness in man and man's knowledge *of* God, which proceeded to man's self-knowledge *in* God." This further means, as Theodore Geraets observed: "There are not two kinds of reason and two kinds of spirit, one divine and the other human" (Theodore Geraets, "The End of the History of Religion 'Grasped in Thought'" *Hegelstudien* [1989]: 64).

135. LPR111, p. 330; VPR111, p. 253.

136. Ibid.

137. Ibid.

138. LPR111, p. 332; LPR111, pp. 254–255.

139. LPR111, p. 333; VPR111, p. 256.

140. Ibid.

141. LPR111, p. 335; VPR111, p. 258.

142. Ibid.

143. See our discussion of this in Chapter Three, "The Inner Dynamics of Faith."

144. Ibid.

145. LPR111, p. 336; VPR111, p. 259.

146. LPR111, p. 337; VPR111, p. 260.

147. LPR111, pp. 336–337; VPR111, p. 259.

148. LPR111, 'W(1831)', p. 336; VPR111, 'W(1831)', p. 259.

149. LPR111, p. 337; VPR111, p. 260.

150. LPR111, p. 338; VPR111, 1827; p. 261.

151. See Chapter Three, n. 76.

152. LPR111, p. 338; VPR111, p. 261. As Walter Jaeschke succinctly pointed out, "The *communicatio idiomatum* is nowhere as real as in Spirit" and, therefore, must be thought as "foremost" in the "formation of the community." Indeed, as Jaeschke further pointed out, "Hegel binds the cognition of the God-man unity to the sublation of the sensible individual and to the actuality of Spirit in the community" (Walter Jaeschke, *Die Vernunft in der Religion: Studien zur Grundlegung der Religionsphiliophie Hegels* [Stuttgart: Frommann-Holzboog, 1986], p. 346).

153. LPR111, p. 338; VPR111, 1827, p. 261.

154. LPR111, p. 339; VPR111, p. 262.

155. LPR111, p. 339; VPR111, p. 262.

156. Ibid.

157. It should be noted that Hegel's treatment of the entire third element is remarkably succinct and "relatively brief" because he was running out of the time usually allotted for lectures. See the editor's remarks, LPR111, 1827, p. 328, n. 212.

158. LPR111, p. 340; VPR111, p. 263.

159. Ibid.

160. LPR111, p. 342; VPR111, p. 265.

161. LPR111, p. 340; VPR111, p. 263.

162. LPR111, p. 341; VPR111, p. 263.

163. LPR111, p. 341; VPR111, p. 264.

164. Ibid.

165. LPR111, p. 342; VPR111, p. 265.

166. LPR111, 'W(1831)', p. 342; VPR111, 'W(1831)', p. 264.

167. LPR111, p. 342; VPR111, p. 265.

168. Ibid.

169. LPR111, p. 343; VPR111, p. 265.

170. Ibid.

171. Ibid.

172. LPR111, p. 343; VPR111, p. 266.

173. LPR111, p. 344; VPR111, p. 267.

174. Ibid.

175. Ibid.

176. LPR111, p. 345; VPR111, p. 268.

177. Ibid.

178. Ibid.

179. LPR111, p. 346; VPR111, p. 268.

180. LPR111, p. 344; VPR111, p. 267.

181. LPR111, p. 243–247; VPR111, p. 173–176.

182. See LPR111, pp. 158–162; VPR111, pp. 94–97.

183. LPR111, p. 246; VPR111, pp. 174–175.

184. LPR111, pp. 346–347; VPR111, p. 269.

185. LPR111, 'L;W(1831),' p. 346; VPR111, 'L;W(1831),' p. 269.

186. LPR111, p. 345; VPR111, p. 268.

187. LPR111, p. 345; VPR111, p. 267.

188. LPR111, p. 347; VPR111, p. 269.

189. Ibid., p. 84; VPR111, p. 4.

Conclusion. The Reconciliation of Philosophy and Theology

1. G. W. F. Hegel, *"Über 'Aphorismen über Nichtwissen und absolutes Wissen im Verhältnisse zur christlichen Glaubenserkenntnis',"* in *Sämtliche Werke,* vol. 20

(Stuttgart: Fromman, 1968), pp. 276–277. Quoted in T. Geraets, "The End of the History of Religions 'Grasped in Thought'," *Hegelstudien* (1989): 74, trans. T. Geraets.

2. Ibid., p. 310. My translation.

3. *Phän.*, p. 24; Hegel, *Phenomenology of Mind*, trans. d. Baillie (New York: Harper and Row, 1967), pp. 85–86. Louis Dupré, "Hegel's Absolute Spirit: A Religious Justification of Secular Culture," in *Hegel. The Absolute Spirit* (Ottawa: University of Ottawa, 1984), p. 128.

4. As we have seen in Chapter Three, philosophy passed judgment on Schleiermacher's "theology of feeling." In Chapter Five, we saw that philosophy criticized Enlightenment and Pietism for 'volatizing' the objective content found in the doctrines of consummate religion. In fact, we can also see that Pietism has performed a service for philosophy; it has brought to the forefront of philosophy's contemplation of religion how thinking can misunderstand subjectivity and consequently misapprehend the essential unity of oppositions that arise initially in religious consciousness. Indeed, Pietism enacts, for Hegel, how the unity of oppositions implicit in Christ and attested to by the witness of the Spirit are separated by thinking when it attempts to articulate its knowledge of God totally from the side of finite subjectivity. As we have seen, when theology keeps to finite subjectivity as the measure of all things, it falls away from the objective doctrines of orthodox theology, especially the doctrine of the Trinity.

5. Hegel, "*Über 'Aphorismen über Nichtwissen und absolutes Wissen im Verhältnisse zur christlichen Glaubenserkenntnis'*," p. 302. Quoted in Emil L. Fackenheim, *The Religious Dimension in Hegel's Thought* (Chicago: University of Chicago Press, 1967), p. 193, his translation.

6. Hegel, ibid., p. 302.

7. LPR1, 1827, 'L', p. 404; VPR1, 'L', p. 209.

8. See Chapter Five, "The Story of the Fall."

9. PS, p. 19; PG, p. 30.

BIBLIOGRAPHY

Hegel Primary Sources

Hegel, G. W. F. *Briefe von und an Hegel*, ed. Johannes Hoffmeister, 4 vols. Hamburg: Felix Meiner, 1952–1981. Volume 4 in two parts [1977, 1981], ed. Friedhelm Nicolin.

———. *Encyclopädie der Philosophichen Wissenschaften im Grundnisse*, ed. Johannes Hoffmeister. Leipzig: Felix Meiner, 1949.

———. Foreword. Frederic Wilhelmm Hinrichs, *Die Religion im inneren Verhältnisse zur Wissenschaft*. In *Hegel, Hinrichs, and Schleiermacher. On Feeling and Reason in Religion. The Texts of Their 1821–22 Debate*, trans. Eric von der Luft. Lewiston, New York: Edwin Mellen Press, 1987.

———. *Hegel, Hinrichs, and Schleiermacher: On Feeling and Reason in Religion. The Texts of the 1821–22 Debate*. trans. Eric von der Luft. Lewiston, New York: Edwin Mellen Press, 1987.

———. *Hegel: The Letters*, trans. Clark Butler and Christiane Seiler. Bloomington: Indiana University Press, 1984.

———. *Hegel's Lectures on the History of Philosophy*, trans. E. S. Haldane and F. H. Simpson, 3 vols. New York: Humanities Press, 1963.

———. *Hegel's Lectures on the Philosophy of World-History*, trans. H. B. Nisbet. Cambridge : Cambridge University Press, 1975.

———. *Hegel's Logic*, trans. from the *Encyclopaedia of Philosophical Sciences* by William Wallace. Oxford: Clarendon Press, 1971.

———. *Hegel's Philosophy of Mind: Being Part Three of the Encyclopaedia of Philosophical Sciences (1830)*, trans. William Wallace. Oxford: Clarendon Press, 1971.

———. *Hegel's Science of Logic*, trans. A. V. Miller. New York: Humanities Press, 1969.

———. *Introduction to the Lectures on the History of Philosophy*, trans. T. M. Knox and A. V. Miller. Oxford: Clarendon Press, 1985.

———. *Lectures on the Philosophy of Religion*. vols. 1–3, ed. Peter C. Hodgson, trans. R. F. Brown, P. C. Hodgson, and J. M. Stewart with the assistance of J. P.

Fitzer and H. S. Harris. Berkeley: University of California Press, 1984, 1987, 1985.

———. *Phänomenologie des Geistes*, ed. Johannes Hoffmeister. Hamburg: Felix Meiner, 1952.

———. *Phenomenology of Mind,* trans. d. Baillie. New York: Harper and Row, 1967.

———. *Phenomenology of Spirit,* trans. A. V. Miller. Oxford: Oxford University Press, 1977.

———. *The Philosophy of History,* trans. J. Sibree. New York: Dover Publications, 1956.

———. *Philosophy of Right,* trans. T. M. Knox. London: Oxford University Press, 1967.

———. *Sämtliche Werke.* vol. 20, ed. Herman Glockner. Stuttgart: Frommon, 1968.

———. *Vorlesungen: Ausgewählte Nachschriften und Manuscripte.* Vols. 3–5. *Vorlesungen über die Philosophie der Religion,* ed. Walter Jaeschke. Hamburg: Felix Meiner. 1983–1985.

———. *Vorlesungen über die Aesthetik.* Frankfurt-am-Main: Suhrkampf, 1971.

———. *Vorlesungen über die Philosophie der Weltgeschichte,* ed. Georg Lasson. Leipzig: Felix Meiner, 1944.

———. *Wissenschaft der Logik.* Frankfurt-am-Main: Suhrkamp Verlag, 1969.

Schleiermacher: Primary Sources

Schleiermacher, F. D. E. *Der christliche Glaube nach den Grundsätzen der evangelischen Kirche im Zusammenhange dargestellt,* vol. 1. Berlin: G. Reimer, 1821.

———. *The Christian Faith,* ed. and trans. H. R. Mackintosh and J. S. Steward. Edinburgh: T. & T. Clark, 1976.

———. *The Life of Jesus,* trans. S. Maclean Gilmour. Philadelphia: Fortress Press, 1975.

———. *On Religion: Speeches to the Cultured Despisers,* trans. John Oman. New York: Harper and Row, 1958.

———. *Platons Werke,* Introduction translated into English by W. Dobson. Cambridge, 1836.

———. "Selection from the First Edition of Schleiermacher's *The Christian Faith.*" In *Hegel, Hinrichs, and Schleiermacher. On Feeling and Reason in Religion. The Texts of Their 1821–22 Debate.* trans. Eric von der Luft. Lewiston, New York: Edwin Mellen Press, 1987.

———. *Werke,* vol. 3. Hamburg: Scientia Verlag, 1967.

Secondary Sources

Allison, Henry. *Lessing and the Enlightenment.* Ann Arbor: University of Michigan Press, 1966.

Aquinas, St. Thomas. *The Basic Writings of St. Thomas Aquinas*, ed. Anton C. Pegis. New York: Random House, 1945.

Augustine, St. *Confessions*, trans. R. S. Pine-Coffin. New York: Penguin Books, 1961.

Barth, Karl. *Anselm: Fides Quaerens Intellectum*, trans. I. W. Robinson. Richmond, Va.: John Knox Press, 1960.

———. *Protestant Theology in the Nineteenth Century. Its Background and History*, trans. Brian Cozens and John Bowden. London: SCM Press, 1972.

———. *The Theology of Schleiermacher,* ed. Dietrich Ritschl and trans. Geoffrey W. Bromily. Grand Rapids, Mich.: William B. Eerdmans publishing Co., 1982.

Beck, Lewis White. *Early German Philosophy. Kant and His Predecessors*. Cambridge, Mass.: Belknap Press of Harvard University, 1969.

Beiser, Frederick C. *The Fate of Reason. German Philosophy from Kant to Fichte*. Cambridge, Mass.: Harvard University Press, 1987.

Benz, Ernst. *The Mystical Sources of German Romantic Philosophy*, trans. Blair R. Reynolds and Eunice M. Paul. Allison Park, Pa.: Pickwick Publications, 1983.

Braaten, Carl E. *Principles of Lutheran Theology*. Philadelphia: Fortress Press, 1983.

Brandt, Richard B. *The Philosophy of Schleiermacher*. New York: Greenwood Press, 1968.

Brown, Colin. *Jesus in European Protestant Thought, 1770–1860*. Durham, N.C.: Labyrinth Press, 1985.

Chemnitz, Martin. *On the Two Natures of Christ*, trans. Jacob O. Preus. St. Louis: Concordia Publishing House, 1971.

Collins, James. *The Emergence of Philosophy of Religion*. New Haven, Conn.: Yale University Press, 1967.

Copleston, F. *A History of Philosophy*. Vol. 7. *Fichte to Nietzsche*. Westminster, Md.: Newman Press, 1963.

Crouter, Richard. "Hegel and Schleiermacher at Berlin: A Many-Sided Debate." *Journal of the American Academy of Religion* 48 (March 1980).

———. "Rhetoric and Substance in Schleiermacher's Revision of *The Christian Faith*." *Journal of Religion* 60 (July 1980).

d'Hondt, Jacques. *Hegel in His Time*, trans. John Burbridge. Peterborough, Ontario: Broadview Press, 1988.

Dawson, Jerry F. *Schleiermacher. The Evolution of a Nationalist*. Austin: University of Texas Press, 1966.

de Nys, Martin. "Negativity and Mediation in Hegel's Phenomenology of Religion." *Journal of Religion* 66 (January 1986).

Descartes, René. *Discourse on Method and Meditation*, trans. Laurence Lafleur. Indianapolis: Bobbs-Merrill, 1960.

Dickey, Lawrence. *Hegel. Religion, Economics, and the Politics of Spirit, 1770–1807*. Cambridge: Cambridge University Press, 1987.

Dunning, Stephen N. *The Tongues of Men: Hegel and Hamann on Religious Language and History*. Missoula, Mont.: Scholars Press, 1979.

Dupré, Louis. "Hegel's Absolute Spirit: A Religious Justification of Secular Culture." In *Hegel. The Absolute Spirit*. Ottawa: University of Ottawa, 1984.

Eckhardt, Meister. *Meister Eckhardt. Mystic and Philosopher,* trans. Reiner Schürman. Bloomington: Indiana University Press, 1978.

Elert, Werner. *The Structure of Lutheranism*, trans. Walter A. Hansen. St. Louis: Concordia Publishing House, 1962.

Erdmann, Johann Eduard. *A History of Philosophy*, vol. 3, trans. W. S. Hough. London, 1890–1892.

Fackenheim, Emil. *The Religious Dimension in Hegel's Thought*. Chicago: University of Chicago Press, 1967.

Findlay, John. "Hegelianism and Platonism." In *Hegel and the History of Philosophy*, ed. John O"Malley, K. W. Algozin, and Frederick G. Weiss. The Hague: Martinus Nijhoff, 1974.

Gadamer, Hans-Georg. *Truth and Method*. New York: Continuum Publication Co., 1975.

Geraets, Theodore. "The End of the History of Religions 'Grasped in Thought.'" *Hegelstudien* (1989): 55–77.

———, ed. *Hegel. The Absolute Spirit*. Ottawa: University of Ottawa, 1984.

Gerrish, B. A. "The Secret Religion of Germany: Christian Piety and the Pantheism Controversy," *Journal of Religion* 67, no. 4, 1987.

Gillespie, Michael Allen. *Hegel, Heidegger and the Ground of History*. Chicago: University of Chicago Press, 1984.

Hägglund, Bengt. *History of Theology*, trans. Gene J. Lund. St. Louis: Concordia Publishing House, 1968.

Harris, Errol E. *An Introduction to the Logic of Hegel*. New York: University Press of America, 1982.

Harris, H. S. "The Hegel Renaissance In the Anglo-Saxon World Since 1945." *The Owl of Minerva*, 15, Fall, 1983.

———. *Hegel's Development: Toward the Sunlight, 1770–1801*. Oxford: Clarendon Press, 1972.

Harvey, A. *A Handbook of Theological Terms*. New York: The Macmillan company, 1964.

Haym, Rudolph. *Hegel und seine Zeit*. Berlin, 1857; reprinted at Hildesheim, 1962.

Heick, Otto W. *A History of Christian Thought*, vol. 2. Philadelphia: Fortress Press, 1966.

Heidegger, Martin. *The Basic Writings of Martin Heidegger*. New York: Harper and Row, 1977.

———. *Being and Time*, trans. John Macquarrie and Edward Robinson. New York: Harper and Brothers, 1966.

————. *Hegel's Phenomenolgy of Spirit*, trans. Parvis Emad and Kenneth Maly. Bloomington: Indiana University Press, 1988.

————. "Phenomenology and Theology." *The Piety of Thinking*. Bloomington: Indiana University Press, 1976.

————. *Was heisst Denken?* Tübingen: Niemeyer, 1954.

Hick, John. *Philosophy of Religion*. Englewood Cliffs, N.J.: Prentice-Hall, 1963.

Hinrichs, Hermann Friedrich Wilhelm. *Die Religion im inneren Verhältnis zur Wissenshchaft: Nebst Darstelling und Beurtheilung der von Jacobi, Fichle und Schelling gemachten Versuche, dieselbe wissenschaftlich zu erfassen, und nach ihrem Hauptonhalte zu entwickeln, mit einen Vorworte un Georg Wilhelm Friedrich Hegel*. Heidelberg: Groos, 1822; reprint, Brussels: Culture et Civilisation, 1970.

Hoover, Jeffrey. "The Origin of the Conflict Between Hegel and Schleiermacher at Berlin." *The Owl of Minerva*, 20, no 1 (Fall 1988).

Houlgate, Stephen. *Hegel, Nietzsche, and the criticism of metaphysics*. Cambridge: Cambridge University Press, 1986.

Huertas-Jourda, José. Lectures on *Being and Time*. Winter Term, 1979, Wilfrid Laurier University.

Inge, W. R. *Mysticism in Religion*. Chicago: University of Chicago Press, 1948.

Jaeschke, Walter. *Die Religionsphilosophie Hegels*. Darmstadt: Wissenschaftliche Buchgellschaft, 1983.

————. *Die Vernunft in der Religion. Studien zur Grundlegung der Religionsphilosophie Hegels*. Stuttgart: Fromman-Holzboog, 1986.

Kant, Immanuel. *Critique of Pure Reason*, trans. Norman Kemp-Smith. New York: St. Martin's Press, 1965.

————. *Religion Within the Limits of Reason Alone*, trans. T. M. Greene and H. Hudson. New York: Harper, 1960.

Kaufman, Walter, ed. *Hegel's Political Philosophy*. New York: Atherton, 1970.

Kerr, Hugh T., ed. *A Compendium of Luther's Theology*. Philadelphia: Westmister Press, 1956.

Kierkegaard, Søren. *Concluding Unscientific Postscript*, trans. David F. Swenson and Walter Lowrie. Princeton, N.J.: Princeton University Press, 1941.

Kirkland, Frank M. "Husserl and Hegel: A Historical and Religious Encounter." *Journal of the British Society for Phenomenology* 16, no. 1 (January 1985).

Kolb, David. *The Critique of Modernity. Hegel, Heidegger and After*. Chicago: University of Chicago Press, 1986.

Küng, Hans. *Does God Exist? An Answer for Today*, trans. Edward Quinn. New York: Doubleday and Company, 1980.

Lauer, Quentin. *Essays in Hegelian Dialectic*. New York: Fordham University Press, 1977.

————. *Hegel's Concept of God*. Albany: State University of New York Press, 1982.

Lessing, G. E. "The Education of the Human Race," in *Harvard Classics*, vol. 32. New York: Collier, 1910.

Luther, Kem, and Hoover, Jeff. "Hegel's Phenomenology of Religion," *Journal of Religion* 61 (July 1981).

Luther, Martin. *The Bondage of the Will*. Grand Rapids, Mich.: Baker Book House, 1976.

———. *Large Catechism*, trans. Robert H. Fischer. Philadelphia: Muhlenberg Press, 1959.

———. *Luther's Works*, 55 vols. General ed. H. T. Lehman. St Louis: Concordia Publishing House, 1958–1986.

———. *Selected Political Writings*, ed. J. M. Porter. Philadelphia: Fortress Press, 1974.

Mackay, James P. *The Christian Experience of God as Trinity*. London: SCM Books, 1983.

Maier, Gerhard. *The End of the Historico-Critical Method*. St. Louis: Concordia Publishing Co., 1974.

Otto, Rudolph. *The Idea of the Holy*. Oxford: Oxford University Press, 1969.

———. *Mysticism East and West*. New York: Macmillan, 1932.

Pascal, Blaise. *Pensées*, trans. W. F. Trotter. London: Dent, 1908.

Pattman, Robert. "Commitments to Time in Reformation Protestant Theology, Hegelian Idealism, and Marxism." In *Hegel Today*, ed. Bernard Cullen. Brookfield, Vt.: Gower Publishing Company, 1988.

Pelikan. *The Melody of Theology. A Philosophical Dictionary*. Cambridge, Mass.: Harvard University Press, 1988.

Pfleiderer, O. *The Development of Theology in Germany Since Kant*, trans. J. Frederick Smith. New York: Macmillan Press, 1896.

Popper, Karl. *The Open Society and Its Enemies*. Princeton, N.J.: Princeton University Press, 1950.

Pünjer, B. *History of the Philosophy of Religion*, trans. W. Harte. Edinburgh, 1887.

Redeker, Martin. *Schleiermacher: His Life and Thought*, trans. John Wallhauser. Philadelphia: Fortress Press, 1973.

Ritschl, Albrecht. "Prolegomena to *The History of Pietism*." In *Three Essays*, trans. Philip Hefner. Philadelphia: Fortress Press.

———. *Geschichte des Pietismus*, 3 vols. Bonn, 1880–1886.

Ritter, Walter. *Class Manual for Early Church Fathers and Councils*. Camrose Lutheran College, 1988.

Salomé, Lou-Andreas. *Nietzsche*, trans. Siegfried Mandel. Redding Ridge, Conn.: Black Swans Books, 1988.

Schaff, Philip. *The Creeds of Christendom*, vol 2. New York: Harper and Brothers, 1877.

Schlegel, A. W. *Sämmtliche Werke*, ed. E. Böcking. Leipzig: 1846/4.

Schillebeeckx, Edward. *Jesus. An Experiment in Christology.* New York: The Seabury Press, 1979.

Schlitt, Dale M. *Hegel's Trinitarian Claim. A Critical Reflection.* Leiden: E. J. Brill, 1984.

Schmidt, Roger. *Exploring Religion.* Belmont, Calif.: Wadsworth, 1980.

Schweitzer, Albert. *The Quest of the Historical Jesus. A Critical Study of Its Progress from Reimarus to Wrede.* London: Adam & Charles Black, 1948.

Selected Political Writings, ed. J. M. Porter. Philadelphia: Fortress Press, 1974.

Solomon, Robert C. *From Hegel to Existentialism.* Oxford: Oxford University Press, 1987.

Spener, Philipp Jakob. *Pia Desideria,* trans. Theodore G. Tappert. Philadelphia: Fortress Press, 1964.

Spinoza, Benedict de. *Theologico-Political Treatise.* New York: Dover Publications, 1951.

Stace, W. T. *The Philosophy of Hegel. A Systematic Exposition.* Toronto: Dover Publications, 1955.

Stirner, M. *The Ego and Its Own,* trans. Steven Byington. London: Rebel Press, 1982.

Surber, J. P. "Hegel's Speculative Sentence." *Hegel-Studien,* 10 (1975).

Taylor, Mark C. *Journeys to Selfhood. Hegel and Kierkegaard.* Berkeley: University of California Press, 1980.

The Lutheran Hymnal. St. Louis: Concordia Publishing House, 1941.

The Encyclopedia of Philosophy, vols. 1–8. New York: Macmillan, 1972.

Tholuck, F. A. G. *Die Lehre von der Sünde und vom Versöhner; oder, Die wahre Wiehe des Zweiflers.* Hamburg, 1823, 2d ed., 1825.

———. *Die speculative Trinitätlehre des späteren Orients: Eine religionsphilosophische Monographie aus Handschriftlichen Quellen der Leydener, Oxforder und Berliner Bibliothek.* Berlin, 1826.

Tice, Terence N. "Schleiermacher's Concept of Religion: 1799 to 1831." *Archivio di Filasofia* T11, vols. 1–3 (1984): 334–356.

Tillich, Paul. *Dynamics of Faith.* San Francisco: Harper and Row, 1957.

———. *A History of Christian Thought. A Stenographic Transcription of Lectures Delivered During the Spring Term, 1953.* (Also published as: *A History of Christian Thought*). Philadelphia: Fortress Press, 1968.

———. *Perspectives on Nineteenth and Twentieth Century Protestant Theology,* ed. Carl E. Braaten. New York: Harper, 1967.

———. *The Protestant Era,* trans. James Luther Adams. Chicago: University of Chicago Press, 1948.

———. *Systematic Theology,* vol. 1. Chicago: University of Chicago Press, 1951.

Toews, John. *Hegelianism. The Path Toward Dialectical Humanism, 1805–1841.* Cambridge: Cambridge University Press, 1980.

Westphal, Merold. Introduction to "Reason and Religious Truth: Hegel's Foreword to H. F. W. Hinrichs," in *Die Religion im Inneren Verhältnisse zur Wissenschaft (1822).* In *Beyond Epistemology: New Studies in the Philosophy of Hegel.* The Hague: Martinus Nijhoff, 1974.

———. *Kierkegaard's Critique of Reason and Society.* Macon, Ga.: Mercer University Press, 1987.

Williams, Robert. *Schleiermacher the Theologian. The Construction of the Doctrine of God.* Philadelphia: Fortress Press, 1978.

Williamson, Raymond Keith. *Introduction to Hegel's Philosophy of Religion.* Albany: State University of New York Press, 1984.

Wyschogrod, Edith. *Spirit in Ashes: Hegel, Heidegger, and Man-Made Mass Death.* New Haven, Conn.: Yale University Press, 1985.

Yerkes, James. *The Christology of Hegel.* Albany: State University of New York Press, 1983.

INDEX